Escape Plan

Published 2024
Printed in the United States of America
Print ISBN: 978-1-64742-778-8
E-ISBN: 978-1-64742-779-5
Library of Congress Control Number: 2024901814

For information, address:
She Writes Press
1569 Solano Ave #546
Berkeley, CA 94707

Interior Design by Kiran Spees

She Writes Press is a division of SparkPoint Studio, LLC.

Escape Plan

Dreaming My Way Out of the Projects

Lynette Charity, MD

SWP

SHE WRITES PRESS

Contents

Part I

Anywhere but Here

Chapter 1
The Porch

"STRATFORD AND ROOSEVELT! Last stop!" the bus driver called out. When he opened the door, Mama grabbed my arm and pulled me down the bus steps. I missed the last one and almost fell on my face, but Mama caught me.

Under the corner streetlight, she glanced at her watch yet again. Like the rabbit in *Alice in Wonderland*, she was late, late for a very important date. Shaking her head, she took off walking real fast.

I was nine years old and had to run to match her long strides. I couldn't keep up.

"Mama, wait for me!" I yelled.

"Come on, girl!" she yelled back without turning around. "It's nine o'clock!"

Our house was the second one on the left from the corner where Stratford Drive met Taft Drive. Every corner in our Portsmouth, Virginia, neighborhood had a streetlight, and every house had a porch light. Every family turned their porch lights on at sundown. The lights lit up not only the porches but the house numbers, too. Sometimes folks enjoyed sitting on their lit porches, observing the goings-on in the neighborhood. That's what I liked to do too, but not tonight.

Mama and I had gone to a barbecue that Saturday afternoon. My aunt Joyce was the host. I had lots of aunts and uncles, even though my mama was an only child. Of all of them, I loved Aunt Joyce the most. When she and Mama would get together, Mama would relax. Mama would laugh. Mama would dance. Mama could tell Aunt Joyce anything. I heard Aunt Joyce ask her once, "Why do you stay with him, Anne? He's no good."

Mama said, "I have to, Joyce." And left it at that.

Daddy didn't like that Mama smiled a lot after she visited Aunt Joyce. He didn't like that Mama hummed a lot after she visited Aunt Joyce. Daddy didn't like Aunt Joyce, period. Even so, he'd said we could go to the barbecue. But he'd also said, "You best be home by nine o'clock. I'll watch the boy till then." The *boy* was my two-year old brother, Kevin. Mama understood the rules. When Daddy said nine o'clock, he meant nine o'clock.

We took the bus to Aunt Joyce's. There was a stop a block away from her house. Convenient.

The homes in the segregated developments in Portsmouth had large backyards, usually cordoned off with chain-link fences. The main streets had no sidewalks, so those who had cars parallel-parked close to their front lawns.

The driveway leading to Aunt Joyce's carport had room for two cars but was empty when we arrived. We walked up the driveway from the street and headed for the backyard. I recognized Aunt Bootsy and Uncle Elmo, a nice couple who'd been friends with Mama for as long as I could remember, right away. Other adults there spoke to me as though I knew them. Maybe I should have, but I didn't. No matter—everyone was nice to me, and I got lots of hugs that day.

One woman grabbed my arm, twirled me around, and said, "My oh my, Lynette! How you have grown. Do you like your new house?"

A little dizzy from the twirling, I replied, "Yes, ma'am." But that was a lie. I wanted to return to the projects to live with my granny. You didn't have to worry about getting hit by a car while playing hopscotch or jacks in the projects. There were sidewalks there.

Aunt Joyce had two daughters, Linda and Brenda, who were around my age. With so many adults, it was nice to see some children. But I admit that even with Linda and Brenda there, my plan was to entertain myself by eating all the delicious dishes that were spread out on the aluminum tables covered with vinyl tablecloths. This gathering was a potluck, but we hadn't brought anything. Aunt Joyce had told Mama to "just come."

I filled my plate with Aunt Joyce's fried chicken and homemade rolls, plus yams, green beans, and potato salad. Linda and Brenda joined me sitting in the grass. As children, we knew that the folding chairs and the chairs from the dining room table were meant for the adults, especially the older folks who couldn't get down on the ground easily and certainly wouldn't be able to get up without assistance.

I was sitting there, cradling my paper plate filled with deliciousness, when Aunt Joyce said, "Lynette, don't forget to have some of my sun tea."

"Yes, ma'am." I placed my plate on the grass and bounced up to get a cup.

Sun tea was simple to make—a bunch of tea bags in a pitcher of water left out in the sun to steep, then diluted with ice cubes when ready. Simple, but Aunt Joyce's was so good, especially with all the sugar she added. It was sweet tea like no other.

We were having a good time at the barbecue. There was music and dancing. Linda, Brenda, and I commented on the grown-ups dancing, especially the men. Even with a few Budweisers in them, they could still cut a rug. To me, these men seemed so nice. I didn't know how they acted in their homes, but at this barbecue, they danced, laughed, and attended to the women there like perfect gentleman. I got caught up in the gaiety of the event. Time, for me, had stopped.

I was on my fifth piece of fried chicken, a drumstick, when Mama snatched it right out of my hand and said, "Lynette, it's almost eight. We gotta go. Last bus will be coming soon."

As I watched my drumstick sail through the air and land in the nearby trash can, I wondered how five hours had passed so quickly. Mama hurriedly gathered up our things and said goodbye to people on the way out, saying, "This was fun, but I gotta get back home to Kevin."

That was a lie. Well, maybe not a *lie* lie, but not the whole truth, either.

She grabbed my arm and pulled me through the gate of the chain-link fence, down the driveway, and in the direction of the bus stop. She let go when we were almost there. Her grip had left an indentation in my wrist and I rubbed at it as I followed along after her.

Upon arrival, she began to pace. Her smile was gone. Her laugh was gone. Her brow furrowed as she searched the street for any evidence that the bus was coming. There was none.

The sun was setting. The streetlight turned on and the crickets chirped. While pacing back and forth, Mama lit up a cigarette. She looked at her watch and said, "It's 8:10. Bus should be comin' 'long any minute."

Was she speaking to me? Was she trying to convince me? Was she trying to convince herself? I wasn't sure, so I said nothing. Besides, it was wishful thinking. She knew full well that the buses ran late all the time, especially on Saturday nights.

She took a long drag off her cigarette and blew out slowly through her nose. She didn't smoke much, and usually only at home. Mama was wearing her *worry* face: forehead wrinkled, eyes scrunched up. She kept looking at her watch, mumbling to herself and chain-smoking her Marlboros. Daddy had given her a curfew: she knew she was going to miss it, and she knew there'd be *hell to pay*.

How much hell, exactly, was up to Daddy. Last time he'd given her a busted lip.

"It's eight thirty—where's that damn bus?" she whispered as she dropped her sixth cigarette butt on the ground and smashed it with her shoe.

Until that moment, Mama had never cussed in front of me. Until that moment, I'd never counted how many cigarettes she smoked. Now I was wearing my *worry* face too.

Will Daddy blame Mama for the bus being late?

I already knew the answer: *Yep, and there's gonna be hell to pay.*

The bus finally came. Real late. We arrived at our stop past nine o'clock. The bus route did not extend all the way down Stratford to Taft. There were two blocks to walk once we got off.

Mama wasn't walking those two blocks, but she wasn't sprinting, either. All I know is that I ran to keep up with her and I couldn't.

She reached our street ahead of me and came to a sudden stop at the intersection.

"Damn it!" she swore as she began moving again.

I looked up to see that our porch light was off. I didn't know exactly what that meant, but I knew it wasn't good.

As we walked toward our house at 512 Taft Drive, I noted that every other house on the block except ours had its porch light on.

"Mama!" I gasped. "I cain't see the house!"

I must have been yelling because Mama reprimanded me in a loud whisper, "Lynette, hush up and come on!"

With the absence of a lit porch light, our house appeared non-existent. I knew it was somewhere in the void between 510 and 514 Taft Drive, but looking at the spot was like looking into a black hole of nothingness.

Mama arrived ahead of me. She groped into that darkness for the hand railing and made her way to the top step of our three-step porch.

Afraid I'd fall, I stood near the nothingness, waiting for her to tell me what to do.

"Lynette, come up here," she whispered.

"Yes, Mama." I strained to see shapes. *Is that a railing? Is that the screen door?* I swung my hands out in front of me like I'd seen blind people do on TV. My hands banged into a railing and I grabbed it. I kicked at the steps with my shoe to get my bearings and made my way to the top, where finally I leaned against the house and waited to see what would happen next.

I didn't want to go inside for sure. I felt safe on the porch. Inside, there would be yelling and screaming. Inside, the argument would end with my daddy's fist hitting my mama in the face. I was so tired of this violence between my parents. I hated my daddy for being so mean. I hated my mama for taking his abuse.

Inside the house was dark and real quiet. Daddy was home—he had to be. Was he asleep? He wouldn't have left, because Kevin was only two years old. I didn't understand then the ways that men punished their wives for transgressing their rules, or the ways that the women tolerated their husbands' beatings. All I knew was that this wasn't the future I wanted for myself.

Mama pulled the screen door handle up and then down. Locked. She knocked quiet-like.

"Chairdy, it's Anne," she whispered. "We're home. Let us in."

She waited. No response.

Daddy's real name was Clarence Charity, but no one called him that. He was known as Chairdy. But he wasn't responding to any name tonight.

Mama, you gotta knock harder than that.

Mama must have heard my thoughts, because she knocked louder and raised her voice a little. "Chairdy, come on now. Let me and Lynette in."

"Where you been?" There was Daddy's mumbling voice, coming from inside the house.

"Come on, Chairdy. Remember? Me and Lynette went to Joyce's barbecue. You said we could go. You said be back by nine o'clock. We left at eight o'clock, plenty of time to catch the last bus, but it came late. We walked as fast as we could. Let us in, now. Don't be that way, Chairdy."

I heard her fiddling with the screen door handle while she justified our tardiness. She was breathing hard.

Still no response. Then a commotion arose from inside the darkness of the house as Daddy bumped into some furniture—likely the piano stool, the coffee table, and the corner of the couch—and cussed his way to the front door.

He turned on the lamp by the front door and clicked the front door open. He pressed his face into the screen door but didn't unlock it. He did not turn on the porch light. I could smell him from where I stood leaned up against the house—cheap whiskey and Camel cigarettes.

I'd seen this Daddy many times before. He was "shit-faced

drunk," as Mama had called it when she didn't think her children were listening. This Daddy acted ugly and never remembered it in the morning.

Finally, Daddy turned on the porch light and unlocked the screen door.

All of a sudden, I could see. Even though Daddy was drunk, the porch was back. I was so happy to see it, I let go of the railing. I'd been holding on to it so tight my hands hurt.

I opened and closed my fists and shook my hands, feeling the ache, as Mama grabbed the screen door handle and pulled the door open.

It might have been a *WHAP* sound, or maybe a *POW*—I wasn't sure, it happened so fast. Daddy's fist came out from the door and hit Mama straight in the mouth while I stood outside at my post on the porch. Her head snapped back, spit flew out and up, and she went limp. The railing that was supposed to keep people from falling into the bushes didn't stop her. She fell backward and flipped over the railing, headfirst. Her feet went up in the air. Her head almost hit the edge of the concrete porch on her way down. She landed in the bushes, on her stomach, face down.

She didn't move.

I didn't move. I couldn't. I need to help Mama, but I was frozen in my spot. Was she dead? I couldn't move. I yelled, *Mama, MOVE!* But the words were only in my head. Nothing came out of my mouth.

Daddy done kilt my mama!

Daddy stared out past me into the dark for a moment. Then he just turned and went back inside. The screen door slammed behind him. I heard him mumbling in his drunky talk.

I was a statue, frozen in place on my porch. I replayed Mama's fall over and over again.

Mama didn't move. She was dead. I knew she was dead lying in those hedges because I'd seen a dead person before, lying face down in the street, just like Mama. Not moving.

Then, by the grace of God, I saw her head move. I heard a moan. She lifted her head.

A dark liquid poured from Mama's mouth. I knew it was blood. I'd seen it before oozing from her busted lip after Daddy hit her. But there was more of it this time.

Mama kept spitting while she wrestled herself out of the bushes. She turned her body until her feet touched the ground. She held on to one of the bushes and got up, all wobbly. I stood in silence, watching, as she shook her head, wiped her mouth with the bottom of her blouse, and shook her head again, then she picked at her hair, her face, her clothes. She picked off most of the bush branches that were poking into her. There was more blood.

Mama was not Mama when she came back up the steps and grabbed me. She shook her head again and I thought about how my granny said that you had to shake your head to get the cobwebs out.

"Get inside," Mama said, already pushing me through the door. When I walked inside, Daddy was just sitting there on the couch, head down, passed out.

I kept going farther into the house. Mama followed behind me and peeked into Kevin's room. I knew he was asleep when she came out without walking all the way in.

My older brother, Butch, whose real name was also Clarence, wasn't home. He was spending most of his weekends these days at friends' houses. "I don't like seeing Daddy drunk," he'd told me recently. I wished I had someplace else to go. I had no real friends. My *friends* lived in my head.

"Go to bed, girl," Mama said.

I went to my room and closed the door. I sat on the edge of my bed, still not quite understanding what had just happened.

Back in the living room, I heard Mama talking to Daddy.

"Chairdy, why you do that, huh? In front of the child. She don't need to see you act ugly. Get up now and go to bed. I be there after I wash up a little."

I heard Daddy mumble and stumble into the bedroom. I listened to the sounds of Mama in the bathroom. I heard the water running in the sink. I imagined she was using a washcloth to clean the blood from her face. She was probably looking in the mirror to see what damage had been done while she thought about how she'd explain the way she looked to the neighborhood ladies. "Oh, girl, this bruise? I walked into the wall. Clumsy me."

She used the toilet, washed her hands, turned out the light. The living room lamp and porch light were still on. Before tonight, the porch light was always turned on at dusk and turned off by the first person awake in the morning. Before being sent to my room, I was certain that Mama had continued the routine. It was Daddy who'd broken the rule.

The light coming from the living room lamp came in through the crack underneath my bedroom door. Mama passed my room, entered her bedroom, and closed the door behind her. She left the living room lamp on.

I waited until I felt it was safe to leave my room. Then I tiptoed out to the living room, straight to the front door. Escaping the house was not an easy feat—I had to hold the screen door just right so it didn't squeak or slam shut—but I managed to slip out without alerting anyone.

I sat on my porch. Now that it was fully lit it was mine again. Where I sat, a creepy crawler was making its way from one side of the top step to the other. I tried to help it out by flicking it in the right direction—but instead of helping, I flicked it right off the porch. *Sorry, bug.*

I took in a deep breath and let it out real slow. All manner of flying bugs, attracted by the porch light, joined me while I again tried to make sense of what had happened.

Those fluttering bugs felt like my thoughts: flying all around, making no sense. I looked at the smushed hedges where Mama had lain, so still I thought she was dead. I looked up at the dark, starless sky. I looked at the light post down the street, flickering in the darkness. I looked up and down the street at all the lit porches. Quiet. Still. I wondered if anyone had heard or seen what had happened. If they had, would they have come out to help?

I already knew the answer was no. I was old enough to know that the neighbor ladies let their husbands hit them and said nothing. These women had no place to go, no money of their own. They couldn't make their own choices. I closed my eyes, hugged myself, rocked back and forth, and tried to think of the barbecue and all the fun we'd had that day. I remembered the smells and the tastes of the food. I dwelled on the fried chicken.

One of the voices that lived in my head spoke to me: *Whatcha gonna do, Lynette?*

"I don't know," I said quietly. "Maybe just run away." I'd wanted to run away for a long time. I knew no one would miss me. I kept rocking myself back and forth as I played out the plan.

Where ya gonna go?

"Maybe Granny's. Maybe . . . maybe Oz!" I'd first seen *The Wizard of Oz* when I was six and had watched it religiously ever since. *Wouldn't it be nice to laugh the day away in the merry old land of Oz?* I thought.

Well, you cain't stay here! That's for sure!

You damn right! I shouted this, but only in my head. I knew enough to stay quiet. If I woke my parents up, who knew what hell there'd be to pay. And it wouldn't be Daddy. He was out for the night. It would be Mama meting out the discipline. She had no control over her husband, but she had control over her children. For us, Mama was the punisher.

In that moment, it occurred to me that I could save my mama by killing my daddy. It wouldn't be that hard to stab him to death while he was in a drunken stupor. But I somehow understood that I couldn't save her. I could only save myself.

Chapter 2
Growing Pains

MY LEGS HAD begun to hurt soon after our move to Portsmouth. They had a mind of their own. They ached. They cramped. They kept me up at night.

In the middle of the night, I'd wake Mama, crying, "My legs hurt, Mama."

She'd get out of bed and take me back to my room.

"Where do they hurt?"

"All over."

She'd rub them for a few minutes, and that made them feel better.

"Now go to sleep," she'd say, and leave me alone.

Not once did she hold me or say, "There, there, does that feel better?" She just sat on my bed and rubbed my legs in silence, then left.

On two occasions, her silent attempt to help me didn't work—the pain was unbearable—so she called our neighbor, Mr. Epps.

Mr. Epps had a car, and he helped Mama from time to time by taking her places. One time I overheard him tell her that he would be happy to beat up Daddy for her.

"That's okay, Epps," she told him. "No need to get into trouble for me."

You can get into trouble for me, I thought.

On those two occasions, Mr. Epps and Mama took me to the ER

at the colored hospital. Daddy wasn't interested in helping. All he said was, "Nuthin's wrong wit dat girl!" And the doctors agreed. The diagnosis was the same both times: "Mrs. Charity, we can find no reason for Lynette's leg pains."

As an adult, I'd learn there was a reason. It was psychosomatic pain manifesting itself in my body. The pain subsided over time. It's hard to know exactly why. Maybe it was because I was better able to deal with my life once I found a reason to live. Maybe it was Ben Casey's inspiration. Maybe it was because I needed to be well in order to escape.

My stomach pains were a different story, though, especially when I vomited up blood. The leg pains Mama saw as a nuisance—"Lynette, ain't nuthin' wrong wit your legs, so stop it!" she'd chide—but when she saw her nine-year-old daughter writhing on the floor and spewing blood from her mouth, she took it seriously. And she took me to see Dr. Newby.

Mama knew Dr. Newby. They'd gone to the same high school. He was a tall, good-looking man, especially in his suit and tie and his long white coat. I imagined Mama saying, "That James. Um um um. He's a tall drink of water and a sharp dresser."

When Mama saw him, she smiled a big smile—and he smiled back.

Why didn't Mama marry him? Then he'd be my daddy.

After Mama told him what had happened, he was visibly concerned. "Anne, I want to do some tests on Lynette if that's okay. Her vomiting blood is a concern."

"Okay, James," she said. She must have been special to him because I never heard anyone else call him James. Everyone else called him *Doctor.*

My Mama saying, "Okay, James," gave Dr. Newby permission to poke and prod me. Would anyone have stopped if I had said no? I already knew the answer. I was a child; I had no say.

"Anne, I want to give Lynette a barium swallow," Dr. Newby finally said. "We can look at her esophagus and stomach and see what's going on."

"Okay, James." And this time she gave him goo-goo eyes.

"What's a sofagus?" I asked.

He turned toward me and smiled. "It's the food pipe to your tummy, Lynette."

"Oh?" is all I said. I'd had no idea I had a pipe in my body. When I closed my eyes I imagined it straight and metal, leading from my throat to my stomach.

"James, do what you think is best for Lynette," Mama said, looking dreamily into his eyes.

I still didn't know what a *bar-i-um swal-low* was, but when I thought about Dr. Newby's smile, I didn't care. I would do anything for him. He was nice to me.

On the day I went to swallow a barium down my sofagus pipe, Mama wouldn't let me eat breakfast.

When she checked me in at the hospital, a nice nurse dressed in a white uniform came over to me and said, "Hello, you must be Lynette."

"Yes, ma'am."

She walked me down the hall and pushed open the door. We entered a room with lots of machines, some hanging from the ceiling. There were cabinets on the walls full of bottles and more gadgets. A metal table stood in the middle of the room.

"Lynette," she said kindly, "we need to take off your top and put you in this gown. It's going to be big on you, but I'll make sure it covers you. You can keep your pants on, okay?"

"Yes, ma'am."

Once I had the gown on, she handed me a glass full of a white liquid.

"Now, I need you to drink all of this, okay? It doesn't taste real good, but you need to drink it all. Okay?" She held it to my mouth. "Drink it."

I tried to do what she asked, but it tasted like chalk. I'd once eaten a piece of chalk while using it to write on a blackboard at my great-aunt's school. I'm not sure why I had the urge to bite into it and chew it, but I did and regretted it. Now, in front of the nurse, I couldn't hold the liquid in my mouth. I spit it out and it went everywhere—onto my gown, the floor, and even on the nurse's uniform. She frowned and said "shit" out loud, and I knew I was in trouble. She was no longer a nice nurse.

"Call Dr. Newby!" she yelled to someone not in the room. She looked at her uniform. "Shit!" she said again.

Dr. Newby came into the room and took in the scene.

"Young lady, do you know how much this medication costs?" he scolded. He then paused. It seemed like he was sorry he'd yelled at me. He took a deep breath and exhaled slowly. He put his hand on my shoulder after first pulling the gown up over it. "Listen, Lynette, I want to help make your tummy pain go away. Don't you want that?"

I nodded silently. I felt horrible for what I'd done.

A second glass of chalk was prepared. This time it was handed to Dr. Newby. He brought it over to me. "Let's try this again, okay?"

I don't know how I did it, but I drank the whole thing and kept it down. Maybe I wanted to please the doctor so he'd tell Mama I was a good girl and he was going to take me home to be his daughter. I wanted that very much.

"Good girl, Lynette," Dr Newby said with a smile when I finished the last bit, and then he hugged me. My real daddy never hugged me. If Dr. Newby had taken me home to be his daughter, I would have drank chalk every day.

A week later, we went back to get the report, and Dr. Newby never mentioned to my mama that I'd spit up the first glass of liquid chalk, never mentioned that I'd made the nurse say "shit" out loud. Why couldn't my daddy be as nice as Dr. Newby?

"Anne, the barium swallow showed that Lynette has a stomach ulcer! I've never seen this in someone so young." He stood up, walked over to Mama, and put his hand on her shoulder.

"A stomach ulcer? How'd she get an ulcer in her stomach?" she asked. Now she put her hand on his and started stroking it, looking up at him—maybe for comfort, even though I was clearly the one who needed to be comforted.

"Good question." He looked at her, not removing his hand from her shoulder. "She's only nine. Hard to say. Anyone else in your family have a history of ulcers?"

"No, I don't think so."

"Has she been under any stress lately? At school? At home?"

"No, not that I can recall."

Finally removing his hand from Mama's shoulder, he said, "Well, the good news is that she will be fine—but no fried foods for a while. The ulcer needs to heal and then her pain will go away."

"Thanks, James." That was Mama's response, it seemed, to every-thing Dr. Newby said.

"Let her decide what she wants to eat for now. Don't force her to eat anything she doesn't want, okay?"

"Thanks, James."

For the next few months, I ate peanut butter and jelly sandwiches on Wonder Bread. I liked milk, so I only drank milk. I poured milk on my Kellogg's Corn Flakes and Frosted Flakes. Like Tony the Tiger said, "They're grrreat!" I was also *cuckoo* for Cocoa Puffs with milk, just like the TV ad said. I ate cereal for breakfast, lunch, and dinner. I ate mashed potatoes with lots of butter on them and potato salad and macaroni salad and green beans. No collard greens for me! I missed eating fried chicken, but I was glad I didn't have to eat chitlins or pig ears or pigs' feet! Dr. Newby said that I didn't have to, and Daddy and Mama couldn't do anything about it. I was a nine-year-old with a stomach ulcer, and for once I got to eat what I wanted to eat.

For once, I was in control.

Chapter 3
Ben Casey

FOURTH GRADE AT the elementary school in my new neighborhood started September 5, 1961.

It had only been three months since our big move from a unit in Roberts Park Housing Project in Norfolk, Virginia, to a house in a city across the Elizabeth River called Portsmouth. Only three days since Mama had last *clumsied* herself into a fat lip and a sore jaw.

I'd heard a few people ask, "Anne, what happened to your lip?" and I'd heard her reply: "I fell. Clumsy me."

I knew better, of course. For Mama to survive all these moments of indignity, there was nothing to do but forget. Out of sight, out of mind. I think Mama had hoped the move would change things between her and Daddy. But if she had, she'd been disappointed. Different city, same life.

For me it was a different story. I'd been hatching my escape plan ever since that night on the porch a month earlier.

The first inklings of an actual plan arose for me while watching television.

It was September 27, a Thursday, when Mama said, "Lynette, come watch this new show with me. It's called *Dr. Kildare*."

"Okay, Mama." I was confused but also intrigued. It was a school night, and I was in my nightgown getting ready for bed. Besides, Mama rarely asked me to do anything with her.

Dr. Kildare aired in black and white at 8:30 p.m. on NBC and was an hour long. By 9:30 p.m., I was usually out like a light. Not that night, though. I sat down on the floor in front of the TV while Mama sat on the couch and eagerly waited.

The show opened with a frantic-looking woman entering the emergency room holding an unconscious boy. She started explaining why the boy was unconscious but got interrupted during the opening credits. *This kid is unconscious! He needs help! Help him!* The episode elicited a sense of urgency in me, so the credits flashing on the screen were upsetting. The scene played out far too slowly for my taste.

Mama didn't seem to mind. At the end of the episode, she said, "I like this new show."

I thought what she *liked* was Richard Chamberlain, who played the lead. But she didn't ask me for my opinion, and I didn't offer one. I went to bed with no comment.

The following Monday was October 2, and another black-and-white medical doctor show aired, this time on ABC. This one was called *Ben Casey*. Mama let me stay up again, probably since she'd let me watch *Dr. Kildare* the week before. Did she have a premonition of things to come?

I took my same spot on the floor. Mama was in the kitchen.

"Mama, the show's starting!" I yelled, thinking, *I hope this is better than that* Dr. Kildare *show.*

"I'll be there in a minute!" she yelled back.

Ben Casey opened with syncopated background music—*Duh duh duh duh duh duh duh duh!* A man pushed a gurney through double doors in a hospital. I leaned into the opening song. *BEN CASEY* appeared in white capital letters, momentarily obscuring the man, but unlike in Dr. Kildare, the scene continued. The man was in a big rush as he pushed that gurney through the hospital hallway.

I was immediately intrigued by the drama. Someone was on that gurney covered in a sheet. Who was it? Was the person alive or dead? *Must be alive*, I reasoned. *No reason to be in such a hurry for a corpse.*

I moved closer to the TV set. Mama stayed in the kitchen.

Hospital personnel looked at the man as he pushed the gurney past them. A woman dressed in a white uniform looked on. She wore a cap like the one I'd seen on a nurse on one of my ER visits. A man with thick black-rimmed glasses appeared. He wore a top like the ones worn by the doctors who'd examined me. He quickly glanced at the gurney as the scene changed to a view from the person on the gurney.

I knew it! They're alive!

I saw what he, or maybe she, was seeing: the ceiling, the overhead lights. The gurney stopped and a dark-haired, dark-eyed, serious-looking man appeared and looked down. The person on the gurney was his next patient. I looked into the doctor's eyes. I felt he was looking back at me!

Starring Vince Edwards appeared across his chest in white letters. Next, an older man appeared on the screen. He had bad teeth and looked like Harpo Marx. *Sam Jaffe* appeared on the screen as he scrubbed his hands at a sink.

The final scene was an operation in progress. Everyone wore scrubs, scrub caps, and masks, even those who observed from seats looking down into the room. The syncopated *duh duh duh duh duh duh duh duh* theme music continued.

Mama's "minute" lasted the entire length of the show, but I barely noticed. I was hooked. At the end of that first episode, I turned away from the TV and yelled, "Mama, I'm gonna be a doctor!"

"That's nice, child," she replied.

She had watched none of that *Ben Casey* episode while she piddled around in the kitchen, yet she'd let me watch it when I should have been in bed on a school night.

By the end of that first episode, I wanted to be Dr. Ben Casey. It was an epiphany like none I'd ever experienced. Becoming a doctor was my way out! I didn't know how to make that happen, or who to even talk to about it. Maybe the library would have answers for me. If they were there, I knew I'd find them.

The next day at school, I knew my mission. I went to the library and found books on becoming a doctor. The path was pretty clear: Go to college. Then go to medical school.

No problem! I was motivated.

Mama had gone to college for two years but had dropped out to marry Daddy, have kids, make peanut butter and jelly sandwiches wrapped in wax paper for our brown-bag lunches, and get fat lips and black eyes from *walking into walls*. That was not going to be my life—no, siree!

When I told Mama I was going to be a doctor, I thought she wasn't really listening. But about two weeks later, a toy medical kit appeared on my bed. It was a red plastic box with a white cross on it. Inside was a black stethoscope, a plastic syringe, a yellow rubber hammer (to test reflexes, it said in the directions), a thermometer, and an otoscope (to look into ears).

Armed with my new instruments, I rounded up the neighborhood kids. I took my stethoscope and listened to their chests. I hit their knees with my reflex hammer. I looked in their ears with the otoscope. They were my patients, and I was Dr. Charity.

It didn't take long for them to start running away when they saw me with my doctor kit, especially after the neighbor girl across the street from me, Celestine, told on me.

"Don't you let Lynette give you a shot," she yelled. "She sticks you with a pin!"

I admit it. I used a safety pin that Mama used for my little brother's diapers to give shots. It was quick: one little poke and I was done. I even put a Band-Aid on afterward. I knew what I was doing. Between the pains in my legs and my tummy aches, I'd been to the local hospital's emergency room a few times. I'd picked up many doctoring tips as I watched all the goings-on there.

"Nurse, draw some blood and send that patient to x-ray," I'd observed the doctor command.

"Yes, Doctor," the nurse replied.

Yep, I was going to be a doctor, just like Ben Casey, MD, and just like those doctors in the ER. Finally, people would listen to me. I would stop being invisible and unloved.

Yet there was a difference between my reality and the world of TV make-believe. I'm not sure when I first noticed that all the real doctors and nurses who took care of me were colored and all the make-believe doctors and nurses on TV were white, but eventually, it dawned on me.

Did it make a difference? Not to me.

Dr. Ben Casey gave me hope for something, though I couldn't have said exactly what it was at the time. I read the *Encyclopædia Britannica* and the *World Book Encyclopedia* for guidance. A door-to-door book salesman had talked Mama into buying them the year before. I was so glad he had, because now that I was nine I saw college in my future. I was going to be a doctor!

I read my *Weekly Reader*. I read about an eleven-year-old orphan girl who was sent to a farm at Green Gables to live. I read about a young girl who lost her parents and went to live with her grandfather on a mountain in the Swiss Alps. I dreamed of traveling there someday. I was eager to explore the unknown. Did I care that these two girls looked nothing like me? Did I care that Ben Casey was a man and also had no resemblance to me? No.

One day Mama came to my room and said "Here." It was a globe of the world. She never talked to me about my dream, but she knew, as soon as I spoke it out loud that night watching Ben Casey, MD, that I wanted to get away. Why else would she have first given me that toy medical kit and now a globe of the world?

In hindsight, these small acknowledgments of my dream were her way of saying, "Lynette, you will not suffer the same fate as I did." She'd fallen into a life of spousal abuse with no apparent way out, but she didn't want that for me.

Later, when I was a young woman, Mama finally told me that she left me alone back then because she knew that I would be able to take care of myself. She called me "tenacious."

Chapter 4
Matches

IF DR. NEWBY wondered how a nine-year-old developed a stomach ulcer, I never heard about it. It's possible he mentioned something to Mama about how unusual it would be for a nine-year-old to have enough stress in their lives to manifest such symptoms. Then again, maybe he followed the tried-and-true custom of not butting into other folks' business.

I wondered whether he speculated about my daddy's drinking, if my mama ever told the good doctor how her husband used her as a punching bag. If he had known, would he have rescued us and taken us home to live with him? Maybe.

My first memory of seeing Mama get punched in the mouth by Daddy was when I was three years old. It was so scary. Crying, "Mama! Mama!" I ran to her, grabbed her around her waist, and tried to hold her tight.

She pushed me away as she wiped her bloody lip with a dishtowel. "Go on, Lynette. Go outside and play."

I wanted to help her, but I didn't know how.

The next time Daddy was liquored up again, he hit me. Not in the mouth or stomach like Mama; he took off his belt and hit me on the backs of my legs while he shouted, "Don'tchu *ever* do that again! Ya hear me!"

"Ow, Daddy! Me and Steve were just playin' Matches," I tried to explain.

He wasn't listening. *Whack! Whack!*

We still lived in the Liberty Park Housing Projects in Norfolk, Virginia, back then. I had two older brothers, Butch and Steve, and the three of us were always sent to bed around eight o'clock and Daddy and Mama would stay up in the living room watching TV.

The night of that whupping to the legs was a Friday night, a drinking night for Daddy. When we went to bed, I saw that Mama was drinking a beer with him.

I fell asleep only to be woken up by Steve saying, "Lynette, wake up," and shaking me.

Rubbing my eyes, I said, "Stop shaking me, Steve. Why you in my room?" My bedroom was dark except for a light from somewhere outside that came through the slightly opened venetian blinds.

"Wanna play Matches?" he whispered, holding an object close to my face.

I looked closer. It was a book of matches. I'd seen them all over the house. Mama and Daddy both smoked.

I didn't know this game, but it was my big brother asking me to play with him. He *never* wanted to play with me. Whenever I asked him to he'd say, "I can't play wit you. You're a girl!"

Now he wanted to play with me, so I said, "Uh-huh."

"Okay, let's go in the closet." He grabbed my arm and pulled me out of bed.

Inside the closet was real dark. He left the door open just enough so a little light could get in. I blinked my eyes a few times, trying to see better.

"Sit down on the floor," he ordered.

I sat down with my legs tucked under my light-blue nightgown with flowers on it. Steve had on his pajamas too.

"Just do this," he said as he tore a match out of the matchbook and ran it across the bottom. It made a scratchy sound and burst into flame. The flame was yellow. I could now see his face. He was grinning. Then he blew it out.

Darkness again. There was some smoke and a stinky smell.

"Your turn," he said. He tore a match out and handed it to me.

I scratched my match on the matchbook like Steve had showed me. It burst into flames. I grinned. It was pretty.

I dropped it in my lap, but I forgot to blow on it first. The lit match began to burn a hole in my nightgown. I jumped up. Steve jumped up. I opened the door to the closet and ran into the living room screaming, "Help! Help!"

Daddy was snoring on the living room couch. I didn't see Mama. "Daddy! Daddy!" I screamed.

He woke up. He saw me. The first thing he saw was the big burnt hole in my nightgown. Instead of pulling the nightgown up over my head to get it off of me, he grabbed the collar and pulled straight down. It ripped apart and fell to the floor. I stood in the living room wearing only my panties.

He turned me around, first looking at the back of me and then the front. "You burnt?" he asked.

"No, Daddy," I said, calmer now. "Me and Steve were playin' a game called Matches and I dropped my match before I blowed it out." I was about to find out that it wasn't necessarily a good idea to tell the truth.

"Playin' wit matches! Playin' wit matches! Steve! Where you, boy?"

He took off his belt and started in on my legs—*whack, whack, whack*—while I hopped up and down trying to get away. No such luck. He had a tight grip on my left arm. I finally stopped moving and sat on the floor crying. Steve was crying over in a corner even before Daddy gave him his whupping.

"Playin' wit matches! Anne!" Daddy shouted.

Mama was already standing in the hallway; she startled when she heard Daddy call her name. She must have heard the commotion and come out of the bedroom, but she'd made no move to interfere.

Daddy had never punished me before, and I couldn't remember him ever having punished Steve or Butch before, either. Doling out whuppings was Mama's job—but not this particular night. She just stood there and didn't say a word. I wonder if she thought he would give her a whupping too. After all, it was her job to manage the children and keep them from playing with matches and potentially getting burned.

"I'm here, Chairdy," Mama said. She walked to where I stood shivering and handed me another nightgown. "Lynette, put this on."

It was my second favorite. Light yellow with no flowers. She picked my favorite one up from off the floor, now torn up and with a big burnt hole in it. I watched as she balled it up and threw it in the trash.

Now I was crying hard. The whupping hurt, but seeing my nightgown thrown in the garbage hurt even more. I had three nightgowns and two sets of pajamas, thanks to my granny. Granny had taken me to the department store to get my favorite one. I loved that nightgown because I'd picked it out. My other sleepwear had been purchased for me without any input from me. I wore them all without a complaint, but that nightgown was the only one I'd loved.

Steve was still crying too. Daddy had hit him more times than he had hit me. And harder.

"Steve, you know better," Mama said. "You older. Serves you right. Now y'all go to bed."

And that was that. Daddy sat down on the couch. He was breathing hard and sweating and mumbling.

After that, Daddy never hit me again. Whether or not he was distressed by his own behavior, I'd never know. But after that, he left the whuppings of his children to their mama. He saved his whuppings for her.

Mama later told me that my daddy was deeply upset about his behavior that night.

"He was so scared that you had been burned, and when he realized you were okay he lost control," she said. "He decided at that moment that he would never hit his children again."

I wonder if he ever thought about giving me a hug and comforting me. Probably not.

Also, you won't hit your children, but it's okay to hit your wife? Made no sense.

The next morning, I looked at the belt marks on my legs. They didn't hurt. I went into Steve's room. Butch was still asleep, or at least he was acting like he was asleep. My guess is, he wanted no part of what had happened the night before. He wouldn't have asked me to play with him. He was convinced that boys didn't play with girls, not even a game called Matches.

Steve was sore at me for snitching. "Why you tell Daddy we was playin' wit matches?" he demanded, scowling.

"I told him that we were playin' *Matches*!" I protested. "That's what I called it."

I didn't understand that in Daddy's eyes there was probably little

difference between "playing wit matches" and "playing Matches."
Steve's either, it seemed.

He folded his arms over his chest. "I'm never gonna play wit you
again."

I was now feeling sad about telling Daddy the truth. I didn't have
any friends. My one chance to become friends with my brother, and
I'd blown it! Why did I forget to blow out the match before dropping
it? Why did I run out of the bedroom and scream? It's not like I was
on fire. The match burned a hole in my nightgown and put itself out.
Was it my fault that I didn't know how to keep a secret? I was only
three years old.

Regardless, now there would be no more playtime with Steve. He
meant what he said and said what he meant, and he was as true to
his word this time as he was any other: we never played anything
together again.

Mama was in the kitchen cooking breakfast. I thought about asking
her to buy me another nightgown, but I didn't. Daddy was now in
the bedroom sleeping. There was fried bacon on a paper towel on the
counter. It smelled good. She took some scrambled eggs and poured
them into the skillet filled with the grease from the bacon. That
smelled good too.

Mama wasn't smiling, but she wasn't crying, either. She was just
being Mama, acting as if nothing had happened.

When she noticed me, she said, "Lynette, go tell yo brothers
breakfast is almost ready. And don't wake your daddy. He fell asleep
late. You scared him last night. He thought you got burnt."

Daddy had looked scared. I'd sure been scared too, though.

After he tore off my nightgown and saw I wasn't burned, I wanted him to hold me close and say, "There, there. It's okay." Instead, he beat me. It made no sense.

I didn't much like my daddy. He was mean to Mama, and he didn't seem to like me much. He never picked me up or gave me a kiss on the cheek or told me, "I love you, Lynette."

I didn't much like Mama, either. She wasn't like any of the mamas on TV, or even like Miss Bea next door. Miss Bea hugged her children. Sometimes I wanted to be hugged, too.

The next week Mama told us, "I'm having a baby."

That didn't stop Daddy from hitting her.

Chapter 5
Leavin'

"I'M LEAVIN' CHAIRDY, Bea! I cain't take it no mo!" Mama whispered as she hung a wet sheet on the clothesline.

I quickly looked up, then back down at the blanket where I sat in the backyard of our unit. Mama had told me to stay put and play with Gwendolyn, Miss Bea's daughter, while she hung laundry she'd washed, rinsed, and squeezed through the wringer to get out as much water as possible on the metal clothesline that stretched the length of our small swatch of grass. That *line* was nothing more than two metal poles about six feet apart with two thick metal wires strung between them, a mesh bag filled with wooden clothespins attached at one end. Just two short lines for a husband who drove a truck and sweated a lot, two young sons who were always getting dirty "rippin' and rowin,'" and a daughter who sometimes played like a boy.

For once I was happy to *stay put*, but I knew there'd be *hell to pay* if Mama noticed in the slightest that I was listening to her *conversating* with her friend and our next-door neighbor Miss Bea. The grown-ups in our neighborhood, at our church, and even at the grocery store constantly reminded us children that we should be seen and not heard. To speak out of turn would result in a slap across the mouth or a whack on the butt. And this could be done by anyone without creating a ruckus. The neighborhood raised the children, not just the parents.

In my three years on the earth, I already had spent a lot of time being *seen and not heard*, and in doing so I'd heard a lot myself, all of which I had recorded closely. I had heard the yelling between Daddy and Mama after Daddy had been drinking. I had seen the bruises and black eyes on my mother when the yelling turned to one-sided fighting. And I had seen and heard my Mama tell the *I'm gonna leave him* story more than once.

Will she really do it this time? I wondered. *Where would we go?*

"He's hit me one too many times, Bea!" she whispered as she touched a swollen, dark purply spot on the right side of her face just above her puffed-up eyelid and simultaneously rubbed her belly. Baby number four was due in a few months; she rubbed her belly a lot these days.

She stood by her clothesline as she looked into the twin yard of her friend while she too hung wet clothes to dry in the sun.

Mama was dressed in a sleeveless pink button-down blouse—too big on the top, but just right where it draped over her middle and stopped below her bulge. She had on white pedal pusher pregnancy pants. She was tall and bony-thin other than her pooched-out belly. Her light sweat-covered skin glistened as the sun reflected off the tiny beads building up on her face and arms. She was beautiful despite the black eye.

Mama never hugged me or grabbed my cheeks and said "I love you" like I'd seen other mothers do, so I decided that it was true what I'd heard her say more than once to my brothers—"If you two keep acting up, I'm gonna give you back to that lady down the street!" I felt that I was part of the return policy, even though I did very little to make her mad.

Though my mama was just trying to get us to behave, most of the time I was ready to go live with that lady down the street. Why had she given us away in the first place? Would she take me back if I asked her to? Where did she live?

I wasn't really sure if I wanted to go back with *that* lady, who might hug me or say "I love you," or stay with *this* mama, who didn't seem to love me but did feed me and buy me coloring books and clothes to climb trees in, though. I knew I was better off not to *act up* and to just *stay put.*

This Mama, who didn't love me, was going to have a baby girl—a little sister for me! I knew it even if no one else did. She had to have a girl, because my little sister would love me and I would love her back and we would be together forever. She had to have a girl, because I was tired of being the only girl with two older boys.

"I toldya, Anne, 'specially with dat baby coming. You gotta go." Bea spoke in a muffled voice distorted by the clothespins she held in her mouth as she hung a man's gray uniform shirt on her clothesline. Her husband and my daddy worked together at the Norfolk Naval Shipyard.

For a three-year-old, I knew a lot—because all the time I was seen and not heard, I was also listening and remembering.

I sat on that blanket in the backyard, braiding, unbraiding, and rebraiding my doll's hair. Gwendolyn sat across from me dressing one of her doll babies. It was a hot, humid Saturday morning. It was laundry day for all the mothers in the neighborhood, just like the next day, Sunday, was church day. I knew my days of the week real well. I knew a lot of things that maybe a three-year-old shouldn't know. I knew how to read and write and color within the lines, thanks to my older brothers, who showed me the homework they brought back from school. I could count to one hundred and add and subtract too. I never shared this knowledge with anyone, however, because no one seemed interested in what I could or couldn't do. The only one I shared it with was my friend who lived in my head. She listened to me count or read and told me, *Good job, Lynette!* She was always there for me.

"Why you keep doin' dat, Lynette?" Gwendolyn asked when she noticed that my doll baby's hair kept getting a do-over.

Gwendolyn was almost five and I played with her only when my Mama insisted. She didn't like to do anything I wanted to do, like climb trees or read books or count clotheslines that ran from one end of our building to the other end.

There were only three clotheslines — one-two-three — but Gwendolyn wasn't interested.

"My mama says that I'll learn how to count when I start school," she told me.

"But I can teach you just like my brothers teached me, Gwendolyn."

Not. Interested.

So, I pretended to like playing dolls with her, as I needed the distraction so that I could hear more of Mama's conversation as she hung another sheet on the clothesline.

"I want her hair to be real pretty, Gwendolyn," I lied as I unbraided the doll's hair again.

"Where you gonna go, Anne?" Miss Bea asked, and my ears perked back up.

"I'm gonna take the chilren and go live with my granny. She says she can get a bigger place for all of us to live in."

"Well, good," Miss Bea whispered. She leaned in and spoke close to Mama's left ear, but I still heard what she said: "Next time he might kill ya!"

* * *

On a Saturday in mid-August, we moved from Liberty Park to Roberts Park, another housing project, to live with Granny—Mama, Butch and Steve, and me. We moved and left Daddy behind. Mama washed all of Daddy's clothes a few days before we moved. She hung them on the clothesline to dry and ironed his work uniforms.

Daddy didn't make a fuss about us leaving. I think he knew he wasn't a nice man when he got drunk. I think he knew he didn't deserve such a wonderful wife who never fought back. I think he knew he might someday kill her if she stayed.

Daddy stood in the doorway of our unit, smoking one of his Camel cigarettes. I knew the word, *C A M E L*, that was written in block letters on the carton he kept in the kitchen. The word was just above a picture of a camel in the desert with pyramids. Steve had explained it to me. Steve didn't play with me after that night we both got whupped for playing Matches, but he did continue to teach me stuff like words on cigarette packs.

Mama smoked Marlboros. It took me a while to learn how to pronounce that word. I couldn't ask Mama—I knew she would probably just say, "Never you mind, girl!"—so I just listened real close when she'd ask Daddy, "Chairdy, you seen my Mall-bur-ros?"

Daddy was wearing a white undershirt, his gray uniform pants, white socks, and his steel-toed work shoes. I wasn't sure why he had on his work clothes since it was a Saturday. *Probably 'cuz he slept in them*, the friend inside my head said.

I had no one else to talk to, so when this voice showed up, I welcomed the company.

Daddy took a long drag and looked down at the front steps as we passed by him and blew out a smoke ring without looking up. He smelled like Aqua Velva rather than his usual "likker" smell. He had shaved. He looked like a nice daddy. We piled into my great-aunt Hunter Sue's big light green Oldsmobile—three children in the back seat and Mama in the front with Hunter Sue. My brothers took the windows, so I sat in the middle.

Hunter Sue was the only family member who owned a car. She was a school principal and she made lots of money, I thought. How else was she able to own a car *and* a house?

I liked her car. I sounded it out—"O's-Mo-Beel"—while I sat stuck between my smelly brothers waiting to leave. *Good job, Lynette!* my friend said.

"Bye, Chairdy," Mama said quickly from her rolled-down window as we drove away. She sounded like she was saying goodbye to one of the church ladies—"Bye, Doris" or "Bye, Miss Alma"—rather than Daddy.

We children said nothing. There was no "Bye, Daddy," or "I'll miss you, Daddy." I don't know about my brothers, but I was happy to get away from him. He hurt my mama. He hurt Steve. He hurt me.

"I'm sorry, Anne," Daddy said before we drove away. He dropped his cigarette on the porch, stamped it out with his shoe, and went inside and closed the door. And that was that.

Mama sat straight up in her seat and didn't say a word during the trip to Roberts Park. Butch and Steve made goofy faces, sticking out their tongues and crossing their eyes at each other but were otherwise also silent. I was unable to see anything in my middle-seat position, so I just talked to my friend in my head. If we had been alone, I would have talked out loud to her, but for this ride, I talked inside my head so no one would know my secret.

You think we gonna come back here? I asked.

No, Lynette, she replied.

It didn't stick, but at least Mama tried to choose her children and herself over her abusive husband. Thank goodness for the strong women around her. If they had not intervened, Daddy likely would have killed her.

The day that Mama and Miss Bea were outside hanging clothes, Mama already had a plan to get away, and it was devised by Granny and Hunter Sue. I heard Mama whispering to Granny on the phone—"Okay, Granny, I'll come live wit you. I sure can use your help wit this baby coming." I heard Mama whispering to Hunter Sue on the phone—"Hunter Sue, thank you for the money. I don't know if Chairdy will give me any money if I leave him." They convinced her to leave, offering housing and financial support. And she followed through.

But something unforeseen occurred while Mama and her fellow escapees lived a reasonable life with Granny—something no one, not Granny or Hunter Sue or anyone else, could have imagined.

She told me later in life, "I made my bed and had to lie in it." Yet her mother, my nana, had left my abusive grandfather, divorced him, and remarried. Maybe she was able to escape because she had only one child in the situation. My mother, meanwhile, had three, with a fourth on the way.

Chapter 6
Granny's Place

MY GRANNY LIVED in the Roberts Park Housing Project in a one-bedroom upstairs unit. Before moving in with her, I only knew that my nana, her daughter, lived in New York City. The day Mama left Daddy, Hunter Sue dropped us off at the bottom of the stairs. She didn't stay. Hunter Sue was the sister of Nana's ex-husband, my maternal grandfather, whom we called Grandpop. Enough said.

Granny opened the screen door when she heard us coming up the stairs. It was summertime and we were drenched from the humidity. Most people kept their front and back doors open during the summer to get a breeze. Granny's unit was one way in and one way out through the front door. There was no breeze.

"Come on in," she said.

"I'm sorry, Granny," Mama said. "I had to get away."

"Shush!" Granny interrupted. "Not in front of the chilren, Anne."

Granny was a diminutive, very dark-skinned woman. Mama towered over her. It was evident that her characteristics came from her daddy. Grandpop was light-skinned and tall. And my nana, Granny's daughter, was also light-skinned. Granny never spoke of a Mr. Cotton, and no one ever asked. She was born Mary Elizabeth Cotton in 1893, which put her age at sixty-three years old when my pregnant mother, my two brothers, and I moved in with her. She was Mama's grandmother and we were her great-grandchildren, but we called her Granny just like Mama did. Even as a great-grandmother, "Granny" suited her.

Granny was no-nonsense. And she didn't put on "airs" like some of the church women. She didn't have to, because whatever she wore was covered by the dark purple choir robe. Granny sang in the choir, and I loved hearing her sing. She was down-to-earth and a respected member of her neighborhood and our church. If Granny suggested something, it behooved you to listen.

Before moving in with her, we saw Granny in church and every other Sunday for dinner. Now we saw her all the time. And it was crowded at Granny's place. Hot, humid, and crowded. Two adults and three children. No breeze.

Under their breath, my brothers said, "There ain't enough room in here and it's hot!" They knew if they spoke too loud, Granny or Mama would knock them *pizzle upwards* for their back talk. Granny had some strange sayings she never explained—and we never asked. None of us ever wanted to be knocked pizzle upwards *or* downwards. Both sounded scary.

When we first got to Granny's place, I looked up and thought, *That's a lotta steps.*

I counted them as I climbed up. I took my time.

One, two, three, four, five, six, seven, eight, nine, ten, eleven, twelve, THIRTEEN! I finished triumphantly. *Granny's got thirteen steps from down on the ground to her front door. I can count them every time I go up and then back down. Thirteen plus thirteen equals twenty-six.*

I loved numbers and counting. I sometimes heard neighborhood ladies tell Mama, "That Lynette of yours, she smart."

Mama and Daddy never said that to me. They never said, "Lynette, you are our pride and joy! So smart! You're only three and you can read, and you know your multiplication tables. We are so proud of

you! Let us give you a hug." Nope. There were no *I-love-you*s in our
household.

I wanted Mama to be more like some of the neighbor ladies. Why
couldn't Daddy stop drinking and just be nice? Why couldn't either
of them play with me and read to me? All they ever said was "wash
your hands" or "go to bed" or "go outside and play until I call you for
dinner."

I thought maybe now that we were away from Daddy, Mama
might pay more attention to me.

Maybe, said the friend inside my head.

At Granny's we all slept in the living room. Mama got the sofa. The
boys slept on the floor. Mama made me a bed by putting two chairs
together and using pillows to make a mattress. It was okay. I knew
that soon I'd be able to sleep in my own bed, because Granny told us
we were going to get a bigger place.

"I talked to the housing manager about it," she told Mama.

"Okay, Granny," Mama replied. She took in a deep breath and let
it all out as she plopped down on the sofa that doubled as her bed.

It took a few months, but Granny did it. She got us a bigger place.
It was a three-bedroom, two-story unit located down the street from
where we were. Granny got some neighbor men to help us move.
They even went to Daddy's and picked up furniture from there.
When moving day came, we walked down the sidewalk, and when
we reached the new place, I memorized the address.

"Two Seven Four Six Li-ber-i-a Drive," I sounded it out quietly.
"Two Seven Four Six Liberia Drive, 2-7-4-6 Liberia Drive!"

Granny opened the screen door and walked in. She looked
around.

Mama was right behind her. "This is nice, Granny."

Butch, Steve, and I pushed in after them.

"It has an upstairs, Mama!" Butch shouted.

The living room and kitchen were on the first floor. The kitchen had a door. I decided to go take a look. It led to the backyard. I opened the door and the screen door. There was an audible whoosh as a breeze entered the stuffy unit. With the front door open in anticipation of the movers, opening the back door started a noticeable temperature decrease. The stuffy, hot, humid air changed. The air now beckoned me to step outside and explore the backyard, but I hesitated when I heard Steve ask Granny, "Can we go upstairs?"

Granny said, "Y'all go on up. I'll be there in a minute."

Steve and Butch raced each other to the top of the stairs. I followed very deliberately, counting the steps as I went. There were thirteen. I remembered that Granny's upstairs unit had thirteen steps outside to get to the front door. This unit had thirteen stairs inside to get to the second floor.

"Mama, it's got three bedrooms up here," Steve yelled down. "Which one's gonna be ours?"

"Mama, the bathroom's up here too!" Butch shouted.

"Granny, which bedroom do you want?" Mama asked. Granny got first dibs, she knew that.

"Let me see," Granny said.

She climbed the steps one at a time, holding on to the railing. Mama followed.

"I'll take this one," Granny said, pointing to the bedroom next to the bathroom that looked out onto the backyard.

"Well then, boys, you can take that bedroom," Mama said, pointing to the one closest to the stairs. Its window looked out onto Liberia Drive.

"And I'll take this one for me and the baby," she said as she peeked into the bedroom farthest from the stairs. It also looked out onto Liberia Drive.

I ran into the bedroom that she chose for herself and my soon-to-be baby sister and looked out the window. Liberia Drive was full of activity. There were kids riding bikes and roller skating. There were people sitting outside their units just signifying. (That's what Granny called it when people were being nosy, getting all up in your business.)

This bedroom had plenty of room for Mama, her furniture, and me since the baby wasn't even born. Why couldn't I sleep in it with her?

And if not with her, then where? I did the math. There were three bedrooms. The boys had a room. That's one. Granny had a room. That's two. Mama had a room. That's three.

"Lynette, you gonna sleep wit Granny," Mama said as if she'd heard my thoughts.

My brothers snickered. They were used to sharing a bedroom. I was the only girl in our old place, so I'd had my own room, with its own tiny closet. It was just big enough for my bed and my dresser. I'd also had a tiny table and chair where I colored in my coloring books and read my picture books and talked to my friend inside my head or to my dollies. Now I was going to sleep with Granny.

I sighed, wishing I could just sleep on two chairs put together with pillows as a mattress in Mama's room.

I moped my way downstairs and went out to the backyard. There were no trees like in Liberty Park and no permanent clothesline on the grass. Our yard was separated from the yards on either side of us by a tall hedge. I couldn't see over them. There was a metal tube in the ground in the middle of the yard.

I walked out of the yard and onto a path that stretched the full length of the backyards of the units. I peeked around the hedge to my left and saw a lady hanging clothes on what looked like a metal umbrella that the wind had caught and turned inside out. The long metal handle was inserted into that metal tube. It had three rows on which to hang clothes.

"Hello, little girl," she said.

"Hello," I said back. Then I ran back into the house.

Granny had propped the front screen door open. We heard a commotion outside and then a man appeared at the opened door.

"Where you want the couch, Miss Mary?"

Miss Mary was what everybody called my Granny. All the adults in the community were called "Miss" or "Mr." by children and many adults. It was the custom, like saying "Yes, ma'am" or "No, sir." This was taught at an early age, and if you forgot, there'd be trouble—a whack up the side of the head or a butt whupping. Maybe someone had been knocked pizzle upwards for forgetting.

"Put it up against that back wall, Mr. John."

Granny stood in the middle of the living room area, hand on hip, and pointed to the wall farthest away from the front door.

"That's a good place for dat couch don'tcha think, Anne?" Granny said to Mama—not really expecting an answer, I think. No matter what Mama said, the couch was going to stay right where it was.

Granny didn't own much furniture. For the living room, she had a couch, two end tables with lamps, a big, upholstered chair, a coffee table, and a rug big enough to cover most of the concrete floor. For the kitchen, she had a metal table with a yellow top and four metal chairs with yellow vinyl seats. Since there were five of us, a neighbor gave her a mismatched chair. For her bedroom, she had a full-size bed, a chest of drawers, a rocking chair, and a dresser with a mirror.

While they were moving in Granny's furniture, more friends of Granny's came with Mama's furniture from our old place. They took her bedroom set and put it in her room. I guess Daddy had let her keep it.

Where Daddy gonna sleep now? I wondered—then thought, *I don't care, as long as it's not here!*

A man took a crib up to Mama's room. Next came my brothers' bunk beds, their dresser, two desks, and two chairs.

My furniture never arrived.

The last piece of furniture was Mama's piano—black, shiny, and really big. It came with a bench that opened up. Inside were pieces of paper with scribbles on it. Mama called it sheet music. I remembered Mama playing her piano a couple of times at our old house. It sounded nice, but she never played it when it arrived at the new house. It became part of the living room décor. The piano bench became extra seating when Granny had company and we children were not allowed to lift the cover that protected the piano keys.

Though Mama never played her piano after we moved, I later learned that after the baby was born, she found work at a juke joint nearby where she played for tips. She had a built-in babysitter in Granny, so she could stay out late on Friday nights. We had church on Sundays, so she didn't do much playing on Saturday nights.

I walked into the kitchen and saw something moving in the sink. It peeked out at me and then disappeared. I went over to the sink, stood on my tippy toes, and looked in.

"A roach, Granny! Granny, there's a roach in the sink!"

"Oh, pay them no nevermind, child. They just as a-scared of you as you a-scared of them. I'll take care of it in a minute."

Roaches were part of the way of life in Virginia—here and at the other place we'd lived too. No getting around it.

* * *

By Saturday evening, Granny had killed some roaches, Butch and Steve had gone to sleep in their bunk beds, and Mama had gone to sleep in her bed alone without Daddy. The bed-in-waiting for the baby's arrival stood empty against the wall by the window.

As for me, I prepared to sleep with Granny.

Granny's bed was plenty big for the both of us. I don't know which one of us fell asleep first once the light was out. As I fell asleep, I thought, *Is Daddy gonna give my bed and dresser to another little girl?*

I couldn't have known it at the time, but I would be Granny's roommate for the next five years.

I awoke Sunday morning and Granny was not in bed. I heard her and Mama downstairs. Now Sunday was church day, but no one appeared to be making any preparations. I went downstairs and there were Mama and Granny, putting kitchen items away.

"Mama, we goin' to church?" I asked.

"No," she said, "we gotta clean this place up. Since you up, you can help. Put this in the pantry." Mama handed me a big bucket. I didn't have time to find an excuse not to do it.

My brothers probably knew better. I didn't hear a peep out of them from upstairs. When they finally came down, Mama put them to work too. It was unusual not to go to church, but I wasn't gonna complain.

We cleaned all day. After dinner, Granny stood. "Anne, I'm gonna go to bed early. Tomorrow is a workday," she told Mama.

Granny worked for a white family as a housekeeper. Mama said that Granny's official title was "laundress." Sounded fancy.

We went upstairs to bed together, and this time I heard Granny snoring before I fell asleep. I guess she was plum tuckered out.

I was awakened Monday morning by Granny yawning and stretching. She turned on a lamp on her bedside table. She had set all her clothes out the night before and started to get dressed. I peered over the top sheet and watched her. She put on a gray uniform dress that buttoned in the front over her undergarments. Next came her stockings and black shoes with a low, broad heel. She had a work wig and a church wig to cover her almost-bald head; today, she put on her work wig. Next she put in her dentures, and lastly she applied some facial powder, a little lipstick, and some clip-on earrings. She took one quick look at herself in the dresser mirror before turning off the lamp, grabbing her purse, and leaving.

After she closed the door behind her, I heard the *clomp, clomp* on the floor as she went first to the bathroom and then downstairs. I knew she would have a soft-boiled egg, two strips of bacon, toast, and a cup of coffee with lots of cream for breakfast. That's what she had every morning.

When she finished, I heard the front door open and close and the screen door screech open and then slam. Mary Cotton, the laundress, was headed to the bus stop. She'd make a right on Liberia Drive and then a left on Grand Bassa Drive, which she'd walk down to Princess Anne Road. The bus would come, she'd get on, and have a seat.

I'd see her that evening.

Chapter 7
Settling In

FRIDAY NIGHT, GRANNY didn't come directly to bed the way she normally did. She and Mama had been talking for a while when Mama said, "Lynette, go upstairs now."

I did what I was told and tucked myself in under the covers. It wasn't long before I heard the sound of a pop-top can opening woke me. And then I heard Granny slurp from the can and say, "Aaahhhh."

I turned under the covers to see what was going on. The room was dark except for light coming through the window from the streetlight on Grand Bassa Drive. Granny was sitting in her comfy rocking chair, looking out the window. She had raised the venetian blinds just enough to see out.

I stared as Granny pulled something out of her house coat. She struck a match and held the flame to what was in her hand. She took a puff. It turned red. It was a cigarette! Now I knew Mama and Daddy smoked, but not Granny! And when she put the can back up to her mouth, it wasn't soda, it was Schlitz Malt Liquor. Mama had bought it. I remembered her asking Granny, "Where you want the Schlitz Malt Liquor?"

"In the icebox," Granny had replied.

I'd thought it was Mama's at the time. But that couldn't be right. Mama was pregnant. She had given up smoking and drinking because of the baby. So, it was Granny's?

I watched as she made smoke rings in the room, illuminated only by the streetlight outside. When she inhaled, the end of the cigarette glowed red, and when she exhaled, she blew smoke out of both nostrils. She was good at making smoke rings, just like Daddy. When Mama did smoke, she never got the hang of making a smoke ring. She would watch Daddy do it, but just couldn't quite do it herself. I loved the way Granny held her cigarette between her thumb and index finger, her palm turned up. Daddy and Mama held theirs between their index finger and middle finger with the palms turned toward their chests. Granny looked elegant when she smoked, like this white lady I once saw on TV who was sitting in a chair wearing a pretty dress and pearls.

Granny heard some activity outside. She picked up the blinds a little higher. "Look at them chilren rippin' and rowin'. Wey dey parents? They should be in bed." She spoke to no one in particular and obviously didn't care that her three-year-old great-granddaughter was in her bed and could hear everything.

My church-going Granny, who loved her God, had a secret. She was a member of the choir. She sang hymns every Sunday, two days after, a brewski and a cig. Had she been doing this all along? In church, I loved watching her sway from side to side, caught up in the syncopated rhythm of songs such as "That Old Rugged Cross." She was a Nubian goddess dressed in a dark purple robe with gold trim, wearing her black-framed cat-eye eyeglasses, her sparkling white dentures, and her *Sunday-go-to-meetin'* wig.

Granny often talked about people being *trifling*. When husbands "stepped out" on their wives or when they didn't pay the rent on time because they spent it drinking or when some of the moms let their kids run around in dirty clothes, Granny would say, "They are just trifling, that's all that is! Trifling!" She'd say about someone—"He ain't got a pot to piss in or a window to throw it out of." That night, for the first time, I saw Granny piss in a pot in the bedroom! It was a white metal pail that she kept under the bed. I knew it was there, but I hadn't known its use before that moment. We had a bathroom. But why bother to walk from the bedroom into the hall to the toilet when you had a place to go right by your bed?

Mama told me later that Granny had grown up without an indoor bathroom. They'd had something called an "outhouse." I guess that meant Granny was used to peeing without a seat. It seemed that way to me when she pulled out that pot, lifted her nightgown, squatted over that pot, and did her business like it was nothing. The pee hit the sides of the metal pail and made a *ping-ping* sound. She wiped herself with some toilet paper. I guess she kept a roll in the bedroom for this reason.

When Granny was done doing her business, she eased back into her viewing throne. She puffed. She slurped. She observed.

Eventually, I fell asleep.

When Granny woke up in the morning, she took her pot straight to the bathroom to empty it, clean it, and replace it under the bed. She made sure our bedroom didn't smell like a bathroom. Our regular bathroom stayed stinky because of my two trifling brothers, who sometimes missed the toilet and never cleaned up after themselves.

The Sunday after I saw Granny's pee in the pot for the first time, about an hour after we got home from church, there was a knock at the door.

Granny was cooking, so I went to the door and opened it.

A short, really old man was standing there. I thought Granny was old, but this man seemed twice her age. He was bent over and couldn't seem to straighten himself. He was dressed in a suit, white shirt, and tie and wore a straw hat.

"Hello there, young lady. My name is Mr. Ash. Is Miss Mary at home?" He carried a grocery bag in one hand.

Granny must have heard him because she yelled, "Ash, come own in!"

Mr. Ash removed his hat before entering and stood at the door until Granny said, "Ash, take off your coat and have a seat on the couch. I'll get you a glass of sweet tea."

He put the bag down on the coffee table and removed his suit coat, revealing his long-sleeved white shirt. "Thank you, Mary," he replied as he sat down. "It's still a hot one out there. How was church? Oh, and Mary, I brought you some white potatoes and some collards. Next time let me know what I should bring."

I wondered why, if Mr. Ash thought it was so hot, he decided to wear a long-sleeved shirt. Did he only own long-sleeved shirts?

Granny went over and took the grocery bag into the kitchen. "Thanks, Ash."

I was curious who this Mr. Ash was, but there was no way on God's green earth I was going to ask Granny. So I waited for Mama to come downstairs.

"Anne, Ash is here!" Granny yelled up the stairs.

"Okay, Granny, be right there," Mama called back.

My brothers had changed out of their church clothes and would be outside playing until Mama called them for dinner. When we got home from church, she changed clothes, set the table, and started cooking. Mr. Ash had arrived at the right time. The chicken was fried and sitting on a platter, the potatoes were mashed and displayed in a pretty blue bowl, the potato salad was in a yellow bowl in the icebox covered with Saran Wrap, and the green beans sat in a smaller blue bowl on the table with a big dollop of butter melting over them. All Granny had to do was pop the rolls in the oven.

"Hi, Mr. Ash," Mama said as she came downstairs. She had exchanged her church dress for a pair of pedal pushers and a loose-fitting sleeveless blouse. She went over to him and gave him a hug. "It's been a while. What do you think of Granny's new place?"

"It's bigger, for sure," he said cheerfully. "But since the furniture is the same, I feel I'm still in her old place. I've missed coming by for dinner these past few Sundays while you got settled. Mary thought it best. I'm looking forward to doing this again starting today. Your grandmother is a mighty fine cook, Anne."

"Stop it, Ash!" Granny interrupted.

"It's true, Mary. I should know. You've been feeding me for a while."

The adults were talking, so I just sat on the lowest step of the stairs and said nothing, just listened, in hopes of finding out more about this Mr. Ash. That didn't happen.

Later, when I was a teenager, I learned that Mr. Ash was a widower. After he and Granny met, they'd started having dinner together on Sundays.

Mama went to the front door and opened it. "Butch! Steve! Dinnertime!"

They were playing right out in front. "Yeah! I'm hungry!" Butch said.

"Me too!" Steve said.

My brothers had dinner roll–eating contests. It was a sight to see. The winner was simply whomever ate the most rolls at dinner. I never participated. Wasn't asked to. But even if I had been, I would certainly have lost. I could never eat more than one; my brothers, on the other hand, could eat ten or more—and this was in addition to other fixings!

Granny had gotten another chair and the six of us sat tightly around the kitchen table meant for four. Mr. Ash wasn't a big eater, either. His eyes were set on Granny. I watched him watch her. He had kind eyes. Granny never mentioned a Mr. Cotton, and yet Mr. Ash seemed like the perfect mate for her. Granny could do no wrong around Mr. Ash. She didn't have to put on any airs. Granny was Granny: bra off, wearing a duster, and stockings rolled down to her ankles. He, dressed always in a suit, was the perfect gentleman around her. I was able to see a different kind of colored man in Mr. Ash. I could never imagine him hitting a woman.

We were living in a housing project. I had to share a bed with my great-grandmother. There were roaches. Yet life at 2746 Liberia Drive was nirvana compared to the life we'd had with my father. We didn't have much, but we had peace and quiet, and that was priceless.

Those years we lived with Granny, we let our guard down, relaxed, and started to live a more normal life. My brothers made friends. Mama made friends. My friends continued to live in my head, and we spent many days at the neighborhood community center reading and coloring while we all awaited the baby.

My sister.

Chapter 8
Beverly

IN LIBERTY PARK, my brothers were in school all day, and when they weren't, they did *boy* stuff. "You cain't play wit us," they told me, "yer a girl!"

I wanted so much to play with them. Sometimes, I'd hide behind a tree and watch them. Once I *borrowed* a truck and they yelled at me, "Yer a girl, Lynette! Go play wit your dolls! Leave our toys alone. They for boys. Um gonna tell Mama!"

Like I said, after that game of Matches where we both got in such trouble, Steve never played with me again. He wanted nothing to do with me.

I was relegated to play doll babies with Gwendolyn, but I mostly entertained myself. My doll babies had voices, which I alone could hear.

Those boys are mean, Lynette, Susie said. She was my oldest doll. She had black hair and wore a pink dress.

"Uh-huh," I said.

I wanted Mama to play with me, but she before we moved, she was always busy washing clothes or making beds or picking up after my brothers and Daddy. Maybe she kept herself busy so she didn't have to pay me any attention. I wondered if she would ever find time to play with me.

After we moved, Mama still didn't play with me. "Lynette, I'm big as a house! I cain't play with you," she said whenever I asked, which was less and less frequently.

My future playmate and sister, Beverly Joanne Charity, was born on January 6, 1956, at Norfolk Community Hospital, the Negro hospital. Butch and I had also been born there. Mama hadn't made it to the hospital in time for Steve. She'd had him at home with Granny's help.

All Mama said of Beverly's arrival was, "The doctor got there in time to cut the cord. That's it!"

A friend of Daddy's who had a car brought Mama and my sister home.

"Anne, she is a beautiful baby," Granny cooed as she grabbed Beverly out of Mama's hands.

"Let me see! Let me see!" I shouted, jumping up and down. "I have a sista! I have a sista!"

My brothers were still in school, so I had her to myself. Well, almost. Until Daddy showed up.

"Look at my baby girl," he said, all smiles. He paid me no nevermind.

Beverly was so tiny, and after Daddy had had his turn, Mama let me hold her.

"Go sit on the couch and scooch all the way back," she instructed me.

I got on the couch and pushed myself back until my legs stuck straight out. My back was right up against the back of the couch, creating a perfect spot on my lap for my little sister.

Mama handed me Beverly, who was wrapped up in a blanket. I knew she had arms and legs, but I couldn't see them. Mama put Beverly's head on my arm and the rest of her in my lap. She'd been making a fuss, but as soon as she was in my lap, she stopped.

"Now, hold her head up," Mama told me. "She cain't do it herself yet. You don't want her head to go backwards, okay?"

"Yes, ma'am."

I loved Beverly from day one. I told Susie that I needed to take care of my baby sister for a while and wouldn't be able to play with her as much. She stopped talking to me. I think she was mad.

Over the next few weeks, Mama let me dress Beverly and give her a bath with her help. It was fun, except when she had a stinky diaper. When she cried, I'd rock her back and forth and hum like Granny did, *um um um ummm,* and say, "*There, there,*" and she'd stop—at least sometimes.

"It's okay, Beverly," I'd say, "your BIG sista is here"—and she'd look at me and smile.

When Beverly got bigger, we spent our days having tea parties with our dolls. Susie was talking to me again. We made mud pies that we baked in the sun. I was so happy to have a sister. We were going to do everything together. I didn't need my mama, my daddy, my brothers, or Granny. I had Beverly.

Beverly and I never fought. One time she did hit me—don't know why. She was two. She hit me on the head with a toy baton while we were watching TV—*WHACK!*

"Beverly! Why you hit me?" I asked as I rubbed the sore spot on the top of my head.

"Don't cry, baby, don't cry, baby," she said. She held my face in her tiny hands and looked into my eyes, and I could tell she was real sorry.

She didn't mean it, I thought. *But if I cry, Mama will come and rub my owie and hold me and say, "There, there."*

I tried to act like I didn't need Mama, but her comforting me would have still been nice. There were so many times I could have used a hug. But she never did hug me.

In Roberts Park, just across the street from our unit, was a concrete playground. No grass. The swings, the monkey bars, the one basketball hoop, and the see-saw had been cemented into the concrete. I once ran to Mama after scraping my knees falling on the cement in the playground. I'd been on the swing, trying to touch the sky, and decided to jump. I'd done it lots of times before, but this time, I didn't stick my landing. I fell over onto my knees.

"Mama, look!" I said, showing her my bloody knees.

"Oh, it's just a scratch," she said, and she licked her fingers and wiped the blood away.

That did nothing. The blood oozed out of the scratches again.

She wiped them again.

"You'll be fine," she said mildly. "Go on back to playing."

No hug. No "there, there baby" like Granny did for Beverly. No "Mama time" for me when I needed to be comforted.

When Beverly hit me, I saw a chance to get Mama to pay attention to me.

So I began to cry.

It was just an act, but Beverly didn't know that. "Don't cry, Ninette," she said sweetly, "don't cry." She used her tiny hands made into little fists to wipe away the *tears* that weren't there.

I began to wail—"Owie owie owie!"

Mama came. Finally.

"Beverly hit me, Mama," I whimpered. I gave the best impression of a child hit by a toy baton as I could muster.

"Beverly, why you hit yo sista?" she snapped. "You go upstairs to bed this instant!"

Beverly stopped consoling me and went toward the stairs leading up to Mama's room, where her crib was. Mama swatted her as she went by. Her diaper and rubber pants made a *pfft* sound. In silence, she made her way upstairs, climbing each step using both arms and both legs, almost crab-like. She wasn't tall enough to use the handrail. Thirteen steps—and then she waddled and *swoosh swooshed* all the way to her room. The crib made a creaking sound as she climbed over one side. She'd learned how to do that early on. And then there was nothing but silence from upstairs.

"Ow, Mama, my head hurts," I whimpered as I rubbed the spot where the baton met my skull.

"You okay, Lynette. It's just a toy baton. Go back to watching TV." She returned to the kitchen.

Now I cried real tears in silence. Mama was gone. Beverly was gone. I was alone.

I wiped my tears away as I turned back to watch TV.

I'm sorry, Beverly.

The next morning, Beverly jumped on my bed with a bright, "Hello, Ninette!" Unlike with Steve, all was forgiven. She loved me and I loved her.

I was smart—and Beverly was smart too. In our neighborhood community center, she and I spent most of our time putting together jigsaw puzzles, drawing, and coloring. I read books to her like *Fun with Dick and Jane*—"See Spot run. Run, run, run." She liked Baby Sally and Spot the Dog.

"Dog!" she'd squeal as she pointed to Spot on the page. She was going to be just as smart as me. It was fun.

We never left the neighborhood except to go to church or to see Hunter Sue and Grandpop and Mamma.

Some thought us calling our mama "Mama" and calling our paternal great-grandmother "Mamma" was weird, but no one in my family seemed bothered by it. Mamma was born Annie Noah Seaborn in 1888. Her first husband, Nehemiah Washington, was the daddy of Hunter Sue and Grandpop. Mamma was "cultured" and she could pass for an older white lady. Like Granny, she worked for a white family—though she worked as a cook, not a laundress. She had used her position to elevate her knowledge. She'd helped Hunter Sue attend college, get her teaching certificate, and become one of the first Negro principals of a school. She had groomed her son to be educated too, but Grandpop had gotten Nana pregnant while they were in high school. And they were forced by the families to marry, for the sake of the child.

Mamma didn't like Granny or her daughter. She did, however, love her great-grandchildren. The set schedule of alternating Sunday meals allowed her to stay connected to us without having to communicate with Granny.

Beverly and I spent bad-weather days at the community center and good-weather days playing tea party with our dolls in the backyard. And making those mud pies. Susie sometimes just wasn't in the mood to talk, but I didn't mind because I had Beverly.

On a nice May day, Miss Massey, the activities director at the center, saw me drawing with Beverly.

"Lynette, I want you to learn this poem for the summer recital," she said, handing me a sheet of paper with several lines of words on it. The poem was titled "Smile."

The Roberts Park Community Center had a summer recital every year. Miss Massey would pick children to recite poetry or sing a song or dance. It was an honor to be chosen. It was well attended by the families in Roberts Park, especially if they had one of "the chosen" in the recital.

The poem began, "Smile, smile every day." Over the course of June, I memorized the poem and recited it at home over and over again for practice. The recital was in July. Beverly watched and ran around saying, "Smile, smile everwy day!"

On the day of the recital, I sat in the audience with Mama and Beverly.

Miss Massey stood in front of the audience, clipboard in hand. The stage with three short steps leading up to it was behind her. "Next up is Lynette Charity, daughter of Anne Charity and great-grand-daughter of Miss Mary Cotton. Her poem is titled 'Smile.'"

I stood to make my way to the front but stopped when Mama said, "Where's yo sista?"

I looked around.

Where she go? Oh, there she is.

She'd used her tried-and-true crab-walk method, hands and feet, to climb those three steps and now she stood before the audience. She wore her yellow sun suit with straps that crisscrossed in the back and white sandals.

She started, "Smile, smile . . ."

Miss Massey turned to face the stage when she heard the

imposter. "Little girl, you need to get off the stage," she interrupted, a little perturbed.

"My name ain't widdle girl!" Beverly replied, hands on her hips. "My name is Bewerly Jowanne Chairdy!"

Miss Massey picked her up and placed her in the aisle. She was not pleased with my precocious sister interrupting her recital. Mama grabbed Beverly by the arm and plopped her back in her seat. She sat quietly, swinging her pudgy legs back and forth. "Smile, smile ewery day," she said very softly.

"Shh . . . " Mama said.

I walked up the stairs and recited the poem. Miss Massey clapped. Mama clapped. And then others in attendance clapped. Beverly clapped as she rocked back and forth in her chair. "Smile, smile, everwy day!"

We walked home, Mama holding each of us by one hand. It was a short walk, and Beverly repeated "Smile, smile, everwy day, smile, smile everwy day," until we reached the back door and went inside.

Chapter 9
Sorry Ain't Gonna Bring Her Back

It was another hot, humid summer day in Roberts Park. A Friday. Beverly would be three years old in five months. I was six. We played in the backyard while Mama hung clothes on the clothesline. Granny was at work being a laundress. Our brothers, now nine and ten, were *rippin' and rowin'* somewhere in the neighborhood. The sun was high in the sky and my green sleeveless blouse stuck to my back as the sweat rolled down from the top of my head. Beverly wore her favorite yellow sunsuit with the straps that crisscrossed in the back and her red Keds with white anklets.

Butch and Steve came running toward us.

"Mama, can me and Steve take Lynette and Beverly to go get ice cream? Puhleeze?" Butch begged, eyes closed and grinning from ear to ear.

Mama turned to Butch. She held a wooden clothespin in her mouth, dangling like one of her Marlboros.

"All right, but you two watch out for yo sistas, ya hear? Hold their hands."

"Yes, ma'am," Butch and Steve said in unison. She said this every time. We knew the drill. Butch held my hand and Steve held Beverly's hand as we left home.

"Ice queem!" Beverly squealed.

We knew the route well. Right turn on Liberia Drive to Grand Bassa Drive, left at Grand Bassa and one block to Princess Anne Road, a four-lane street split in two by a median strip. This was the street where Granny got on and off the bus for work. We arrived at Princess Anne Road. We were four happy siblings, hand in hand, as we crossed the first two lanes and stood in the median strip. We all looked left and then right. We were skilled at street-crossing. There was very little traffic that day. Butch and I, Steve and Beverly, still hand in hand, watched the traffic for our chance to cross.

"Beverly, what kind of ice cream you gonna get?' I asked, even though I knew the answer.

"I get manila. I want manila ice queem!" she squealed.

THUD!

"Beverly!" Steve shouted.

It happened so fast. A car, a big black one, came up onto the median strip and ripped Beverly from Steve's grasp. It carried her forward.

"Stop the car! Stop the car!" someone screamed.

The car abruptly stopped, then lurched forward again.

"Oh my Lord!" another person cried out.

The car tried to keep moving forward, tried to escape, but a crowd formed quickly in front of it and on its sides and blocked it.

A man in the crowd banged on the hood of the car.

"Hey, mister! You done run over a li'l girl! I think she dead!"

While people yelled and screamed, blocking the front of the car, a small figure lay motionless on the asphalt, face down, at the rear of the car. It wore the same yellow sun suit with straps that crisscrossed in the back as my little sister. But it couldn't be Beverly, because those straps, as well as the body wearing it, were blackened by tire dirt. The body wore one red Ked on the left foot. The right foot was shoeless. The other shoe lay in the gutter nearby.

Butch stood on the median strip, shaking and making a sound like a hurt dog. I had heard an injured dog once. I think someone had beat it or hit it with a rock. It was making a *yow-oooh* sound over and over again. Butch's crying sounded like that dog.

I looked at him, not able to register what had just happened. *What's wrong, Butch?*

Steve stood exactly where he'd been when Beverly had been ripped from his grip, wailing and hitting himself.

Steve, why you doin' that?

I heard people yelling, "She dead! She dead!"

What is dead?

"Where's Beverly?" I asked no one in particular.

Someone in the crowd spoke: "Mr. Jackson, will you take these chilren home and fetch Anne?"

"Yes'm. Come own, chilren."

A man I didn't recognize grabbed my hand. My brothers walked alone behind us. We left the median strip and crossed the two lanes that headed back toward the house. There was now no traffic in either direction. All cars had stopped. Butch was crying so hard that his tears met his snot and everything rolled down his face onto his T-shirt. Steve continued to inflict punches to his head as he cried. He was mumbling to himself.

I stared up at the man as we walked. He wore gray pants and a gray shirt. He smelled good. *Who's this man? He knows where we live? Does he know my mama? Maybe he knows Granny?*

Mama came up the street toward us. Her face didn't look like Mama's. It looked like a mask. Steve saw her and cried more. Butch looked down at the ground.

What's wrong wit Mama?

"Mama, where you goin'?" I said as I tried to grab her.

Her mask face turned back into her Mama face, but it was a sad Mama face. "Go home, Lynette. Go home wit yo bruthas."

The man took us back to the house and left right away. My brothers went straight to their room. They left me downstairs alone. I sat in the chair by the window. I looked out through the blinds in the living room window, looking for Mama. She was gone a long time.

Eventually, a knock came at the door. I opened it and found Mr. Red, a good friend of Granny's, standing there. He came inside.

"Where yo bruthas, Lynette?" he asked in a soft, kind voice.

"Dey upstairs in dere room," I said. "I think dey cryin'."

"Well, um gonna stay wit ya 'til yo mama comes back, okay?"

I nodded.

Mr. Red was a *high-yeller* Negro with freckles and red hair. That's what the grown-ups called him. I listened even though I wasn't s'posed to.

They said, "Yeah, Red could pass if he wanted to. Yeah! He *light-skinned* enough to *pass* for a white man."

I wanted to ask Mr. Red why he'd want to pass for a white man, but I remained *seen and not heard*.

A while later, Mama walked through the door with her mask face on. She became Mama again when she saw Mr. Red, though.

"Hi, Mr. Red. I had to stay up there until the ambulance came. It took her away. They said there was nuthin' they could do. I talked to the white man who was driving the car. He said he was sorry. Well, sorry ain't gonna bring her back now, is it? His sista was in the car wit him. She was yellin', 'You nigras get away from our car!' I tell you, Mr.

Red, I thought those men were gonna turn over that car and beat up that man, so I had to stop it. I didn't want them gettin' into trouble over this. Now, Mr. Red, you gotta meet Granny's bus, okay? Don't let her hear about this from nobody but you, okay? This probably gonna kill her. I don't know what we gonna do." Mama sighed and shook her head side to side.

"You 'bout right 'bout dat, Anne. Beverly was *her* baby! It's a cryin' shame!" Mr. Red shook his head just like Mama did. "I'm gonna go up dere right now and just wait. She be 'long soon."

Mama and I knew when Granny was on her way home because she was screaming, wailing, screeching, and moaning long before she reached the front door. When Mama opened it, Mr. Red was holding Granny under her left arm and another man was holding her under her right arm. They entered and helped her to the sofa.

"Oh, Lordy, Lordy! Oh, Lordy, Lordy! My baby! My baby!" Granny wailed. She plopped down and immediately fell over onto her left side. Mr. Red put her feet up, shoes and all.

Ooooh, I thought, *Granny don't like no shoes on her couch! But dey's her shoes. I guess dat's okay?*

The attention centered on Granny while the three surviving Charity children were ignored. No one asked us, "Are you kids, okay?" No one explained to me that being dead meant that my sister was never coming home. Butch and Steve were older. Maybe they knew. Or did they?

I sat in the chair in the living room. Granny lay on the couch, moaning and saying, "Lord have mercy" over and over. Butch and Steve were still in their room.

"Mama, where's Beverly?" I asked.

"She's in heaven."

"Can I go see her?"

"Lynette, go upstairs and go to bed," she said wearily. "Don't worry me right now."

I left that chair in the living room and went upstairs. I waited for Beverly to make her way upstairs the way she did, crab-walking and *swoosh-swooshing* all the way. I waited to hear the creak of the crib as she climbed in.

I fell asleep waiting.

In the morning, there was no Beverly.

Beverly Joanne Charity: born January 6, 1956; died August 15, 1958.

Beverly's funeral was held at Graves Funeral Home, a Negro-owned establishment, on August 19, 1958. It was a Tuesday. The room where the funeral was held was an ample-size area near the entrance. A few rows of folding wooden chairs, divided by an aisle, faced a lectern and a tiny pink coffin elevated on a stand. There were flowers all around and a wreath at the foot. Mama and Daddy talked to people while I watched. I watched everybody.

A woman wearing a big hat covered with flowers approached Mama. Her dark-colored dress stopped just below her knees. Dark-colored heels and dark-colored stockings completed the outfit. She grabbed Mama's hands—she had big hands too!—and held them between hers as she looked at Mama with tears in her eyes. "Anne, she's wit her Father up in heaven now."

Huh? Wit her father? In heaven? Daddy's right over dere. He ain't in no heaven. I frowned and gave my head a little shake. *Where's heaven, anyway?*

A man dressed in a dark suit, white shirt, and dark tie followed the big-hat lady. When he spoke, I jumped. His voice sounded like Reverend Freeman's when he used a microphone. But this man wasn't holding a microphone.

He pointed upward and said, "She's wit the Lord, God Almighty! Amen! Hallelujah!"

What dat mean?

Daddy had said something to me about God the day I woke up and realized Beverly wasn't coming home. He said, "Why didn't God take you instead of my Beverly? She was my girl!" He was crying, and I could see he was angry. Even though I was only six, I also knew he was drunk.

Truth is, I agreed with him. I didn't really know what death was, but I thought I'd prefer it over having to live with the fact that my father and maybe others felt that the wrong daughter had died. I had always felt disconnected from my family; something was just not right when it came to my relationship with all of them. Beverly, though—she'd been special in a way that I could never be. I had felt the calmness she'd brought to our world. She was not just a ray of sunshine; she was the whole sun. And now she was gone, and I had to live in the aftermath of her brief presence.

I kept trying to worm my way into my parents' grief, but all my attempts were unsuccessful.

I tugged on Mama's dress and tried to get in her lap. "Mama, why did Beverly go away?"

Mama pushed me away. "Lynette, you need to go sit down over dere with your bruthas. The service is 'bout to start."

I sat beside Steve. There were tears in his eyes that he didn't bother to wipe away. Butch was crying too as he sat next to Mama. Daddy was on her other side.

My brothers wore dark suits and bow ties and white shirts. They wore the same clothes they wore to church. Daddy wore a suit too. I wore a light pink dress with a wide collar, patent leather shoes, and white anklets. Mama had put a bow on one of my plaits.

It was unusual to see Daddy all dressed up. He didn't go to church with us anymore; I hadn't even known he owned a suit before today.

Mama wore a dark dress. Granny's dress was black. She sat across the aisle from us, her face hanging down. She took off her glasses and wiped her eyes with a white handkerchief. The tears flowed faster than she could wipe. The moles on her face looked bigger and darker than usual.

Nana had come all the way from New York City. She had visited when Beverly was born, just as she had for all the other Charity grandchildren. This visit, in contrast, had not been planned.

Nana sat beside her mama, my granny. Grandpop sat beside Nana. Mama told me they used to be married, but Nana now had another husband. Grandpop's real name was Kenny. He was from a place called the West Indies, and I knew he spoke funny—"with an accent," Mama told me. Aunt Hunter Sue sat beside Grandpop.

My other great-grandmother, Annie Holloway, whom we called Mamma, was there too. It was confusing for me to have two people I called *Mama*, so in my head I always called her by her full name, Annie Holloway. Before she sat down, she came over to speak to Mama. I noticed she smelled good. I loved how she smelled.

After talking to Mama, Annie Holloway sat in the last seat in the row. She sat stiff-like. She held a fancy handkerchief in her lap. It was white, but the edges were a light blue.

Some of Daddy's folks sat in chairs behind us, but they were strangers to me. It was Mama's people who helped us.

Reverend J. Jasper Freeman—the pastor of our church, Queen

Street Baptist—started to speak. He wore his robe from church. He read from his Bible. He preached like he was in church. He said "God's will" and how "Beverly touched so many lives in her time amongst us" and how "Beverly was too good for this Earth." I wasn't really listening. I stared at the small pink box.

Beverly's in dere?

The sermon and singing of hymns finished. It was now time to view the body.

Mama and Daddy were the first. They walked toward the box hand in hand.

Why were they getting up? What were they doing up there? Why was this happening? How could Beverly be in that box? I knew she wouldn't like being boxed up like that. It wasn't right.

Mama wiped away her tears with Daddy's white handkerchief. She gave it back to Daddy and he wiped his whole face. He was sweatin' and cryin'. He smelled of his cigarettes and the whiskey he'd drunk the night before.

They came back to where we kids were sitting. "Okay, boys, you go now," Mama said. "Take your sista. Go kiss Beverly goodbye."

Butch took my right hand and Steve took my left hand. With me between them, the three of us slowly walked to the coffin. Butch and Steve were crying. They each bent over and mimicked what they saw Mama and Daddy do. I was shorter, so they hoisted me up.

"Go own, Lynette, kiss Beverly goodbye," Butch said.

I tilted my head and looked at him.

"Lynette, just do it, NOW!" he said in a quiet but forceful voice as he pushed me farther into the pink box.

I did what my big brother told me to do. I kissed IT. But the thing in there was not my sister. It was an ugly doll baby. It smelt real bad. It was cold. It was even wearing lipstick and red powder on its face like how Granny did when she went to church. Why?

This ritual of kissing loved ones "goodbye"—whose idea was that? Maybe for adults who can process the event, but not children. It was an image I'd never be able to wipe from my memory, much as I wanted to. Because that thing inside the coffin was not a doll baby but the bloated, embalmed corpse of my once-beautiful sister.

I now know that the smell I encountered that day was embalming fluid and formaldehyde. In an attempt to make Beverly appear presentable for the viewing, face powder, rouge, and lipstick had been applied, though she was just two years old. Just a week before Beverly's death, Great-Aunt Hunter Sue had returned from New York City with matching dresses for me and Beverly. I wore mine for the funeral, just that one time. She wore hers in the casket, and would wear it until she and her dress were no more.

Ashes to ashes, dust to dust . . .

Chapter 10
Seeing Red

No ONE SPOKE of Beverly after her funeral. Any pictures of my sister were put away in the back of some drawer. Memories were put under lock and key. *How could someone so loving be forgotten so quickly?*

Although I have no memory of the actual event, a black-and-white picture was taken of the three surviving Charity children sometime after Beverly's death. In the picture, we're in the living room at 2746 Liberia Drive. Butch and Steve stand behind a chair where I'm seated. They wear dress pants, long-sleeved white shirts, and bow ties. The closed drapes that separated the living room from the kitchen hang behind us. I have been posed by someone—my left leg bent at the knee and placed under my right leg, which dangles toward the floor. The dress I wear has a frilly collar. My white anklets and black patent leather shoes are visible in the shot. We are smiling.

Later, someone cut out a photo of Beverly, sitting in her rocking chair, from another photo and put it into the picture just to the right of us. It looked so out of place. She was dead. In the rocking chair, Beverly is smiling. No one mentioned why this was done. Just like the other pictures, this one found its way into a drawer not long after it was taken.

My brother Kevin Leon Charity was born on April 18, 1959, approximately nine months after Beverly was buried. He was the replacement child. He was created to fill a void left by Beverly. Unfortunately, my father was angry that Kevin wasn't a girl. As aloof as he had been with me, so was Daddy with my new little brother. Mama was behaving as a mother should, but something was missing. I think she loved Kevin, but not like she'd loved Beverly. As for me, I thought Kevin was a cute baby, but I had no room in my heart for him.

Granny, at least, was happy to have another baby to distract her from the loss of Beverly.

If you wonder how a new baby arrived nine months nearly to the day of Beverly's funeral since Daddy didn't live with us, I'll fill you in on what I didn't learn until Mama was in her eighties.

"I was distraught after Beverly was buried," she told me. "Your Daddy was so so sad too. So I let him stay with me for a couple of days. And stuff happened. I was lonely, Lynette."

For me, even though Beverly was gone physically, she remained a voice in my head. I couldn't let her go.

Two weeks after Beverly's death was my first day of school. I attended Bowling Park Elementary School, which was located within walking distance of Roberts Park. Mama and Beverly were going to walk with me on the first day, but I ended up going it alone. Mama didn't seem interested in accompanying me.

"You gonna walk with me, Mama?" I asked hopefully when it was time to go.

"No, Lynette," she said, "you go on. Just follow the other chilren."

As I walked to school on that first day, the kids were so mean.

Why did they think that teasing me about my dead sister was okay? They stared at me and pointed their fingers at me and continued to remind me that I was the girl whose sister got run over by a car. One boy poked me and said, "Your sista is dead. Your sista is dead." I felt the anger bubbling up inside of me. The voices said, "Hit him! Hit him!" So I did. I punched him in the gut.

As soon as we all arrived at school, he told his teacher what I'd done.

"Yes, ma'am, Lynette hit him," the other kids said. "He wasn't doing nothin'. She just hit him."

I told the teacher that he'd poked me, but she told me that I wasn't anyone special and I couldn't go around hitting people. I wanted to tell her that I didn't *want to,* but something inside of me *needed to.* Instead, I said nothing. No one could understand how filled with grief I was. My grief made me angry and made me want to fight. I wasn't special, but I had suffered a profound loss that could never be undone.

Beverly's name was never mentioned at home, and my teachers at school offered me no comfort either. I felt that people wanted to avoid me. It seemed to me that children continued to be seen and not heard, and that included not expressing grief about losing someone to death. So there was no one to talk to. I was alone in my grief, not even understanding that what I was feeling was *called* grief. I just knew that my heart ached for Beverly.

My whole being hurt. It took all my focus and effort to believe that I was going to survive in the world without my little sister.

My acting-out continued into second grade. Teachers whispered about me. They remarked about my angry outbursts. One teacher said she'd heard that I'd given a boy a bloody nose. (She was correct; he'd teased me about my sister.)

When were people going to stop reminding me that my sister had been hit by a car and killed right in front of me? They just kept reopening that wound. One day, I overheard two teachers talking about "that Charity girl."

"If you ask me, the wrong sister died," one teacher said to the other.

"You right about that," the other replied.

Maybe they were right. Beverly never would have bitten a girl in her forehead over a damn crayon! I got a spanking with a paddle for that one and was sent to stand in the corner of the classroom. I didn't care.

When Mama found out that I had bitten Theresa Tripp in the forehead, she also gave me a whuppin'. I shed no tears. I felt numb.

No Beverly. No feeling.

I spent hours and hours praying to God to give me back my sister. I made promises that I would *be good*, and that I would *go to church and like it*. I wanted him to give her back. When he didn't, I became mean. I wanted everyone to go away and leave me alone. I just wanted to go be with my sister.

That night after the biting incident and my whuppin', Mama sent me to bed without dinner.

"Anne," I heard Granny say, "I don't know what you gonna do wit dat girl. She's got the devil in her! I need to talk some sense into that child."

"I don't know, Granny," Mama said. "I punish her and she don't even cry. She don't even care."

She was at her *wits' end*, as Granny would say.

Granny tried to talk some sense into me. She told me that I

needed to stop this nonsense. I needed to *pay them no nevermind.*
"You need to get the education, child," she counseled me. "Dat's goin'
to make things better. You cain't do that if you always fightin'."

I couldn't listen. I felt so much rage, and I didn't know how to
control it. I wanted to fight. I wanted to scream. I wanted to disappear. No one understood what was happening to me, including me.

At the beginning of second grade, Kevin was five months old. Granny
had another baby to help raise. At the end of second grade, Great-
Aunt Hunter Sue went to Mama and asked, "Would it be okay for
Lynette to come live with me for the summer?" She must have seen
that Mama was overwhelmed, and perhaps she was responding to the
rage everyone saw in me. She told Mama she had things that would
keep me busy—new books to catalog at the school where she taught,
and classrooms to clean. "I think she'll enjoy it," she said. "And you
have the boys to deal with."

"Hunter Sue, you sure you want that?" Mama asked. "She's
become so ornery."

"Yes." Hunter Sue nodded briskly.

No one asked me. I was just told that I was going to go live with
Hunter Sue for the summer. But I didn't care. There was nothing for
me in Roberts Park. Without Beverly, I didn't go to the community
center anymore. I stayed inside or in the backyard, talking to my
voices while coloring or reading or doing my numbers. I had no
friends. And my brothers, including the baby, ignored me.

So, on a Friday evening shortly after the end of second grade,
Hunter Sue picked me up and off we went to her house.

* * *

I didn't live with Hunter Sue for very long. In fact, I never actually *lived* with her. Juju, her decrepit, blind German shepherd put the kibosh on that!

I knew Juju—we had spent time together before—but he was old and probably senile. I entered Hunter Sue's house behind her that night and watched as she greeted Juju. She patted him and then walked past him. He focused his opaque eyes on me, stared, and growled.

Hunter Sue turned around. "Now, Juju, that's Lynette. She's going to stay here, okay? Be nice."

Juju growled louder, this time baring the few teeth he still possessed.

I moved to his left. He moved to his right. I moved to his right. He moved to his left. He never took his unseeing gaze off of me. I couldn't get past him. He guarded his territory with ferocity.

"Hunter Sue, Juju won't let me by," I said. I was now scared of him. It seemed my great-aunt hadn't gotten permission from him to have another person in the house.

Looking worried, Hunter Sue walked back past Juju and said "Lynette, come on."

We went down the front steps, made a right turn, and went up the steps of the adjoining house. Hunter Sue knocked on the door and Annie Holloway soon appeared.

"Juju won't let Lynette come in," Hunter Sue told her. "I'm worried he might bite her, so I need to leave her with you and Bubba."

Bubba was Grandpop, Annie Holloway's son. They lived together.

"Come on in, Lynette," Annie Holloway said. "You can take your suitcase up to my bedroom. Put your things on the bed closest to the door."

I did what I was told and a few hours later found myself sleeping with another great-grandmother in the same bedroom. At least this time I had my own bed. But still, I had no room of my own.

I spent the summer helping Hunter Sue at her school. She was the principal at Liberty Park Elementary. I cleaned blackboards and erasers. I swept floors and pasted library card pockets in new books. I replaced old library cards in some of the books in the library with new ones. I was paid in Coca-Colas and peanut butter crackers out of the vending machines. It cost ten cents each for those delights for those who didn't have a key. Hunter Sue let me use the key and I felt special. It turned out to be a perfect way to pass the summer, and sometimes I even managed not to think about Beverly.

Annie Holloway, however, was the antithesis of Granny. I imagined Granny would say, "I don't care about setting a table. I cook the food, I put the food on the table, and you eat it!" Which we did. Mismatched utensils. Chipped serving bowls. Mason jars as drinking glasses. Paper napkins. That was Granny. And at Granny's we could eat with our fingers!

At Annie Holloway's? Absolutely not! We ate off of fine china and used matching silverware. Do you know how hard it is to eat fried chicken without using your fingers? How are you supposed to suck the bone to get that last bit of meat? I felt a lot of good chicken was wasted at Annie Holloway's.

While I stayed with her, she was determined to make a lady out of me. At first I wondered if she realized that I was only eight years old. Then I realized it wouldn't make a difference. She had worked as a cook for a white family for many years and had learned a thing or two about how to set a table properly. She was determined to teach me etiquette.

"Sit up straight, Lynette," she'd carp. "No slouching! No elbows on the table!"

Once I learned how to properly put on the linen tablecloth, we started Utensils 101.

"Utensils are placed in the order they're used, Lynette," she instructed. "Forks to the left of the plate and knives and spoons to the right."

Just when I thought I had it, she jumped to Utensils 201 and added a small spoon and fork above the plate, an additional plate she called the bread plate, and a water goblet. Lord have mercy! When would I ever drink out of a water goblet in anyone's house but Annie Holloway's?

Annie Holloway never hugged me, but her sternness and her etiquette teachings molded me. She grew on me over time, and as the summer waned, I really didn't want to return home.

I started third grade while living with Annie Holloway and being kept busy by Hunter Sue. I don't know what other kids did that summer, but I read lots and worked on my writing and my arithmetic. Steve and Butch were now in sixth and seventh grades and continued to show me their lessons when they came over to Hunter Sue's every other Sunday for dinner.

I thought I would stay with Annie Holloway forever. I would have been okay with that. Unfortunately, it was not to be.

After first grade, the school had wanted to skip me to third grade, but Mama said no. If she'd let me skip, Theresa Tripp never would have gotten those teeth marks in her forehead—at least not by me. If she'd let me skip, perhaps what happened next might have never happened either.

Miss Mignon Cooke was my third-grade teacher. She was not much taller than me. Mama said I was tall for my age, but I thought Miss Cooke was short for *her* age. In her class, I received E's for Excellent on all my schoolwork and she would sometimes say, "Class, look at Lynette's paper. See how neat it is." I loved the attention.

One day, Miss Mignon Cooke said, "Class, open your books and do the writing assignment."

I opened my writing book and saw a paragraph. The instructions said to properly copy the paragraph. It was in boring block letters, so I decided to impress Miss Cooke with a new writing skill I'd mastered: cursive.

I turned that assignment in with a big grin on my face, thinking, *She's gonna be hoopin' and hollerin' over this when she sees it. She's gonna show it to all my classmates and say, "Look at this, class. Look how neat Lynette wrote this paragraph."*

When the graded papers came back, I was dismayed. Instead of the E+++ I was expecting, instead there was a *circled* big fat U in red magic marker in the right upper margin.

I looked at the grade. I looked at her. She was frowning. Something started happening to me. My eyes widened and my nostrils flared as I quickly took in big, deep breaths and then screamed, "Miss Cooke, you gave me a U"!

"Lynette, you didn't do the assignment correctly," she explained. "We don't use cursive letters in this class. You must learn to do what you're told."

Some of my classmates snickered.

"Ooh, Lynette got a bad grade," they chanted. "Lynette got a bad grade."

"Hush up, students," Miss Cooke ordered.

My face felt hot. My palms got sweaty. I jumped out from my desk, stomped up and down, and yelled, "You take it back! You take it back!"

Miss Cooke said nothing at first.

I continued my tirade, screaming at a decibel I didn't know I had in me. "You take it BAAACK!" I screeched like an eagle as I threw my paper at Miss Cooke.

"Lyn-ette Cha-ri-ty, you will not behave in my class like that!" she snapped. "Now you go outside in the hall and stand there until I tell you to come back in."

More snickering came from my peers.

She pointed to the single wooden door that led from the classroom into the long hallway.

I stood in the middle of the classroom, my chest heaving, my fists clenched. I wasn't moving. Miss Cooke wasn't much taller than me, but she was a stocky woman. She grabbed me around my waist with one of her beefy arms and dragged and pulled me toward the door. I resisted, but to no avail. When we reached the door, she used one hand to open it and the other to push me out into the hall. She then closed the door behind her and locked it.

"Let me in! Let me in! Let me in!" I yelled, kicking at the door and banging on the window. I knew I shouldn't, but I couldn't stop myself.

"Lynette, you can't come back in until you stop this nonsense!" Miss Cooke said through the closed door.

I continued my rant, my right hand banging on the windowpane, "Let me in! Let me in! Let me—"

CRASH! The windowpane shattered, with pieces falling into the classroom and some falling onto the hallway floor. My hand went through the jagged opening in the window, and as I pulled it out a shard of glass cut across my right wrist, opening a wide gash. Blood spurted from the wound.

"Ooh, Miss Cooke, Lynette done broke that window," I heard someone say from the other side of the door.

"Oh my goodness!" I heard her say from inside the classroom, following by the clicking of her heels rushing toward the door. She quickly unlocked and opened it.

I ran past her into the classroom—covered in sweat, exhausted from my histrionics. I sat in my seat and put my head on my desk. I was breathing in big gasps.

A trail of blood from the door led her straight to me.

"What have you done, Lynette?" she demanded.

I kept my head on my desk. My head was filled with confusion. The voices were all talking at once.

"You're bleeding, child! We got to go to the school nurse!" She raised her voice a couple of notches. "Class, don't any of you leave your seats, ya hear me! There's glass everywhere. I'll send a teacher in here in a minute."

She pulled me out of my desk and wrapped a brown paper towel around my wrist. She held my wrist tightly as we left the classroom. I did not resist.

"Miss Cooke, everything okay?" one teacher inquired as we scurried by.

"Yes, Miss Johnson. Just a small acci . . . accident. Go . . . ing to see . . . the nurse." Her breaths came in irregular gasps. "Can you go check on my students? Oh, and watch out for the glass."

Miss Cooke didn't release her tourniquet hold on my right arm until we got to the nurse's station. By then, my blue plaid jumper and white short-sleeved blouse with a Peter Pan collar were speckled with droplets of blood.

"Miss Cooke, Lord have mercy, what happened here?" the school nurse exclaimed when she saw us. The paper towel was soaked through with blood.

Miss Cooke explained through pants what I'd done while the nurse removed the blood-soaked paper towels and washed the gash, then applied mercurochrome into and around the wound and covered it with a Band-Aid.

As she finished up, the principal entered the nurse's station. "Mrs. Goodman is on her way," she announced.

Hunter Sue had dropped me off at Bowling Park that morning on her way to her school. She would have planned to pick me up at around 3:00 p.m., if not for the call from the principal.

I heard her arrive before I saw her. Her heels made a distinctive *click-clack* sound. She entered the room and looked at me, lying there on the examination table. I looked back, hoping for some sympathy. I was cut and was bleeding and it was all Miss Cooke's fault. She'd given me a U!

"Lynette, get up, right now! Go get into the car!" She looked angry. No, she *was* angry.

"Yes, ma'am," I said before scooting past her and out the school doors and into her big light green Oldsmobile 98.

I wasn't alone in the passenger seat for long. Once she got in, Hunter Sue was silent. She removed her right shoe as usual, started the car, put her shoeless right foot on the gas pedal, and drove off.

When we arrived back at Liberty Park, Hunter Sue parked in the principal's parking spot and said, "Get out, Lynette," as she put her shoe back on.

I obeyed.

We walked from the car to the side entrance of the school in silence. I looked down at the asphalt. We walked up the steps. Hunter Sue opened the large door and we entered.

Miss Pittman, Hunter Sue's secretary, welcomed us cheerfully at first, but then she got a look at me. "Lynette, what's that on your clothes?" she asked, brow furrowed.

"Blood," I replied as I gazed down at the floor.

"She cut herself at school, Pittman," Hunter Sue said. "That's why they called me to come get her." She turned to me. "Lynette, go to the library and see if Miss Smalls needs any help."

My head jerked up. I felt a sense of relief. Whatever punishment lay in wait for me, I had been given a reprieve for at least this moment in time. Hunter Sue had a school to run, so for now my punishment was to go help out in the library—which for me was no punishment at all.

"Yes, ma'am," I said, and quickly sprinted out the door.

Miss Smalls was a diminutive woman, not much taller than the students at Liberty Park. She seemed to enjoy my company on days Hunter Sue brought me back there once my school day ended. I wondered what her plans would be for me today.

"Hi, Miss Smalls," I said in a tiny voice when I walked into the library.

"Why, Lynette, child, what you doing here so early on a school day?" she asked.

"I cut myself at school and Hunter Sue had to come pick me up," I said, not meeting her eyes.

"I see." She looked at my blouse and jumper. "Soak that in cold water when you get home."

I stayed in the library the rest of the school day. Ms. Smalls had me reshelve some books, pick up trash, and dust. Whatever she wanted me to do, I did it. After she went home around 4:00 p.m., I avoided Hunter Sue until she called me to leave around 5:00 p.m.

In the car on the drive home, Hunter Sue addressed the incident for the first time. "Your grandpop will not be happy when I tell him about what you did, Lynette," she warned me. "You know how mad he sometimes gets."

Yes, I knew, and I knew I was going to get a whuppin' from him.

When we arrived home, Grandpop was sitting in the living room reading the paper.

"Bubba," Hunter Sue said, "Lynette got mad at the teacher at school today and put her fist through a glass window. They called me and I had to stop what I was doing and pick her up. Her teacher was very upset with her."

I just stood there, head bowed, waiting.

Grandpop rose from his chair, let out a sigh of frustration, took off his belt, and hit my legs a few times. "Don't you do that ever again," he thundered as he whipped his belt.

I just stood there in silence, taking it.

"Now go to your room," he commanded when he was done. "No supper!"

Annie Holloway was setting the table. "Bubba," she said, "you should let her eat something."

"No, Mama!" he called out.

I don't know why he felt that what I had done warranted physical punishment and no supper. He never asked me for an explanation. If he had, I might have said that Ms. Cooke gave me a U on my paper and the kids in the class were teasing me, and I just lost it! I couldn't control myself once the anger arose. I just couldn't. But he never asked me about my wrist or the blood on my clothes.

Children should be seen and not heard.

As I stomped up the stairs to the bedroom, I groused, "I was tired anyway and I ain't hungry!"

I half expected Grandpop to come bounding up the stairs after me to hit me a few more times for my back talk, but that didn't happen. Still fuming, I took off my clothes, put on my nightgown, and got into bed. Eventually, though, I calmed down, and I realized that I still loved him. I decided I would try to never put him in the position of disciplinarian again.

I didn't know it yet, but Hunter Sue had been talking to a psychologist, and he'd told her that what I most needed was to keep busy. Despite my family's sometimes harsh way of dealing with me, they were looking out for me.

As soon as I got into bed, I forgot about soaking my blouse and jumper in cold water, and even though I was hungry, I fell fast asleep.

Chapter 11
The Psychologist

AFTER THE INCIDENT, Miss Cooke was different. She didn't smile at me. She didn't call on me to read an assignment. She didn't show my papers to the class as an example.

I wanted to grab her and hug her and say, "I'm sorry, Miss Cooke. I get mad sometimes and I can't control myself"—but the voices said, *NO!* They saw no reason to apologize. They thought *she* should be the one apologizing to *me* for giving me that U! My cursive was perfect, and I should have gotten an E+++ for it!

So I didn't apologize, but I didn't get into any more trouble, either. I just did my schoolwork and kept quiet, and I finished third grade without any further incidents.

On the last day of class, the last time Miss Cooke ever spoke to me, she said "Behave yourself, you hear?" Those were her parting words to me.

She gave hugs to the other children.

School was out for the summer, but there was a lot to do at Hunter Sue's school to prepare for September. I was eager to help.

One day she hauled me off to a big building in downtown Norfolk. We rode an elevator to a floor above ground level. The person we were meeting was important-sounding. Hunter Sue said he was a psychologist, and I was going to spend some time with him over the summer.

What's a psy-cho-lo-gist? I wondered, but I didn't voice my question aloud. I tried not to ask grown-ups "What's that?" or "Why's that?" or "Who's that?" I'd learned by now that asking such questions could be met with a death stare, meaning *don't ask*, or a backhand across the mouth, or a belt lashing. For the most part, I just did what I was told.

The office waiting area was small, with just a few chairs. Most of the chairs were for grown-ups, but two were for children. They were next to a small table. While we waited, I sat in a grown-up chair—I was too big for the kid chairs—and read copies of *Highlights* magazine. The poems and a crossword puzzle held my interest until finally a door opened and a tall, thin, white man came out. He was dressed in a white shirt, dark blue tie, and gray pants. He had wavy white hair.

Most white men in my segregated world were characters on the TV, like the dads on *Father Knows Best* or *Make Room for Daddy*, but here was a white man in the flesh. He walked straight toward me, sat down beside me, and leaned in. "You must be Lynette," he said with a big smile on his face. His teeth were not as white as his hair.

I just nodded.

"I'm going to help you," he said, still smiling.

Help me with what? I thought.

He told Hunter Sue that she could wait or to come back in fifty minutes. Hunter Sue decided to wait. As I took his hand and walked with him through a door, I turned to see Hunter Sue picking up the same *Highlights* magazine I had just finished. *She's not going to be able to do the crossword puzzle*, I thought. I'd finished it already.

Inside his office, which was much bigger than the waiting room, there were games and jigsaw puzzles and stuffed animals and coloring books. He had a wooden desk in the back of the room with lots of papers on it and a clock. On either side of the desk was a bookshelf pushed up against the wall and filled with books, all of them neatly organized from top to bottom. There were so many books that some were on their sides on top of other books, but even those were neatly placed. He had diplomas and certifications on the walls, just like Hunter Sue, but no pictures of him shaking hands with important people. The large window behind the desk had blinds that were closed to shut out the bright sun. There was a couch made out of shiny, dark material under another window to the left of the door. He told me to sit there.

I pushed myself up on it and scooted back until I could no longer touch the floor. I sat quietly while he went to his desk and moved around some papers, looked at a few of them, then returned to me.

"I have lots of games to play in here, Lynette. Which one would you like to try?"

I was confused. Hunter Sue had brought me to this man to play games? I didn't understand, but I decided it was best to do what I was told. I looked around the room and spied an object on one of the walls. "What's that?" I asked him.

"Oh, that's a good game. It's called darts! You want to try it?"

I nodded.

He handed me a dart. It was metal, heavy in my hand, and had a sticky tip.

"Stand here and try to get your dart to stick on that board on the wall. If it sticks, you get the points, okay?"

I threw the dart and it hit the wall to the left of the board with a clunk and fell to the floor.

"Try again," he said.

This time I closed one eye and stuck out my tongue. I was

concentrating. I inched slightly closer to the target. It didn't seem like cheating. I took my time and threw it again. It hit the target and stuck!

I ran over and ripped off the dart. *Three points!* I thought triumphantly.

"You're a quick learner, Lynette." He paused. "So, tell me about how you got that scar on your wrist?"

I ignored him. I returned to my spot and threw the dart again. This time I missed. Frustrated, I said, "I don't want to play this silly game anymore." Then I asked, "Why you wanna know about my scar?"

He sat on the couch and told me to come sit by him. He looked down at my right wrist, which I still covered with a Band-Aid even though the wound had healed a while back.

"Lynette, your aunt tells me that you put your hand through a window at school." He looked me straight in the eyes. "Do you know why you did that?"

I looked down at my shoes. "I don't know . . . I guess I was mad 'cuz Miss Cooke gave me a bad grade."

"You don't like bad grades, do you?"

I shook my head sideways, first to the left and then to the right. "No, sir."

"I bet you're very good on tests, so let's do a few, okay? And then we'll play some other games. And I have a jigsaw puzzle that I've started, and you can help me finish it. How's that?"

"Okay," I said.

He gave me an "IQ test"—that's what he called it. He showed me a picture of a few dice and asked me which one was different. After I answered, he showed me another and another. It was easy. Then he showed me pictures of shapes in different positions and asked me which one didn't belong.

Over time, that IQ test got harder.

Eventually he asked me, "Do you miss your sister, Beverly?"

By that time, my brain was tired, so I just nodded my head up and down. I had no energy to try to avoid his questions. Even the voices in my head were too tired to stop me.

"Lynette, next time we'll talk about Beverly. Will that be okay?"

I nodded again.

"Let's go find your aunt, shall we?'

We didn't need to find her. I knew where she'd be even before he opened the door. She was sitting in the same spot, reading that *Highlights*.

"We had a good session, Mrs. Goodman," he said, wearing that smile again. "Same time next week?"

"Yes," she said.

For eight sessions that summer I visited the psychologist. I called him my "play Daddy," but I wanted him to be my real daddy because he was so nice to me. He smiled at me and told me "well done" a lot. We finished several jigsaw puzzles and I got really good at darts. I told him about the voice in my head I called "Beverly." He told me that sometimes when someone you love dies you still need them to be around, so they become an imaginary friend. He said that was okay. That made me feel so good. But not good enough to make me tell him that I actually had several "imaginary" friends.

At the eighth session, after we finished yet another jigsaw puzzle, he said, "This is our last visit, Lynette."

I didn't remember knowing that before he said so. If I did, I probably I shut it out of my mind. I didn't want to stop coming to see him. I wanted him to take me home with him and to be my *real* daddy. Later, when I understood something more about therapy, I'd understand that I was experiencing transference. I had no daddy, at least not one I wanted, and so I redirected all my emotions at his substitute, my therapist.

When he walked me out to the waiting room that day, he told Hunter Sue, "Lynette is a smart young lady. The tests show that. She acts out because she's bored. She should be in a higher grade. Keep her busy with books and duties at your school. She enjoys that the most. I will follow up with you at the end of next month, after she's back in school."

He never mentioned the chats we had about Beverly to Hunter Sue. I think those were just between him and me. Maybe he understood that Hunter Sue might not take the news about the voice in my head as lightly as he had. He seemed to understand what I was going through in a way that most of the adults in my life never could.

So, that late-July day, I said goodbye to a man I would never be able to call daddy but would keep in my heart as one. I cried. It was an odd sensation for me when the tears came, but I didn't fight it. He hadn't solved all my problems, but he'd helped me better understand them, and had provided me with a safe haven in which to speak about Beverly. I'd needed that.

I just wished I could have more time with him.

Hunter Sue was in her kitchen making lunch on the Saturday following my last session with the psychologist. The teal Princess phone on the wall across from the icebox rang, and she picked it up on the second ring after wiping her hands on a dish towel.

I was sitting at the small table in the kitchen, reading. I had free access to both houses by this point and came and went easily. Juju didn't seem to mind me anymore.

"Hello, Goodman residence," Hunter Sue answered. There was a pause as she waited for a response. "Oh, Anne, hello." Pause. "I'll let Fred know that you appreciated his help with the lawsuit. I'm glad you found a place. Good news." Pause. Hunter Sue leaned against the wall. It appeared that she had been gut-punched, but unlike what I'd seen when Daddy hit Mama, the fist was invisible.

"Do you think that's a good idea? Lynette really is no bother. She's a big help at the school. She can continue to go to Bowling Park and stay next door with Mama and Bubba." Pause. "Well, if you think it's best. All right. Goodbye."

Hunter Sue hung up the phone, then stood up straight and turned to me. With tears in her eyes and a faltering voice, she said, "Your Mama wants you back, Lynette. You're moving to Portsmouth with her, your daddy, and your brothers."

The book I was reading fell from my hands to the table. My eyes grew wide and my jaw dropped. *I'm moving where? Daddy's coming? Why can't I just stay here?*

A voice said, *RUN!*

Another replied, *Where?*

That voice was right. Where could I run to avoid this fate?

Nowhere, it answered.

Hunter Sue cared about me . . . just me. It wasn't the gooey, squeezy, squishy love of a mother or father hugging you so tight that you can't breathe as you soak up the sensation. Not even my parents gave me that. No, Hunter Sue's love was just being there for me, guiding me through my existence. She knew what I was enduring and was trying in her own way to help me as best she could.

I later learned that my uncle Fred, Hunter Sue's husband, had urged my parents to get a lawyer and sue the man who killed Beverly, since no criminal charges had been filed. The case had taken a while, but with the help of Steve's testimony, the judgment had been in favor of my parents.

The lawyer had gotten a third of the $10,000 award and Daddy had taken the remaining funds, along with a VHA loan, and purchased a brand-new house in Portsmouth, just across the Elizabeth River from Norfolk, at a purchase price of $11,000.

In that house—a three-bedroom, one-bathroom, single-story structure—would live Mama, Daddy, Butch, Kevin, and me. Daddy told Steve he couldn't come. He told him that he had to stay in Roberts Park with Granny so she could remain at 2746 Liberia Drive. The unit needed three occupants. Those became Granny, Steve, and an older woman, also named Mary.

Steve's testimony had won the case. He deserved to live in the house that he'd helped get. But Daddy blamed him for Beverly's death, and he wouldn't budge.

My parents had discarded one child in a pink box in a hole in the ground; now they left another in a housing project to live with two old ladies.

Me—I didn't want to go with Mama and Daddy. But I did go that summer of 1961, the same summer Daddy hit Mama so hard that she lost consciousness and fell backward over the porch railing.

My voices helped me deal. Deal with the image of a little girl in red Keds and a yellow sunsuit that crisscrossed in the back as she was struck and killed by a big black car; deal with the image of Mama getting coldcocked and doing a somersault over a railing. Images that nightmares are made from; images that never go away. Images that keep you going forward with your escape plan.

This was not my family. I wanted no part of them. They were stuck in a life with no exit strategy—but not me. I thought of my psychologist and how he'd boosted my confidence, telling me how smart I was. He'd seen potential in me. He'd told Hunter Sue to keep me busy. He'd told me that having an imaginary friend to cope with the loss of my sister was okay.

Without the validation I received from that psychologist, what came next might have taken me off my path of escape entirely. His words were what kept me sane during those trials.

To this day, I'm grateful for that.

Interlude:
Then and Now

AS A CHILD, teenager, and young adult, I felt no love for my mother. I wanted to love her; I wanted to be loved by her. So what was the issue? Was I so difficult to love?

Our relationship improved when I became an AARP-aged adult and she became a *senior* senior citizen. On her eighty-fifth birthday, when I was visiting her at the fifty-five-plus community in Mesa, Arizona, where she now lived, I just came out and asked, "Mama, why didn't you love me when I was growing up?"

She stared at me in silence for a moment and then plopped down on her couch in her double-wide Cavco home. She sighed—and then told me her story:

Lynette, I was an only child. My mama got pregnant by my daddy in high school. They both dropped out and got married. Mama didn't love Daddy. She didn't want to marry him, but what was she supposed to do? Those were the times. They lived with his mother—your great-grandmother Annie Holloway—but Mama couldn't take it. Annie Holloway was mean to her. She blamed Mama for getting her Bubba in trouble. And my daddy was mean to her too. So Mama went to live with Granny. She took me with her. I was around three at the time.

Daddy wanted her to come back. She knew he wouldn't leave her alone, so she decided to run away. A friend of hers got her a job as a housekeeper in New York City, but she couldn't take me.

I remember the night when Mama boarded that Greyhound bus to New York. It was raining hard. Granny held me as Mama got on that bus. She was crying. Granny was crying and I was crying. Mama took off on that bus, and I didn't see her again until I was around eight. That's when I went up to New York to live with her. Daddy had let me live with Granny after Mama left. I guess he didn't want me.

When I got to New York, I didn't like it there. It was noisy and dirty. So Mama sent me back. I lived with Granny until I married your daddy. I married your daddy to get away from my daddy. He tried to control me more and more as I got older. He would say, "You ain't gonna leave me like your mama."

Well, I quit college and married your daddy on my eighteenth birthday, February 28, 1947. Granny signed for the license because I was seventeen when I applied. Your daddy was twenty-two. I had my first baby at nineteen; my second at twenty; my third at twenty-three; my fourth at twenty-seven; and my fifth at thirty. I didn't know about your daddy's drinking and mental health problems until after we married. He started beating me soon after I said "I do" at the justice of the peace. I just tried to survive. I tried to leave him, but I couldn't make it stick. I stayed with him because he kept a roof over our heads and food in our stomachs. I stayed because of all of you. I didn't work.

So, I'm sorry about all that back then. I didn't know how to love back then. But, Lynette, I love you now.

Part II

Plan in Motion

Chapter 12
Science vs. Art

I TURNED NINE IN May of 1961. I finished third grade that June. By the end of June, or maybe early July, we moved to Portsmouth. One thing's for sure—by August, Mama had resumed her role as battered wife.

In October of that year, after seeing *Ben Casey*, I hatched my plan to escape. I would get an education; education was my ticket out! I remembered what the psychologist had told Hunter Sue: "Lynette is a smart young lady. She should be in a higher grade. Keep her busy."

In the fourth, fifth, and sixth grades, I continued to find my way, alone. There was no one to help me. The segregation and regimented structure of the educational system was the antithesis of what I needed to grow and reach my academic potential. I was attending colored schools in a colored neighborhood. I was forced to *follow the rules*: no skipping ahead in the curriculum, no extra-credit work. More of Miss Cooke's *no writing cursive* approach.

If I wanted to write cursive, why not? Was there a law that said, *If the child shows advanced learning abilities, nip them in the bud?* But there was no use complaining. For school, I did the grade work to pass—and behind my closed bedroom door, I did a little extra to excel. I had a summer reading list to keep my brain occupied. The local library was a daily adventure; I wasn't old enough to work there, but I became familiar with the Dewey Decimal System, and sometimes when the librarians weren't paying attention, I'd reshelve books.

The psychologist had been a blessing. He'd helped me understand some of my issues. But telling Hunter Sue to keep me busy worked only to a certain extent, especially after we moved. I no longer spent after-school days at Liberty Park Elementary. I no longer spent summers helping get the school ready for the fall. I no longer had the motivation provided by Miss Smalls, the librarian. It was all gone.

Instead, between trips to my local library, I spent the summer after fourth grade becoming the Marble Champion of Taft Drive.

I observed the game first; then I became a fanatic. The science of it all fascinated me—what types of marbles to use (I especially loved my shooter, a cat-eye); how to hold the marble; the angles to aim for to ensure the marble I was targeting got shot out of the circle and became my trophy. After a while, the boys didn't want to play with me anymore. They even begged Mama to make me give them back the marbles I'd won off them.

Mama just shook her head. "Listen, boys. You know better than to play marbles with Lynette! You gonna have to live without them marbles. She won them fair and square."

Word got around, and after that no one would let me play with them. My marble career was over after one summer.

I tried to stay out of trouble. However, sometimes trouble found me. In fifth grade, a boy named Ronald called me flat-chested, so I punched him in the gut. Reflex. It was undeniably the truth that I had no boobs—but who lets someone get away with saying that? I made him cry and didn't care that I did.

He told the teacher, of course, and I was made to write on the blackboard one hundred times, "I will not hit people." It was supposed to be a punishment, but it was actually fun! I wrote it first using my right hand, then gave it a try using my left hand; that took too long, so I returned to writing it right-handed. I divided the job into ten segments, since 10 × 10 = 100. I wrote as tiny as I could. I'm not sure how long the teacher thought it would take me, but when she came into the room to check on my progress, she looked at the board and said, "Lynette, go home." I had only two segments left to go. Twenty more *I will not hit people*s, and I would have been done. My hand wasn't even tired. I wanted to show her that I could finish. Still, as I walked home, I still felt pretty darn good—despite having no boobs.

In sixth grade, I got into a fight with Maria. What was I thinking? Maria, who must have been in the sixth grade for the second time— *or was it the third?*—was a big girl, and when I say *big* . . . she was tall, built like a longshoreman, and definitely *not* flat-chested.

Maria pummeled me good, and when she ripped off my shirt— revealing a boy's undershirt covering two nipples and nothing much else—my truth was officially revealed.

Ladies and gentlemen, it was official!

"Oooh—Lynette ain't got no titties!" one observant of the fight announced.

So what if I *was* flat-chested? Who needed boobs to go to college? If you'd ripped open my skull, you'd have found two cerebral hemispheres the size of double-Ds! I wasn't a pugilist, but sparring with me on any school subject at the time was a losing proposition. I easily knocked out my opponents when it came to subjects that mattered.

After my fight with Maria, I hung up my gloves. Fighting when provoked was not the answer. Fighting even when not provoked was a bad idea. I had to put a lid on my anger. I had to lock it away. Getting my ass kicked by Maria helped me see that.

I turned my focus to starting middle school.

The one advantage to attending middle school was that there were class periods with subjects taught by different teachers. Having to sit through a full class day with only one teacher was onerous and boring. Multiple teachers per day was a welcome relief.

S. H. Clarke Junior High School was where I attended seventh and eighth grades. Mrs. Jenkins was one of my teachers there.

"Good morning, class," she drawled. "How y'all doin'? Did you have a good summer?"

Mrs. Jenkins introduced me to the joy of science, and I'd have her for the next two years. Her husband, Mr. Jenkins, was the band and orchestra director. I played the E-flat horn, a smaller version of a tuba, in the marching band. I could play the tuba, but it had to remain on its stand because it was too heavy for me to lift. In the orchestra, I played the French horn. For two years it was the battle of the Jenkinses, with me as the musical scientist in the middle.

Imagine a boxing arena. The referee comes out to center stage and grabs the microphone:

"Welcome, ladies and gentlemen! In this corner we have Mrs. Jenkins, Lynette's science teacher. Mrs. Jenkins is skilled in all things science and has worked with Lynette on a project to look at the effects of heat and cold on copper. She wants Lynette to present her findings at the Science Fair.

In this corner we have Mr. Jenkins, Lynette's music teacher. He is a master marching band teacher. His band is one of the best in the city.

He wants Lynette to play her E-flat horn in the parade. The Science Fair and the parade are on the same Saturday. Who is going to be the winner of this bout?"

The bell rings. Mrs. Jenkins yells, "Lynette's science project is a winner! She's gonna bring home the first-place trophy!"

BAM! Ding ding ding!

"Mrs. Jenkins wins by a knockout!"

Mr. Jenkins was never a match for his wife. Being in the band was fun, but learning science was my ticket out!

The Science Fair for seventh and eighth graders was in Lawrenceville, Virginia, about four hours from Portsmouth. We didn't own a car. There were so many things to hate about my daddy, but on rare occasions—okay, two occasions—he acted like a father. On this one of the two, he borrowed a friend's car to take me to the fair.

The Science Fair began at 9:00 a.m. on that Saturday morning. We set out at 4:00 a.m.—Daddy driving, Mama serving as his copilot with a map. Cubby Lee, now six and an irritating pest, was in the back seat on the passenger side. I sat in the back seat on the driver's side. My science project rested on the seat between us.

For four hours I begged, "Mama, make Cubby Lee stop touching my science project!"

And for four hours Mama yelled, "Cubby Lee, leave your sister's science project alone!"

I still didn't have a nickname, but all my brothers did. Kevin Leon Charity had become Cubby Lee after watching the *Mickey Mouse Club*. There was a character on it named Cubby, and *Lee* was short for *Leon*.

Mama never turned around and Daddy never threatened to

stop the car those whole four hours, despite the yelling. He drove in silence. He was sweating a lot. Friday and Saturday nights were his *drinkin' with the boys* nights. But he hadn't gone drinking the night before we took off for the Science Fair. Mama had asked him not to. She'd said, "Chairdy, can you stay home tonight? We have a long drive tomorrow and I don't want you to oversleep."

When my daddy tied one on, he slept in, sometimes until noon. Mama knew that I could kiss that Science Fair goodbye if Daddy went out drinking that Friday night. I was surprised when Daddy said okay. He rarely did what Mama asked, but that Friday night, he stayed home and didn't drink.

We arrived with about an hour to spare for me to set up my project. I was tired—it had still been dark when we left the house that morning—but I managed to set up my poster boards and do my presentation on the effect of temperature on copper. The gist: cold contracts, heat expands. There you go.

During the awards presentation, I fell asleep.

I was shaken awake by Mama.

"Lynette, Lynette! Wake up! You got second place! Wake up!"

I had been sleeping *hard*, and I woke up with drool running down my mouth and onto my blouse. Mama continued to hit me on the shoulder. I rubbed my eyes and shook my head, trying to get those cobwebs out.

Finally, I stood and slowly made my way to the podium to receive my second-place ribbon and trophy. A few people clapped.

After I shook the hand of the award presenter and returned to my seat, Daddy stood up and said, "We gotta go. It's four hours of driving and I want to get back before dark."

It was only noon. I think he wanted to get back to his buds and his bottle.

We all headed for the door, picking up my project on the way out. This time we threw it in the trunk.

Cubby Lee and I slept most of the way. Daddy just drove. We made it home in no time.

Mama must have fallen asleep, because when we got there Daddy said, "Wake up, Anne, we home."

Not once did he say, "Good job, Lynette," or "That's my girl!" But I guess I didn't really expect him to.

"I'm gonna take the car back and go down to Big John's house," he told Mama.

Mr. Big John was one of Daddy's drinking buddies who lived down the street within walking distance. None of the men in our neighborhood left the neighborhood to drink. They just rotated houses every weekend—and I do mean every weekend.

At least Daddy had driven me to the Science Fair and returned us home safely. I think I wanted to tell him thank you, but I couldn't form the words looking at him. He hit my mother. He drank too much. And he didn't really give a rat's ass about me. One fatherly act couldn't change that.

"Congratulations, Lynette!" Mrs. Jenkins shouted in her thick southern accent when I returned to her class on Monday.

"Thanks, Mrs. Jenkins," I said, producing the trophy from my backpack.

"My goodness! Looook at thaaat!" she dragged out without her southern drawl as she held the trophy up to the classroom light. "This is so niiicce. May I keep it for the week? I want to display it for all the classes."

"Yes, ma'am." This was Mrs. Jenkins's trophy, too. She'd seen my potential and pushed me to do the science project. I loved her for that.

She put the trophy on her desk and taped the ribbon to its front.

My parents might not care about my achievement, but my favorite teacher did. I smiled all through class.

In band class that day, Mr. Jenkins's welcome was, "Take your seat." There were no congratulations.

A bandmate came up to me and said, "Lynette, you lucky you wasn't in the parade. Dey put us behind the horses again! My band shoes smell like horse poop. There were some really big piles this time. Our lines got all messed up."

An eight-hour round-trip to attend a science fair didn't seem so bad after hearing the story of playing *dodge the horse manure*. Mr. Jenkins probably would have disagreed. I was just happy he wasn't angry enough to pull me from my French horn solo for the concert the following Thursday night.

The song I'd be playing was "Moon River." I had practiced and practiced. I put my mouth on the mouthpiece and waited for Mr. Jenkins's cue.

Dah dat dah; dah dah dah dah dah . . .

After I performed my solo the next week, I never again picked up the French horn. The marching band and the orchestra were fun, but not necessary for my future. Science, not music, was my love.

Mrs. Jenkins and I continued our relationship going into eighth grade. She never questioned my decision to drop band and orchestra. I think she knew that I had lost interest. I also chose not to enter the Science Fair again so I wouldn't have to beg my parents to take me. That was okay. I remained focused and eager to start high school, where my science classes would have a real impact on my escape plan. Good grades in chemistry and physics would be a necessity. I was ready.

Chapter 13
Don't Go There!

DIDN'T LIKE MY family. Didn't like my neighborhood. Didn't like my school. Didn't like my life. I sensed being deprived of something as I trudged along in school. Our books seemed outdated. My education seemed stagnant. My escape plan moped along as I finished junior high school with stellar grades.

On my last day as an eighth grader, Ms. Jenkins grabbed me in a big bear hug and said, "Lynette, I loved teaching you. You're gonna do great things!"

Caught up in the wonderment of her statement, all I could think to say was, "Thank you, Mrs. Jenkins."

I was going to do *great things*, according to Mrs. Jenkins. She was only the second person in my short life who'd seen my potential. The first was my psychologist. But he'd spent only part of a summer with me; Mrs. Jenkins had spent two years molding me and helping me hone my capabilities, especially in science. And she done it with such enthusiasm!

But what did "You're gonna do great things" mean? Would it happen while attending high school? I was about to find out. Despite the 1954 Supreme Court decision in *Brown v. Board of Education of Topeka*, which clearly stated that racial segregation of children in public schools was unconstitutional, Virginia just kept on segregating students for twelve more years. I had heard that a few coloreds had been allowed to integrate some of the white high schools, but I hadn't seen evidence of that. And if that were the case, why didn't the system give me the option to attend a white school?

The white school in our town was in the white neighborhood that was separated from my neighborhood by a four-lane highway called Victory Boulevard. When I walked from my house to Moffitt Elementary School during sixth grade, I had to walk on my side of Victory Boulevard to get there. I saw people on the other side—white people—doing what all people did: going about their business. I was curious about that neighborhood, and I wanted to go to that school.

Instead, my school choices were Woodrow Wilson High School, Churchland High School, or I. C. Norcom High School. Not a white school in the bunch. Norcom was the closest to Victory Park, so the *system* enrolled me there.

My first day at Norcom went as expected. I signed up for ALM French 101 elective because moving to a foreign country fit into my escape plan strategy. I asked to take a test for advanced placement into English, but the school office manager said, "We don't allow that. You must stay with your age mates. It's for the best."

If that was true, why was someone "held back" if they didn't pass a course? Why was Maria still in sixth grade when her age mates were in seventh or maybe eighth grades? This made no sense to me.

Since I wasn't allowed to take a test for advanced placement English, I was signed up for the obligatory ninth-grade English. Boring. Boring. Boring. How could I do great things if the school was holding me back? I felt deep down that my intelligence was being wasted on regurgitated knowledge I had already acquired. I was better than that, but no one could see it.

I wanted to go to the white school. I felt that there, I would be challenged. I was convinced the education there would be better than what I was receiving at a school that was dismissive of my capabilities. I had become *uppity*, in colored-folk vernacular. I knew I'd have to work hard not to be bored.

At the end of the day, I got off the school bus and looked down the street that led to my house. I stood in the middle of the street and shouted, "Somebody help me, please!"

Other kids walking with me looked at me, startled by my outburst. No answer to my cry for help was forthcoming.

I reached my house and sat on the porch, my thoughts spinning: *Lynette, all you need to do is pass these grades and go to college. You can do that!*

After that self-administered pep talk, I went back to school the next day and dug up some old English textbooks in the school library. While coasting through ninth grade English, I'd review tenth-, eleventh-, and twelfth-grade English on the side. I would be prepared if at some point the rules changed. There had been talk about school integration coming to our area. The first chance I got, I was going to that white high school.

Meanwhile, I settled into a routine at Norcom and kept my head down.

During the second semester of my freshman year, in mid-March, I was startled out of a writing exercise while in my language arts class. "Lynette Charity, please report to the principal's office," a female voice announced over the PA system.

I didn't care why I was being summoned. It was a chance to get out of the tedium of this writing exercise.

My teacher, upon hearing my name, said, "You're excused," even before I could ask.

I speed-walked down the hall to the office and approached the school clerk's desk.

"I'm Lynette Charity," I said.

"Have a seat." She pointed to the row of chairs against a back wall in the office, then walked over to the principal's office.

When she returned, she said, "Mr. Johnson will see you now."

There were not many reasons that a student would be called into the principal's office. The most egregious might be cheating on a test. Or having an altercation with another student. But neither of those things had happened, so I couldn't fathom why I was there. I entered the principal's office tentatively.

Principal Johnson looked up from his desk. "Have a seat, Ms. Charity," he said, pointing to a wooden chair facing his desk.

Mr. Johnson was a tall Black man with a very deep voice. He wore a nice suit with a white shirt and tie. I had been at I. C. Norcom for seven months, and except for class assemblies in the auditorium or seeing Mr. Johnson in the hallway, I knew little about this man. I had, after all, been keeping my head down and just doing the work. I was not involved in any extracurricular activities and I didn't attend any sports events. I went to school, trudged through my classes, and went home. So he likely knew very little about me—but he had to be aware of my academic standing. I was a straight-A student.

As he sat reviewing some papers, he said, "You've been selected to transfer to Cradock High School in the fall. It's a new state program called Freedom of Choice. Virginia is going to try to integrate the schools. Right now, the state is picking just a few students to transfer. If you want to transfer to that white school, one of your parents must sign this permission slip." He handed me an envelope that had *Mr. &*

Mrs. Charity on it. He looked me in the eyes. "Now, you don't have to go if you don't want to. Understand?"

Was he trying to discourage me from going? I guess he had to tell me, but he didn't have to condone it. I felt that he didn't.

I, however, couldn't wait to get into that white school, so I just nodded. I was going whether he liked it or not!

I stood to leave, envelope in hand. In a final comment, clearly still attempting to deter me from transferring, he said, "You're getting a great education right here. And the teachers tell me that you're a very good student. Why transfer to another school?"

My response to his last question was a brief silence, and then: "Thank you for the information, Mr. Johnson."

What I wanted to do was jump up and down and say, "I want to go! Yes! Yes!" But I sensed that telling him that I wanted to transfer to the white school was not the response he wanted, so I buried my enthusiasm and scooted out his door.

If I could have negotiated, I might have asked to be allowed to advance to twelfth grade. What was so wrong about pursuing opportunities for growth? I needed to expand my horizons.

I was giddy with anticipation. I had heard about Cradock, the white high school, but I had never seen it. I knew that it was located somewhere across Victory Boulevard and through the white neighborhood. I was told they had more up-to-date books and more resources than our school had. But none of us knew for sure, having never been there.

As I left the school bus to walk home, all I could think about was how to get Mama to sign my permission slip.

Mama was in the backyard when I arrived home. I saw her through the window in the kitchen after I entered through the front door. She was hanging clothes on the clothesline. I went out back to ask her to sign the slip.

"Hey, Mama," I said carefully, knowing I had to present things the right way if she was going to go along with it. "I got a permission slip from school. I need you to sign. Can you do it right now?"

"What's it about?" she asked, holding a clothespin in her mouth.

"I got selected to go to the Cradock next year!" I blurted out. "I wanna go."

Mama pulled the clothespin out of her mouth. She paused. She looked at me with *that look*—the one she gave me when the answer was going to be *no*. The same look she'd worn when Bowling Park Elementary School wanted me to skip second grade and she'd told them, "I don't feel comfortable lettin' Lynette do that."

And just as I expected, she said, "Oh, Lynette, that's not a good idea. Those white folks don't like us. They might hurt you."

"But, Mama, I really want to go," I pleaded.

"Did I ever tell you about these colored kids down in Arkansas—I think it was Little Rock? It wasn't too long ago. Anyway, there were nine of them that went to this white school and the white kids hurt one of the girls. Pushed her down some stairs. Cryin' shame. I don't want that happening to you."

"Mama, I'll be fine," I insisted. "I wanna go. Please. We don't live in Arkansas."

"I cain't see myself signing that piece of paper, child. You are just fine at Norcom."

No, I wasn't *just fine* at Norcom. I was miserable. What was I going to do?

I went to my room and threw myself on my bed. Mama was still outside. *Okay, Lynette, think!* I knew Mama had some papers and some old checks with her signature on them, so I composed myself, snuck into her bedroom, and found an old canceled check and a piece of paper that had *Anne W. Charity* in cursive writing on it. I took it back to my room and practiced writing her name. If she wasn't going to give me permission, I'd give myself permission.

Why was everyone so hell-bent on not letting me escape? I copied my mother's signature again and again. I was willing to risk the wrath of Anne Charity in order to follow my escape plan.

Monday morning, I dropped off the permission slip in the office. The office clerk tsk-tsked as she put it in a tray.

Mine was the only slip in that tray. There were several slips in the tray next to it. I didn't know what it said on those other trays, but I imagined those were the slips of the kids who'd said no. I imagined that my tray was labeled "Hates our school" and the other one was labeled "Loves our school." I didn't care. I was gonna go!

Two days later, on Wednesday morning, another PA summons came over the loudspeaker: "Lynette Charity, please report to the school office."

What now? I panicked, thinking I'd been caught forging Mama's signature. Had they called her and asked, "Did you really sign this permission slip to have Lynette go to that white school? Why on earth would you do that?"

When I entered the office, Mr. Johnson was standing at the counter with this scowl on his face. "So, I guess you're going to Cradock next year, Ms. Charity." Everyone in the office stared at me as though I had cheated on a test or been disrespectful to a teacher.

The tips of my ears burned with discomfort, but inside I was defiant. Why was it wrong for me to want to challenge myself, to face the unknown? It was time for a change—at least for me. I could no longer languish in my colored world. I was focused on my escape!

Word traveled fast after I left the office.

"Lynette, why you wanna go to that white school anyway?" a classmate asked.

"I want to go to college and to medical school," I said. "I hear they got better books there."

"So, you think you better than us now, huh?"

I was miffed that I was being confronted in such a negative, threatening way. What business was it of hers? No one asked her to transfer!

I looked down at the hallway linoleum, running different responses in my head. What if I said "yes"? Would we then come to blows? I didn't want to get into a fight for stating a fact. I did think I was better than them. I wasn't afraid to make a change, even if it might make others uncomfortable. So what if they saw me as "uppity"? But I wanted the cross-examination to end, so all I said was, "No, I don't! I just can't stay here!"

"Well," she said, hands on her hips, "Miss Jones says that you gonna fail and they gonna send you back! She says that you're a traitor to your race!"

I wasn't about to try to understand how wanting to go to Cradock betrayed my race; all I knew was that I would be a traitor to *myself* if I didn't try.

Chapter 14
The White School

Two WEEKS WENT by, and then one day I came home from school to find Mama standing on the porch waiting for me.

"Lynette!" she snapped. "I just got this letter in the mail that says you be goin' to that white school next year! I said you couldn't go. Who signed that slip for you?"

"I signed it, Mama," I admitted, eyes cast down at the ground. "I signed your name."

"You did *what*?"

"I signed your name, Mama," I said. "I practiced writing your signature and then I signed the permission slip." I met her gaze. "I had to, Mama. I just couldn't spend another day in that high school. I need to get away from here! Don't you understand?"

Why were people so concerned with where I wanted to go to school? I sighed and sat down on the porch and lowered my head, shaking my head in frustration. I wasn't afraid. I was determined do it—or die trying.

Mama had long ago stopped whuppin' me, but she could have right then if she'd wanted to. I wouldn't have resisted. I had lied to get my way. I waited quietly for her to give me a talkin'-to.

"Listen, Lynette," she said quietly. "I guess you really want to go. And I know you smart, and you will surprise those white folks when they see how smart you are. I guess I cain't protect you forever. So, you go to that school, and you show them what for, okay?"

She almost sounded proud of me. *Who is this lady?* I thought. *Where is my mama?*

Mama turned and went inside, and she made no mention of that permission slip again. I don't think she ever even told Daddy. Even if she had, though, he wouldn't have cared. I remained invisible to him.

I think Mama finally realized that day that I had plans that didn't include living in Victory Park for the rest of my life. She had seen the signs ever since that night I told her, "Mama, I'm gonna be a doctor!" She'd bought me a medical kit, after all; why would she do that if she didn't believe in me? She saw how hard I worked in school. This was a train that she couldn't stop, and this permission slip had been the last obstacle.

I think after I told her I forged her name, for a moment she thought, *Clever girl.* And that's when she threw in the towel. From that moment forward, she left managing my life to me.

When ninth grade came to an end, I was relieved. The final two months were difficult, with all the finger-pointing and the eye-rolling from my peers and their comments about my being *uppity*. Okay, maybe I was. I did see myself as better than them—not necessarily because I was smarter, but because I was willing to give it a try rather than just sitting by while the world changed around me. I wanted to be out front, and if that meant being uppity, I'd wear it as a badge of honor. Their reproach reminded me of the teasing I received when my sister died. It also reminded me of Granny's advice to "pay them no nevermind."

I knew nothing about what to expect come the fall, but I prepared as best I could.

Mama was informed that there would be no school bus service for me. There was a plan to start a bus route from Victory Park to Cradock, but it wasn't implemented yet. We didn't have a car, so our next-door neighbor, Mr. Epps, volunteered to take me—"You're a brave girl, Lynette," he told me. But the week before I was scheduled to start, Mr. Epps became ill. He told Mama that he would be *good as new soon*, but wouldn't be able to take me the first few days.

That left only one option: I would have to walk. I'd walked to school before. In fact, I hadn't started riding a bus to school until ninth grade. I. C. Norcom had been too far from my house to walk to. But Cradock was really not that far. It was just through uncharted territory.

I would have to walk through the neighborhood in a straight path and the school would appear at the end of the street—at least that's what I was told. Mama was more distraught about this than I was. I'm not sure why she didn't offer to walk with me, but she did have my brother to get ready for school. And maybe she just knew I could do it.

Of course, she had to tell me another horror story the week before school started. This one involved a boy from our neighborhood who took a shortcut through the white neighborhood. ("Lynette, that boy had to run for his life!") I imagined that boy had been very scared. But I was not that boy. I was going to be okay.

I wondered if I should carry the permission slip with me just in case. If accosted, I'd hold it up and say, "Hey, you white folks—I have permission to be in your neighborhood. You can't run me off!"

Would that work? I wondered.

* * *

Monday morning, I had my book satchel ready, permission slip inside. I wore my navy plaid jumper with a white short-sleeve blouse with a Peter Pan collar and my tan and white saddle Oxfords with white anklets. I wore my hair in a flip with bangs, thanks to the sponge rollers that I slept in and the every-two-week beautician appointment for a press and curl. (This bimonthly hair ritual kept my coarse hair manageable. Mama had started the routine when I was six. If she washed my hair and did not get the kinks out before it dried, all was lost. She shared her frustration with Hunter Sue, and Hunter Sue started taking me to her beauty shop.)

I was ready and confident. Mama had cooked me scrambled eggs and bacon, served with a slice of toast. I washed it all down with some milk. Daddy had already left for work. Cubby Lee was still in bed.

School started at nine. I didn't know how long it would take me to get there, so I ventured out around seven thirty.

I knew the route. Out my front door, right turn on Taft, right turn on Stratford, right turn on Cavalier Manor Boulevard. From there it got tricky. Once I reached Victory Boulevard, I'd have to cross a four-lane highway and then continue through the white neighborhood to reach the school. Would they come after me with torches and pitchforks like they did to Frankenstein's monster? Would it be like going through the Haunted Forest on my way to the Emerald City? There was only one way to find out.

I had just seen *The Wizard of Oz* in technicolor—Daddy had finally decided to buy a color TV on credit. I had seen the movie several times before and loved it each time, but this last viewing had been different due to the color. She opened the door and—oh my!

"Mama! Mama! Come look!" I called when that scene came on.

"Look at what?" she said. "Oh, my goodness!" She stayed to watch, with running commentary: "The yellow brick road is really yellow! Look at Dorothy's outfit!" She sat down on the couch. She stared at the TV as the Munchkins sang and danced. When the ruby slippers ended up on Dorothy's feet, she remarked, "Oooh!"—never once moving from her seat. We finished the movie together. I realized as the credits rolled that Dorothy's journey was my journey. The only difference? I wanted to get to the Emerald City and never return home. *There's no place like home* had a different meaning for me.

I made it across Victory Boulevard in one piece. I didn't want to walk all the way up the street to the traffic light, so I jaywalked. Traffic was light.

Where I ended up on the other side was right at the entrance into the neighborhood. Aretha Franklin had just recently released a new single called "Respect." I started singing it as I entered the Haunted Forest, and it gave me some confidence.

So far so good, though I could hear some dogs in the distance. Were they going to be like the flying monkeys and attack me?

And then I saw them. Women sitting on their porches. Porches just like the ones in our neighborhood. They were dressed in paisley dusters and bedroom slippers. Their hair was set in pink sponge rollers and covered with head scarves. Some had cigarettes in their mouths.

At first, they just stared at me, giving me the evil eye. They never took their eyes off me. *Wicked witches!* I thought.

Finally, one cackled, "You don't belong here, Nigra girl!"

"Yeah, we don't want you here," another said.

Yet another chimed in, "Why don't you go back to Africa!"

Was I scared? Not really. Nothing really scared me anymore. Witnessing the death of my sister and Daddy knocking Mama clear off the porch had scared the scare out of me, I think. I'd stopped crying a long time ago. Even when Mama punished me for fighting, I never cried. After a while, she gave up and just sent me to my room— which was my haven, so that really wasn't punishment at all.

So, if not fear, how did this situation feel? *ODD. Nonsensical.* Why did they see me as a threat? I was fifteen.

Why don't you go back to Africa? My rational brain knew that I couldn't *go back* to a place I'd never been. Obviously, this woman didn't know anything about me. In fact, I knew none of these women, and yet they felt quite comfortable yelling at me, a young girl just walking through the neighborhood to get to school.

I knew what to do: I paid them *no nevermind!*

But then one of the witches jumped down from her porch. She took her cigarette, dropped it on the grass, and quickly stomped it out with a pink bedroom slipper. Then, sneering at me, she moved toward me, walking at a slow pace so as to not lose her bedroom slippers in the grass. Something on the ground caught her eye and she stopped to pick it up. Holding that something in her hand, she returned her focus to me. Brow wrinkled, eyes narrowed, grasping that something tightly in her hand, she again rushed toward me as fast as her slippers would allow.

I didn't run right away. I just picked up my pace from a walk to a jog. When she reached the street, she threw whatever was in her hand at me—and for a moment, arm up in the air, she looked more like the evil tree in the Haunted Forest than a witch.

I thought she must have thrown a rock—but when it hit me on the back of the leg with a thud, it didn't hurt. *Not a rock*, I surmised. I kept my pace and glanced behind me at the object on the ground. It was dog poop! Not a wet, squishy, recent deposit but the hard, sun-baked kind you could easily pick up with your hand and throw. I felt sure it had left very little of itself on my leg, seeing as it was still pretty intact after having fallen to the ground.

I couldn't understand why this woman was willing to pick up this dog poop and throw it at me to make her point. She was an adult, and this action wasn't appropriate for an adult—even one running after me in pink bedroom slippers, wearing a duster, and covered with a head full of pink sponge rollers. Honestly, she looked ridiculous.

All I wanted was to attend the white high school. I had no inter-est in living in that neighborhood. *What is the matter with her?* I wondered.

I turned around to see her still staring at me as she wiped her hand on the grass. I picked up my pace from a jog to a sprint and ran straight ahead, my book satchel hitting me occasionally on the leg.

Perhaps this should have registered as a horrific experience, but all it did was make me question the whole concept of what constitutes proper adult behavior. I knew my role as a child. All adults deserved respect. That was the law. But what about children? I thought of some-thing Granny used to say—"Cat fur makes kitten britches." Made no sense, but neither did this behavior.

Rounding the corner, there was the high school, which reminded me of the scene in *The Wizard of Oz* where Dorothy, Toto, the Tin Man, the Scarecrow, and the Cowardly Lion wake up in the poppy field after Glenda the Good Witch makes it snow. They head toward the Emerald City while a chorus sings about stepping into the light and walking up to the gate.

I had made it to my Emerald City.

* * *

The Cradock High School of my imagination was just that—an Emerald City of gigantic proportion. This was The White School. I'd heard so many stories about it that I envisioned it as the Taj Mahal of high schools. So imagine my disappointment when, after escaping the poop gauntlet, I reached a three-story brick building that looked very similar to I. C. Norcom. I felt cheated. My escape plan included getting an almost supernatural education from this neighborhood school, and now here I was, finding out that the only difference between the schools was that almost everyone who attended this school was white, as were the teachers.

My disappointment, however, quickly gave way to a new feeling of determination. I'd show those teachers at Norcom! I'd show these teachers at Cradock! I'd show them all! I was going to TCB—*take care of business*—just like Aretha Franklin sang about in her song. But first I was going to need to wipe off the back of my leg.

I walked up the stairs, bade the double doors to *open, open,* and found the girls' bathroom. I entered, and was once again taken aback by the total lack of contrast between Norcom and this school. No difference.

I grabbed a bunch of paper towels and wet them. I put soap on them using a soap dispenser that could have easily been the soap dispenser at Norcom, then scrubbed my leg with the soapy towel, wiped it off with a wet towel, and dried it with another paper towel. I cleaned my book satchel, too. There was no evidence of poop on it, but it had been in close proximity to my leg, so I wanted to make sure.

When I was done, I looked at myself in the mirror. Nothing about me was any different.

When I reached my homeroom class, boys and girls were kidding around and laughing. They all appeared to know one another, and they probably did, since this was tenth grade. When I walked into the room, they paid me no nevermind, which was a little surprising after my encounter in the neighborhood. I was truly ignored. After hearing the story about the Little Rock Nine from my mama, I'd been prepared for some reaction. To my relief, it never occurred.

"Your name?" the teacher asked.

"Lynette Charity," I replied.

"Go find a seat."

The whole front row of desks was devoid of bodies, so I picked a desk directly across from my teacher's desk. I didn't want to miss a thing. I was very happy that no one seemed to notice the colored girl sitting in the front row in their class. I felt invisible. Maybe they did notice, but it wasn't important for them to react. It wasn't as though I was the only colored student. A handful had come before me, paving the way.

My homeroom teacher seemed as unfazed as my classmates by my presence. She took attendance like a drill sergeant. She asked each kid who walked in after me, "Your name?" and then instructed them to "Go find a seat," just as she'd said it to me, with no difference in speech cadence that I could detect. It was comforting to realize that while I wasn't being welcomed with open arms, I also wasn't being met with violence.

I wondered if the person whose mother had thrown dog poop at me was in my class, but I decided not to ask. My escape plan was proceeding.

"Okay, everyone, take a seat," she said in the classic southern drawl native to our region. "My name is Miss Hinton." She wrote her name on the blackboard, then turned to face us. "I'm y'all's homeroom teacher for the year. And I suspect I will also be the physics and chemistry teacher for some of y'all."

That day Miss Hinton strutted before us like a general review-ing her troops. She was a statuesque, fair-skinned, narrow-waisted woman whose uniform was a teal pencil skirt, a teal blouse tucked into that skirt, stockings, and heels. And I do mean *high* heels—none of those clunky shoes with the stumpy broad heel for her. When she strutted from one side of the room to the other, she pivoted on one heel, not once faltering. Her auburn hair was cropped short, and she wore red lipstick. Her peacock strut said, *Don't mess with me—I'm a woman, a chemist, and a physicist!* And she used *y'all* a lot—as in, "Those who are in my classes, y'all better not forget your homework assignments."

I would be in both her chemistry and physics classes. I felt that she was going to continue where Mrs. Jenkins had left off. It was won-derful to meet a teacher who wanted to teach and not have preset opinions about who she taught. And even if she had such thoughts, what was more important was that she loved science and I loved sci-ence. And science was colorblind, as far as I was concerned.

After leaving homeroom, my first class was French, where I met Madame Bruce.

"*Bonjour*, class!" she greeted us as we entered.

I had taken French 101 at Norcom. I'd already decided that if I ever ran away to France, a distinct possibility in my running list, I'd better know how to speak the language.

When Madame Bruce dropped the French accent, she sounded just like Miss Hinton. She said, "Y'all are going to love this language and I encourage all y'all to join the French Club." She didn't need to *encourage* me. I planned to participate in everything!

I went to every class—Algebra 2, English 10, social studies,

American government—bright-eyed and eager. My last class of the day was chemistry, back with Miss Hinton. She was sitting at her desk as I entered, and I sat in the same seat as I had for homeroom.

She looked up. "Lynette Charity, right?" she asked, southern drawl intact.

"Yes, ma'am," I said.

While we waited for the other kids to file in, she asked me what other science classes I had taken and if I liked science.

"Yes, ma'am!" I told her that I'd had a great science teacher named Mrs. Jenkins in junior high and that my biology class the previous year had been good.

She responded with a nod. "Well, that's nice to hear."

As we wrapped up our conversation, a boy sat at the desk next to me. He wore khaki pants, an ironed white short-sleeved shirt, white socks, and brown loafers. He had brown eyes and a crew cut. He looked over at me and said, "Hi, I'm Paul."

"I'm Lynette," I managed to reply after the shock of his speaking to me wore off. None of the other students had said a word to me that first day. If they had an opinion about me attending their school, none had voiced it. I was invisible.

Maybe it was their coping mechanism for this radical change in their lives, having a colored girl being educated beside them. So when Paul introduced himself to me, I waited for the secret police monitoring the situation to swoop in and grab him for reprogramming—"Y'all aren't supposed to speak to them, ya hear?" *Zap zap.*

While Miss Hinton laid out what we'd be learning, I found ways to get quick looks at Paul. I dropped my pencil, then a piece of paper, and even my chemistry book. I think I was smitten. I was going to love chemistry class! But in order to make it back for a second day, I had to make it home in one piece, or at least not get dog-pooped again.

I chose a different route going home and encountered no resistance. When I crossed over to my side of Victory Boulevard, I looked back and all I saw was what appeared to be a quiet community, albeit a quiet community of white folks. I hoped to figure out a way to walk to and from home in peace, but I was satisfied after my positive first day at Cradock High that the trouble was worth it.

When I reached my porch, I sat for a moment.

Mama came out. "How was school, Lynette?"

I told her about my day but left out the dog-poop incident and Paul. What could Mama do about those witches in the white neighborhood? And why bother her with my being smitten by a white boy on the first day of attending his white school?

As soon as I was done filling her in, I went inside and did my homework. I was never going to be unprepared for school. Never.

The next day, I entered the Haunted Forest via a different route and there were no wicked witches. Yes, there were white women in smocks and slippers, hair in curlers, smoking and sitting on their porches, but these ones appeared uninterested in me. Even so, I essentially ran most of the way to school.

I was overjoyed by how nonconfrontational my second day of walking—well, running—to school had been. I was sweaty by the time I got there, so I went straight to the bathroom again.

I needed to freshen up just in case I saw Paul in the halls.

We saw each other again in chemistry.

"Hi, Paul," I said as I sat down.

"Hi, Lynette," he replied.

I smiled inside. The very fact that he spoke to me and treated me like a regular person made me feel like I had a friend.

I started off the year with straight A's and became a member of the National Honor Society.

Madame Bruce loved my name. "*C'est français*," she told me.

Not only was she my French teacher, she was also the advisor for our French Club. And I was doing well in class.

She approached me one afternoon that first semester and said, "Lynette, *vous devez participer à ce concours de français. Oui?*"

I understood most of that. Something about participating in a French contest.

Turned out she was talking about the French Club's poetry contest. We could choose a poem to recite. I chose "La Cigale et la Fourmi" by Jean de la Fontaine, a poem about a cicada (*cigale*) and an ant (*fourmi*), and I practiced reciting my poem with as much intensity as I had when I recited the poem "Smiles" for Miss Massey at the Roberts Park Community Center back when Beverly was alive.

As I stood at the lectern before my fellow students on the day of the contest, cheat sheet close by, I began reciting. I looked at Madame Bruce and saw the twinkle in her eyes as I shared this French fable, complete with a pretty good accent, to the group.

She clapped when I was done, crying out, "*Très bon! Très bon!*"

Paul, who was not in my French class, was in the audience.

Paul became my first true love. We were two bookworms who loved science. And science, as I said before, was colorblind. If he had asked me, I would have attended prom with him. But that wouldn't come to pass. While on the surface there was a semblance of acceptance of my presence at Cradock, I was never asked to sleep over at a slumber party or attend a party of any kind. That was *verboten*. (*Forbidden* sounds scarier in German than it does in French.) When all things school-related were done for the day, I got out of Dodge and stayed gone until the next school day.

I was content with my platonic relationship with Paul. We could not be boyfriend-girlfriend—no way, no how. But we could go to study hall together and enjoy the library together. I loved being with Paul in whatever capacity was permissible, and I knew he felt the same. There was an occasional touch of a hand and some googly-eyed looks, but nothing overt.

VERBOTEN!

But then one day he stunned me by asking, "Lynette, you want to come over to my house on Friday after school?"

"You sure it will be okay? I don't want any trouble," I replied hesitantly.

"Yeah, sure. I'll just tell my parents that we're working on a science project together and need to work on it. It'll be okay."

"Okay," I said.

This was a bad idea. A really bad idea. I should have said, "No, Paul, it won't be okay! I've walked through your neighborhood. I've seen how white adults react when they see me here." Why would his parents be any different?

But Paul insisted that it was going to be okay. And we *were* science partners at school. But the "working on a science project" thing—that was a bold-faced lie!

Paul smiled and went off to his next class. I watched him walk down the hall. There was such an innocence about him.

* * *

Friday came, and at the end of the school day Paul found me at the bottom of the school steps.

"I don't live far," he said. "Let's go."

On the way to his house, we talked about the periodic table—made jokes about nitrogen and oxygen getting together and saying "NO." We were being silly, and it made us giddy. We were in our own world. I stopped worrying about being in a white neighborhood.

Suddenly, Paul stopped. "That's my house over there."

Just like the similarity between the schools, I was struck that the homes in his neighborhood were so similar to those in my neighborhood. Except the white neighborhood was older. Victory Park was only six years old. That said, it seemed that my neighborhood must have been modeled after the older white neighborhood.

I'd always imagined that the white neighborhood would be nicer than ours, but now I understood that wasn't true. The only real difference was that it had more established landscaping. Our neighborhood was young, and while we had nice homes, our yards had not yet matured. The tree we'd planted when we first moved in was still growing. The trees here were nice and big already. Just as my neighborhood took pride in their homes and yards, so did this neighborhood.

As we approached Paul's front door, my stomach began to ache as though I was forming an ulcer right in the moment. My hands were sweaty, and I had the urge to run. I was turning to do just that when a woman came out of the front door.

The screen door slammed behind her. She stood on her porch, hands on hips, guarding the entrance to her abode. She glared at me over her cat-eye-framed glasses. Her expression was one of disgust. This woman had sized me up and immediately decided she hated me.

"Paul!" she barked. "What you doin' wit dat Nigra?"

"Mama, this is Lynette," he said sweetly. "She's my science partner. We gonna work on our science project together. I invited her over. I told her it would be okay."

"Well, Paul, it ain't okay! You ain't bringin' no Nigra into our house! Your daddy would have a conniption fit if he found out!" She turned her tirade toward me. "Now you, girl. You git on out of here. We don't want yur kind around here. Just because we let you come to our school don't mean we gonna let you come into our homes. Go own, girl. Go back to wherever you came from and don't ever come back here, ya hear."

I wished I had run when I had the chance. I felt so bad for Paul. He was not like his parents, but if he had come to my house, the greeting most likely would have been a version of what I'd just heard. I could imagine Daddy's reaction: "Lynette, why you bring this white cracker boy to our house? He ain't welcomed!"

There was no love lost between the races in our town.

I saw the redness explode on Paul's face. And disbelief. Had he actually thought his parents were going to ignore that he had a darkie girlfriend? I was just glad his father wasn't there. And I hoped that once his mother told his father, there would be no violent repercussions.

"I'll see you at school on Monday, okay?" I said to him quietly.

I said nothing to his mother. What was there to say? I started walking away.

"Paul," I heard his mother say behind me, "git in the house. You wait 'til your father gets home and I tell him what you did."

I glanced back to see Paul stomping up the stairs to his porch, head down, shoulders slouched. He entered the house followed by his mother. The screen door slammed behind her, and then she slammed the front door shut.

* * *

That weekend was one of turmoil in my head. I imagined Paul enduring such awful punishments. Would his daddy beat him with a belt
or a whip? Would his daddy hit him with his fists? All because of me?
What had we done that was so wrong? Why did people have to be so
mean to each other? Yeah, I was a colored girl, and he was a white boy,
but we didn't care. We had mutual interests that attracted us to each
other. We loved science.

If not for the bigotry in the world, I think he and I could have
fallen in love.

Monday came. Mr. Epps took me to school, which had become a
more regular thing now that he was feeling better.

When I entered the building, I immediately went to Paul's locker.
He was talking to a friend, smiling, but when he saw me his smile
disappeared and he looked down at his feet.

I looked him over and saw no visible bruises. I was relieved. But
when I tried to talk to him, he slammed his locker shut and walked
away.

I tried again later in chemistry.

"Lynette, leave me alone," he muttered. "I can't talk to you no
more."

Something had definitely happened at home. And whatever Paul
and I had was destroyed after that. He never spoke to me again—at
least not in the way he once had.

Why couldn't we have been left to figure the world out for ourselves? We never had a chance.

* * *

The rest of high school was devoid of friends and relationships. Paul had been my one and only; having lost his friendship, I put my nose to the grindstone and forged ahead.

Anyway, I was going to college. Who had time for a high school crush?

I told myself that, but I knew that for Paul I would have made time—and who knew what

kind of scientific discoveries we might have made as a team?

Chapter 15

The Accuser, the Denier, the Savior

MR. AUMENT, MY eleventh-grade government teacher, didn't like me from day one. Now, I could state the obvious, but I never had proof that he didn't like me because I was Black—I just knew he didn't like me. And I'm a scientist: I base my assertions on tangible evidence.

Mr. Aument was a short man with wiry, coarse, blondish hair combed away from his forehead.

On the first day of his class, I sat near the back.

"You!" he said. "You sit here so I can keep an eye on you." He pointed to the desk in front of his desk.

I wasn't about to argue with him. He was the teacher. But I often found him staring at me, and it made me feel anxious. I couldn't figure out what he expected of me. He taught. I listened. He gave tests. I passed them with perfect scores.

We were about three months into class when, just after I entered class one day, he told me, "Lynette, you need to take your things and go to the principal's office."

The normal cacophony of students talking over each other and laughing went silent. Everyone stared at me.

What could have provoked this? I wondered.

When I arrived at Mr. Gray's office, it seemed to me that everyone knew the situation except me. When Mr. Gray called me into his office, Mrs. Morgan, the senior class sponsor and my trigonometry teacher, was also present.

"Lynette," Mr. Gray said, "Mr. Aument says you cheated on his last exam. He says that you must've gone into his desk and gotten the master answer sheet. You got all the answers correct and he says that's not possible."

I found it hard to breathe. My stomach hurt. I resisted immediately bursting into tears. "Mr. Gray, I am not a cheater. I knew all the answers."

Mr. Aument entered the office.

Ignoring me, he spoke directly to the principal. "Mr. Gray, I am sure Lynette cheated. I specifically put questions on the test that we did not study in class, and she got them right. The only way she could have known the answers is if she saw my master answer sheet, which I kept in the top drawer of my desk."

"Mr. Aument, I would never go in your desk!" I yelled. I couldn't believe what I was hearing.

"Don't you raise your voice to me, girl," he snarled. "I know you cheated! There's no way you could have known the answer to all those questions."

"Mr. Aument, I did know," I said, eyes wide. "Please, just ask me the questions again."

"Mr. Gray, she cheated," he insisted. "I'm giving her an F!"

An F would certainly upset my almost straight-A average. But it was more than that. I had never cheated on a test in my life. There was no need to. I studied long and hard for each exam. And Mr. Aument always seemed frustrated at how well I did on his tests. He was the reasons I was an *almost* straight-A student. He refused to give me any grade higher than a B on any of my classwork. I compared my work to others in class who had received A's. Our answers were identical, or nearly so. We wrote essays on Virginia history and US government. While other students got full credit, I was always marked down, but I never complained. He was the teacher. He was the authority. Who would believe me over him, anyway? The only person I ever told was Mama.

I liked getting straight A's. How could any college refuse me if I had straight A's and so many extracurricular activities? But an F? That would destroy everything!

"Mr. Aument, let me look into this and I'll get back to you. I want to discuss the situation further with Mrs. Morgan." Mr. Gray put his hand on Mr. Aument's shoulder and led him out of his office.

"Lynette, don't return to Mr. Aument's class," Mrs. Morgan instructed me when Mr. Aument was gone. "Go wait in the library until your next period, okay?" She smiled at me.

"Yes, ma'am."

Mrs. Morgan knew me well, and she liked me. I hoped that she could convince Mr. Gray that I was no cheater.

I left school that day overwhelmed at the thought that I was going to fail Mr. Aument's class. I knew I had not cheated, but how would I prove it? Mr. Aument was adamant, and I believed that a teacher's word superseded any student's word.

When I arrived home, I told Mama.

"Lynette, you don't cheat!" she cried in disbelief. "You don't need to cheat!"

"I know, Mama, but how can I get the school to understand that?"

She shook her head, lips pressed tight together.

I felt powerless.

I returned to school and for two days I sat in Mr. Aument's class while he glared at me. The fact that I was still in school was good, but being in his class was torture.

"Would Lynette Charity please report to Mr. Byrd's office?" the PA announcer requested.

"Mr. Aument," I said timidly, "may I be excused?"

"Go," he said without making eye contact.

I imagined he knew the outcome and was gloating inside.

I walked into the assistant principal's office and found him talking to Mrs. Wilkinson, another government teacher.

Mr. Byrd, the bespectacled, white-socks-wearing second-in-command of the school, smiled at me. "Hello, Lynette. You know Mrs. Wilkinson?"

I nodded.

"We've decided to have you transfer to her class for the remainder of the course. Mrs. Wilkinson will give you another test, and whatever grade you get on that will be your starting grade in her class, okay?"

Yes, sir! I thought. Had Mrs. Morgan convinced Mr. Byrd and Mr. Gray that I wasn't a cheater?

Mrs. Wilkinson gave me a test. I scored 100, allowing me to start in her class with an A, a grade I maintained the rest of the year. By the end of the year, I was a straight-A student again. Mr. Aument sneered at me every time he passed me in the hall, but no one once mentioned anything about my "Aument problem" again.

What did I do to this man? I wondered. Maybe he just couldn't wrap his head around the fact that a colored girl could be so smart. I found it frightening that a teacher would lie about me—and to what end? Did he want to get me kicked out of the school?

What he couldn't have imagined was how dedicated I was to excelling. He didn't know that I had an escape plan; he didn't know how much I had at stake.

I learned later from Mama that my being accused of cheating didn't sit well with Daddy. She told me that my daddy, who'd never before walked into Cradock High School, mustered up the courage to go defend his daughter that week. According to Mama, he got a ride over to the school, walked into Mr. Byrd's office, and told him I was no cheater. He told him that I didn't need to cheat; I was smart. And I guess they believed him.

I wondered if the situation would have had a different outcome if Daddy hadn't stood up for me, or if it was Mrs. Morgan who'd tipped the scales. I couldn't know.

But his action did show that he cared. First the seventh-grade Science Fair, and now this! Still, Daddy never said, "Lynette, I'm going up to that school and tell them people that you ain't no cheater!" And when I found out about his gallantry, I never said, "Thank you for sticking up for me, Daddy." We'd never had a bond, and it was too late to develop one. But, you know, my daddy was brave that day.

I think Daddy and his friends felt safe in our community. These men never ventured outside of it, except to go to work. Like my daddy, they all worked at the Norfolk Naval Shipyard. Most were truck drivers. A bus from the shipyard called the Blue Goose picked them up each day and took them to work, and then returned them at the end of the workday, around 6:00 p.m. Daddy was out standing by our mailbox by 5:45 a.m. each morning, ready to hop on. And it was always on time. On the weekends he was at his cronies' homes, drinking and gambling. Never did he go into the white world for anything except to work, and he was okay with that. Everything he needed was in the neighborhood.

Given all that, the fact that he gathered up enough courage to go up to the white school to plead my case was downright remarkable.

Chapter 16
Golden Ticket

JUNIOR YEAR WAS the time to get busy if you wanted to attend college. Everyone knew that. So why was I struggling with the process? I had the grades, I had the extracurricular activities, I had essay material ready to go. But where should I apply? What about financial aid? And would I need to go for an interview?

When I raised my concerns with Mrs. Morgan, she suggested I speak with Mrs. Pollard. "She's the senior guidance counselor," she told me.

I knew very little about Mrs. Pollard. I prepared questions to ask her about the college application process. I'd taken the PSAT and the SAT and done well. I was ready. But where should I go? *Anyplace outside the great state of Virginia*, I thought. I was willing to consider UVA, since it was up north. Mostly, though, I wanted to go as far from home as possible.

On the day of our appointment, Mrs. Pollard called me into her office.

"Have a seat," she said, directing me to a chair across from her desk. She was a short woman with blondish hair, and she wore cat-eye glasses.

She sat at her desk and ignored me for the longest time. Finally, she looked up.

"Lie-nette Charity," she drawled. "What can I do for you?"

"Hello, Mrs. Pollard. I need some help with my college applications."

She tilted her head. "College? You want to go to college?"

"Yes, ma'am!"

"You thinkin' about Norfolk Community College?"

Norfolk Community College was a Black college in Norfolk, Virginia.

"No, ma'am. I want to go outside the state. Maybe a college in California. I just need some help with the applications.

"Well, Lie-nette, Norfolk Community College is probably where you should go. And work on your typin' skills. Secretaries need to have good typin' skills."

"I'm not going to be a secretary," I scoffed, though I attempted to keep my face as neutral as possible. I knew that any defiance would be met with some form of punishment, with expulsion being the harshest. I had experienced enough injustice from adults to last me a lifetime. Yet here I was, dealing with the ignorance of an adult once again. In Mrs. Pollard's mind, it seemed, despite all of my academic accolades, the best I could do as a colored girl was go to a colored community college, take typing, and eventually get a job as a secretary. Ridiculous! I didn't even like typing!

Maintaining a respectful tone, I said, "I want to go to a good college so that I can get into medical school."

"Medical school?" she repeated, shaking her head. "Now you probably will get into a Negro college, but no medical school's gonna take a colored girl."

I felt my face get flushed. My hands formed fists and then I quickly undid them. Hitting an adult, even a stupid guidance counselor, was out of the question.

Is she serious?

I was an honor student! I had proven myself time and time again scholastically. Why couldn't she believe I was capable? There appeared to be no doubt in her mind that I was *not* college material—unless I chose to go to a community college to become a secretary. Weren't guidance counselors supposed to give guidance?

Clearly, I wasn't going to find any answers here. I excused myself and stalked out the door.

I fumed the whole ride home. We had school bus service now, and there were even enough Black kids at Cradock to fill a bus. It was great not having to walk through the white neighborhood on the days Mr. Epps couldn't take me. And if I had walked, there would have almost certainly been trouble. There was so much anger welling up in me.

By the time the school bus reached my stop, I could barely hold in my urge to scream at the top of my lungs, "I'm going to college, damn it!"

I needed help. But where would I find that help?

Mama had gone to Norfolk Community College in 1945 for one year. Hunter Sue had graduated from Howard University, but I didn't see her as a knowledgeable counselor candidate. Her college experience had taken place so long ago; she'd graduated in 1926! I felt that Howard had been her only choice then, and I wanted options. I did not want to go to an all-Black school; I wanted experiences not tied to my race.

I felt that I needed a white person to help me navigate the world outside of my city, even my state. After all, I was in the South, and no school integration was going to change some folks' opinions. What I wanted, deep down, was a white path to my future. I believed that was the only way I could escape my life. As a Black female attending a white college, I thought, I could show everyone I could do the work.

I welcomed the challenge.

After getting off the school bus, I turned left at the intersection of Stratford and Taft and slogged my way to my front porch. This had been such a disappointing day. What was I going to do? What if Mrs. Pollard told the other teachers to not help me because I was just a colored girl? I reached the top of the porch and was about to sit down to think things over—collect my thoughts before entering the house and falling into a heap of tears and snot—when suddenly the front door opened.

Mama peered through the screen door without opening it. "Lynette, Lynette! I thought I heard you coming up the steps. You won't guess who just called me."

"No, Mama," I moaned. "Who called?"

"This lady from a college in Pittsburgh, Pennsylvania. She wants you to come take a look at the school. Now I told her that we didn't have any money to send you there for an interview. So, guess what she said?"

"I don't know, Mama," I said, still stuck in my funk.

"Well, I'm gonna tell you. She said she was gonna send you a bus ticket to come up there for an interview. She said she's gonna call you tomorrow. I asked her if she knew that tomorrow was Saturday and she said she did. So, she's gonna call you tomorrow! Phew!" Mama was plum tuckered out by the time she got the story out.

At this, of course, my curiosity was piqued, and I immediately rose out of my doldrums. "Who is this lady?" I asked. "What did she say the name of the school was? How did she find out about me?"

Mama had forgotten that information.

She opened the screen door to let me in, but I shook my head; I wasn't ready to be inside.

"I need to sit awhile on the porch," I said.

Mama paused—and then she did something quite unusual. She came out and sat down beside me.

She said nothing for a good long while, and neither did I. We just sat there in silence together.

Eventually, she stood and went back into the house.

At 10:00 a.m. on Saturday morning, Mama's Princess phone in the bedroom rang. I'd been pacing through the house most of the morning hoping that she had not dreamed the whole thing. I picked up the receiver on the second ring.

"Hello, Charity residence—Lynette Charity speaking."

"Hello, Lynette. My name is Peggy Donaldson. Did your mother tell you I would be calling?"

"Yes, ma'am," I said, heart in my throat. "She said that you were going to call me about coming to see your college."

"Well, it's not *my* college, but I am the admissions director here at Chatham College for Women. We're located in Pittsburgh, Pennsylvania. Have you heard of Chatham?"

"No, ma'am." I wanted to tell her that I hadn't heard of a lot of colleges, but I kept that to myself.

"So, Lynette, I'm going to assume you'd like to come see us, so I will be sending you a bus ticket to travel here in July. Do you have any plans for the summer?"

"No, ma'am."

"Okay. So let's plan on you visiting, and I hope you like what you see. We would enjoy you attending Chatham—it's a wonderful liberal arts college experience—but I'll let you decide that for yourself. Do you have any questions?"

I had lots of questions, starting with: "What's a liberal arts college?" But all I responded with was, "No, ma'am."

We finished our phone conversation with me mostly listening. I had no clue what a "liberal arts college experience" meant. Whether it would get me into medical school or not didn't cross my mind at the time. I decided it didn't matter. The first part of my escape plan was to get into college. That was it; I didn't think any further than that. College was college. And Pittsburgh was far away from home, which was what I really wanted.

I felt so great on Monday morning when I returned to school that when I saw a white classmate in the hall, I blurted out, "Becky! I'm going to Pittsburgh to interview at a women's college!"

Looking quite confused, she said, "Okay."

I had no friends at Cradock, but I was bursting to share my news, so I told my Ms. Donaldson story to a bunch of random students who stopped when I called their names. Most just said, "Okay," like I shouldn't be as excited as I was. However, Ed, one of the Black students, asked, "How did she find you, Lynette? I mean, you haven't filled out any applications, right?"

No, I hadn't—and his question made me wonder.

I later found out that colleges at that time were buying up lists of potential minority applicants. I was likely in a database that said FEMALE, HIGH ACADEMIC ACHIEVEMENTS, BLACK, UNDER-PRIVILEGED. A program called Affirmative Action had been introduced in 1961, eight years earlier, by President John F.

Kennedy, as an answer to racial inequality. All I can say is, "Thank you, President Kennedy!" and "Thank you, Ms. Donaldson!"

I finished out my junior year as a straight-A student with no one accusing me of cheating. I did not see Mrs. Pollard again for guidance. I did learn from a classmate that she had heard about Ms. Donaldson. That made me smile. If it hadn't been for that program, there's no doubt in my mind that my only option for college would have been Norfolk Community College.

I hadn't traveled to many places prior to the bus trip to Pittsburgh. There was Washington DC in third grade, when we went to the White House; there were field trips to Williamsburg, Jamestown, Yorktown, and Mount Vernon; there was that trip to Lawrenceville for the Science Fair; and there was the biggest trip, to Niagara Falls, where my seventh-grade class got to ride the *Maid of the Mist*.

Now, bus ticket in hand, I was going "up North" again to get closer to my dream.

Mama purchased me a travel outfit: a beige polyester bell-bottom pantsuit with a red pleather collar and cuff paired with a red pleather hat with a plume. I wore my new platform shoes. Worried that the mayo in a tuna fish or a chicken salad sandwich might go bad, Mama insisted on making me a couple of peanut butter and jelly sandwiches. I carried a small suitcase with enough clothes in it to last me a couple of days.

I was going to arrive late at night on that Friday and return on Sunday.

"You only get off the bus at designated food stops, ya hear?" Mama chided me.

"Yes, Mama."

It was going to be an eighteen-to-twenty-hour ride one way, with several stops along the way. Mama worried that I'd get off and not get back on. I *was* seventeen, I reminded her. I could read and understand directions.

Mr. Epps got us to the Greyhound Bus station in Norfolk in plenty of time for the 4:00 a.m. departure that would get me to Pittsburgh at 11:00 p.m. The bus driver checked my ticket and I boarded. Looking around, I saw a few people I wanted to avoid, so I sat in the middle of the carriage by a window. *I can lean against the window to sleep*, I thought. *And I can use both seats as a makeshift bed if no one sits next to me.*

Mama and Mr. Epps waved to me as the bus pulled away from the terminal bay. Maybe I should have been excited, but all I felt was *calm*. I was in the moment—on a Greyhound bus headed to Pittsburgh, en route to a college that wanted me.

I laid my head against the window, and the drone of the bus motor soon lulled me to sleep.

At each stop, I got off, used the facilities in the terminal, and returned to the bus. Initially, it was dark, so I slept. Once the sun came up, I passed the time looking out the window and taking in the countryside as we traveled farther and farther from my home. I played a game I called License Plates: I had a piece of paper with a column for each US state, and whenever I saw a new license plate, I put it in its proper column.

When we started out, there were a lot of Virginia plates. As we moved along I-95 going north, I saw plates from Delaware, New Jersey, Connecticut, and even New York.

I saw the sunrise at the beginning of my trip and the sunset as we moved farther north. I dozed. I dreamed of a life in the North where I would be accepted. I truly thought that the Mason-Dixon line separated the whites that hated us in the South from the whites who accepted us in the North.

"Pittsburgh, we're entering Pittsburgh," the bus driver finally announced.

It was pitch black outside as we pulled into the bus station. Ms. Donaldson had called me before I left to let me know that she would be picking me up.

"Helloooo, Lynette Charity!" a voice yelled as I exited the bus. "Over here!"

In the distance two women, one a blonde and the other a brunette, waved their arms in the air.

I walked over to them. "Ms. Donaldson?" I asked, looking at them.

"I'm Ms. Donaldson," the blonde woman said. "I spoke to your mother, and she told me to look for a girl in a red hat!"

"Hello, Lynette, I'm Ms. Hofsoos," the brunette chimed in. "Welcome to Pittsburgh. How was your bus ride?"

"It was long!" I said, and yawned.

"Well, it's late! Let's get you back to the campus and settled in. We have a student tour guide to assist you during the weekend," Ms. Donaldson explained as we walked to her car.

I got into the back seat. I was tired, yet I still marveled at the fact that the admissions director at Chatham College for Women and her sidekick were at the Greyhound Bus station in downtown Pittsburgh picking me up, and so late at night!

"I'd love to show you some features of the area, Lynette, but it's too late and too dark tonight," Ms. Donaldson said as we left the bus station. "You'll get a tour tomorrow, I promise!"

Despite my exhaustion, I was wide awake and paying attention to every little detail. I saw a street sign that read FIFTH AVENUE, and noticed that the street it marked was better lit than the others we'd passed. There was a sign that read CARNEGIE MELLON, and once we got past that sign, a building loomed before us. I later learned that it was the Cathedral of Learning, part of the University of Pittsburgh. I had never seen such a tall building before.

A few minutes later, we made a right turn off of Fifth Avenue. I wasn't sure where we were. I couldn't make out any buildings. I did notice lots of trees lining the very narrow road. I think we drove over a bridge.

It was Saturday morning when Ms. Donaldson stopped. I knew that only because as we pulled to a stop Ms. Hofsoos said, "My goodness, it's one o'clock!"

Ms. Donaldson turned to look at me in the back seat. "Well, we're here, Lynette! This is Fickes Hall, the freshman dorm. Ashley should be just inside waiting for you. I may see you tomorrow—well, later today, I guess." She smiled. "Get some rest. You'll get to meet the other interviewees on your tour tomorrow morning."

I exited the car, walked up the steps of the massive dorm, and knocked on the huge door. An energetic blond young lady opened the front door. As she did, Ms. Donaldson drove away.

"Hello, Lynette! Welcome! I'm Ashley!"

She was way too upbeat for that hour of the morning.

"I'll save everything else until later today," she chirped. "Let's get you settled in your room. Follow me!"

In no time at all, Ashley had shown me the dorm room where I'd be staying for the next two nights. She showed me the common bathroom, which had more toilets, showers, and sinks than I'd ever seen in my life, told me where to meet her at 8:30 a.m., and left me alone to get ready for bed.

My room had twin beds, but only one was made. Towels had been laid across the unmade one.

I undressed and donned my pajamas. As soon as I got into bed, I passed out cold.

I awoke at 7:30 a.m., showered, got dressed, and met Ashley at the bottom of the stairs, as directed.

She looked up as I came down. "Great timing. Let's go eat! They have bagels with cream cheese!"

What's a bagel with cream cheese? I wondered.

When we reached the food area in the foyer of the dorm, I chose something I recognized: orange juice and a blueberry muffin. Ashley had the bagel with cream cheese.

We left the dorm and walked to the main road, where we were joined by three other young women interviewees. Quick introductions were made, and then Ashley began the tour.

I couldn't believe how beautiful the campus was! It was so green. Trees, such an abundance of trees that lined the road leading to all the dormitories. Across from Fickes was a sloping area of grass abutting a sidewalk that led up to an elevated part of the campus. There was a building there that looked like a chapel.

"So the entrance into Chatham off Fifth Avenue is called Woodland Road," Ashley explained. "There is a house at the entrance there called Gateway, and that is used by our day students."

Pointing down Woodland Road, she described the dorms of Chatham: Fickes, Beatty, Rea, Laughlin, Berry, Woodland, and

Benedum. Every one except for Woodland, which had been built specifically as a dormitory, had once been the primary home or seasonal residence of a prominent Pittsburgh family.

One family lived in each of these homes before they became dormitories? I thought. *Wow!*

Everything was within walking distance. We went up to the chapel—which, Ashley explained, was used for nondenominational worship and campus-wide functions—and then inspected some of the classrooms.

When I entered Buhl Hall, I knew that if I attended Chatham, this would be my place. This was the science building.

We took a break for lunch and spent time asking each other the usual questions.

One of the other touring potential students asked me, "Where you from?"

"Portsmouth, Virginia," I said.

"How did you find out about Chatham?"

"Ms. Donaldson," I said with a shrug.

"Where else are you applying?"

I hadn't applied anywhere yet and didn't care to elaborate, so I said, "Virginia colleges."

How do you tell someone that you don't know how in hell you ended up at this prestigious women's college after never having filled out one damn college application? I worried that if I asked any questions myself, the others might ask me even more probing questions that I didn't want to answer, so I kept my mouth shut. I wondered if any of them talked among themselves about me when I was out of earshot—after all, I was the only non-white in attendance.

I was surprised to find that while I had taken a twenty-hour bus trip to get here, the other girls on this weekend retreat had all come from surrounding areas of Pittsburgh.

"I don't want to go too far from home, but I do want the living-on-campus experience," a young woman from some place called Sewickley shared.

Well, I wanted that same experience—just nowhere near Portsmouth or Virginia.

My interview with Ms. Donaldson was right after lunch on Saturday. I wondered how much sleep she had gotten once she got home. Maybe she'd gotten to sleep in, since my interview wasn't until after lunch. Did the other young women have interviews?

Ashley directed me to Mellon Hall, another enormous building and once the home of—you guessed it—the Mellons. I entered, walked up a flight of stairs, and found the admissions office.

Ms. Donaldson was sitting at her desk, while Ms. Hofsoos was seated in a chair to her right. They looked just fine. They looked better in the light. They looked rested.

I knocked on the open door.

"Lynette, come in! Come in! Have a seat." Ms. Donaldson pointed to a wooden chair directly in front of her desk.

"Nice to see you in the light of day," Ms. Hofsoos added.

Ms. Donaldson shuffled some papers and scribbled on one of them. "So, Lynette, would you like to attend Chatham?"

"Uh, yes, ma'am, but we don't have the money," I said, looking down.

"You let me worry about that," she said brightly. "Would you like to attend Chatham?"

"Yes!" I said, smiling.

"All right!"

That was my interview with Ms. Donaldson. I was accepted on the spot, with a financial aid package that included a work-study job. I would be part of the incoming class of 1974.

One more year at Cradock and I would be gone—escape plan complete!

As a straight-A student, I did not have to take any senior exams. This was partly to Mama's credit: she promised me that if I got all A's, she would ride naked on a horse down Taft Drive—"Like Lady Godiva."

I believed her, and I got all A's.

To my disappointment, Mama riding on a horse naked down Taft Drive never happened.

Chapter 17
Making My Debut

AS MY LAST year at Cradock began in September 1969, I felt something shifting in me. I had changed from a colored girl focused on getting through a white high school system that tried to hold me back to someone with a concrete plan. Thanks to Ms. Donaldson and Chatham College for Women, I was going to college!

Infused with a new sense of safety and relief, I took new risks that year that had nothing to do with getting into medical school.

Risk #1: Dancing on TV! The top academic students from Portsmouth's local high schools, Black and white, were chosen to be on a local TV station's (WAVY 10) version of *American Bandstand*. Academics over athletics was finally being rewarded.

Initially, I decided against it. There was just one small problem: I told James, a Black classmate who had also been selected, "I'm not going to do it."

"Why not?" James asked.

I looked down at the floor, and in a whisper I said, "I don't know how to dance!"

He laughed. "Listen, girl, you are Black! Of course you know how to dance!"

I guess my dormant dance gene needed to be awakened. James helped me, using the music of Aretha Franklin, the Supremes, Sly and the Family Stone, and many others. I was a quick study.

James and I attended the same school but rarely saw each other. I was into science, and he was into sports. He played football. I didn't have a single class with him. Like most high schools, ours was full of cliques—and I was not interested. But James was willing to help me despite my not being part of his circle of friends, and I was thankful for that.

I enjoyed myself as I did the twist on TV. I even improvised a bit, doing what might have been a combination of the twist, the loco-motion, the Watusi, and the jerk. The show was taped, and seeing myself afterward—all smiles as I gyrated and looked into the camera—made me feel a sense of accomplishment. I was dancing! I wore my white blouse with a Peter Pan collar, a plaid jumper, white socks, and my Buster Browns. Letting my guard down for once, allowing for other opportunities, opened me to this new experience that had nothing to do with my quest but everything to do with shaping me into a different person from that little girl who felt traumatized by her life.

Cradock was swarming with Black students by the time I started my senior year. Just four years prior, you could have counted "the coloreds" on one hand, but now integration was full steam ahead. Being smart made me an academic resource, and I helped many students, Black and white, pass their exams. But I had made no real inroads on the friends front.

After dancing on TV, I did get a bit more attention at school. Barbara, a white girl, said to me the next week, "Hey, Lynette! Saw you on that dance show. You were great!"

Yes, I was, but still not great enough to be invited to your home, I thought with no small amount of bitterness. But even so, the acknowledgment I got from my peers, Black and white, in the days that followed made me feel special.

My notoriety was short-lived. I was okay with that. Dancing on TV was fun, nothing more. I kept my eye on the real prize: getting out.

Paul continued to avoid me, but I decided it was for the best. I was content to finish out my last year drama-free and leave Portsmouth for good.

Before September came to a close, Hunter Sue approached me with a smile that reminded me of the Cheshire Cat from *Alice in Wonderland*. Through her perfect, store-bought teeth, she said, "Lynette, you've been selected to be a debutante."

"Selected to be a *what*?" I asked. I'd never heard this word before.

"A debutante," she repeated. "It's when a young lady is presented to society. You learn etiquette and there's a formal celebration, a debutantes' ball."

Etiquette! I thought. I remembered Annie Holloway drilling etiquette into my brain. "Sit up straight! No slouching. Watch your diction! It's *this,* not *dis.* It's *that,* not *dat.* It's *those,* not *dose.*" Lessons on how to sit, how to set a table, how to speak. And now I was to be *presented to society?*

Hunter Sue told me that a teacher at her school, Mrs. Lattimer, and her husband, wanted to sponsor me.

Sponsor me?

Before I even had a chance to react, she was peppering me with reasons why I couldn't say no—that this was such an honor and how I should be so appreciative of the Lattimers' generosity.

I thought for a moment. I said no.

I could see the disappointment on Hunter Sue's face. She had helped me so much. But being a debutante wasn't going to increase my chances of getting into medical school. It just seemed so irrelevant. I couldn't be bothered to do it.

Then something out of the ordinary occurred: Mama shared the news with Daddy—and he cared enough to get involved.

Apparently Daddy knew the upside of this honor, at least from his vantage point. Turned out there was a hierarchy among us Black folks. The Lattimers and my great-aunt, Hunter Sue, were at the top. The Lattimers belonged to a social club. My great-aunt was a principal of an elementary school. My parents, in contrast, were on the bottom, with no way to move up—except maybe by having a daughter who was a debutante.

Black social clubs were formed in the 1920s. Everything was segregated at the time, so middle-class Blacks who could not join a white club started their own. The Bachelor-Benedict Social Club of Norfolk, Virginia, was organized and founded in 1922. The hallmark of this organization was presenting young Black women to society. These young ladies dressed in white gowns and long-sleeve white gloves and received a bouquet of roses the night they were presented. The highlight of the "debut" was a formal ball.

Daddy came to me to plead his case—and he was even sober when he did it.

"Lynette, please do this," he begged. "Please! I could never be a part of *that* club, but if you're one of their debutantes, I can tell my guys all about it! I'd be so proud!"

So proud?

This was the same man who had once lamented that God hadn't taken me instead of Beverly.

This was the man who used my mother as a punching bag and almost killed her. This was the man who in his drunken stupor would make my mother beg for money and sometimes throw it down so she had to scrabble for it on the floor. This was the man who'd never showed me any love.

On the other hand, this was also the man who had driven four hours to and from a science fair so that I could come home with a trophy. And who had gone to Cradock to go to bat for me when I was accused of cheating.

When I saw how important this honor would be for my father, I reconsidered.

Then relented.

I told Daddy, "I'm not doing this for you, I'm doing this for Hunter Sue!"

But in my heart, I knew I was doing it for the both of them. I just couldn't give Daddy the satisfaction that he'd swayed me. Why should I?

The road to the debutante ball was not easy. I learned how to sit like a lady, how to set a table for six, how to walk balancing a tome on my head. I learned how to curtsy!

In rehearsals, Daddy escorted me to the stage. Once I reached the steps, he released my arm and I walked up the steps unaccompanied. "I now present Lynette Delcine Charity," the rehearsal coach said. I then walked to the middle of the stage, faced the audience, curtsied, received my "flowers," and exited down the steps on the other side, where on the night of the event my escort would be waiting to take me to the back of the auditorium.

Mama splurged on my ballgown. The slip, which was included, had tubing around the bottom, which when inflated made the gown spread out away from my legs. This would prevent me from getting my knee caught and possibly falling over during my curtsy. It was

pretty ingenious, and I was the only one with such a contraption. The gown package also included white pumps and white gloves that reached my elbows.

It did not, however, include an escort.

Hunter Sue found me an escort. His name was Robert, and he was the nephew of a friend of hers. He wasn't Paul and he would never be Paul, but Hunter Sue was content.

I met Robert for the first time at Hunter Sue's home in early April of 1970. There was a knock at the door. I opened it, and there stood a young man.

He was a handsome guy—what Mama and her friends would have called a *tall drink of water*.

"Hello, I'm Robert," he said, sticking out his right hand.

I reached out with my own hand, and we shook. "Lynette," I said.

Hunter Sue motioned us to the couch. "Sit down, you two. I'll get us some iced tea." And off she went to the kitchen.

"So, Robert, it is so nice of you to do this for me," I said. "Thanks."

"Well, my auntie said that she would pay for the corsage and the tux rental," he admitted. "And she's gonna help me with college money."

That's a pretty fair deal if you ask me, I thought. But all I said was, "That's great!"

We talked about college, and I proudly announced that I was going away to Pittsburgh, Pennsylvania.

"I know," he said. "My auntie told me."

Hunter Sue returned to the living room with the iced tea and some cookies.

"So, Robert, did your aunt tell you about the etiquette classes you will need to attend?" she asked.

"Yes, ma'am." He bobbed his head. "She is letting me use her car."

"Sorry to take up time from your Saturdays," I offered. "You won't have much to learn. Just how to open a door and pull out a chair for a young lady to sit. Oh yeah, and how to hold my arm and escort me to the back of the auditorium."

"Yeah, and I guess there's gonna be a party with dancing afterwards?" he asked.

"Oh, yeah, the debutante ball," I confirmed. "There's gonna be food and music and I think we will have to do a waltz as our first dance, and then we can do whatever we want!"

"A waltz? Okay," he said, a puzzled look on his face.

I could see the wheels turning. This might be a little more than he'd bargained for.

The day of the presentation arrived. Daddy was dressed in black tux pants with a shiny strip down the side of each leg. He wore patent leather shoes he'd rented. His rented white jacket with a white shirt and his black bow tie and cummerbund completed his outfit. He cleaned up well, despite smelling like a distillery and cigarettes. I could tell he was nervous because sweat was rolling down his face in torrents and he kept having to wipe it away with the two handkerchiefs he was carrying.

We stood in a line of father-daughter pairings that went down the aisle on either side of the auditorium. The aisles led to a large stage, upon which various social club dignitaries stood. As each of our names was called, we walked to the steps on the arm of our father. The steps led to the stage. Daddy stopped at the bottom step, gave me a kiss on my cheek, and walked away. He'd never kissed me until that moment.

I walked up the three steps to the stage and paused.

"I present to you Miss Lynette Delcine Charity," Mr. Lattimer announced.

Upon hearing my name, I turned to face the audience, paused, smiled, put out my right arm as a counterbalance, and curtsied. I nailed it! Just like I was taught in those damn etiquette classes. I stood upright again and everyone clapped. Mrs. Lattimer handed me a bouquet of red roses. I walked to the opposite side of the stage, where Robert extended his hand and assisted me down the three steps, and our escort-debutante pairing walked down the aisle and out the auditorium door.

It was done.

At the ball that followed, we danced. At the end of the evening, Robert and I said our goodbyes, and that was that. I never heard from him again.

I thought about Beverly more that day than I had in a while. I'd pondered Daddy's question on and off over the years—"Why didn't God take you instead of my Beverly?" I wondered that too. Why had I survived? Why had I gotten this opportunity? Beverly had been loved by all. And yet after her death her memory had been erased; no one ever so much as spoke her name again.

It felt like no one loved me, yet there were forces that seemed to see something lovable within me. In dying, had Beverly saved me by giving me a bigger purpose? Without her around, my singular focus was on getting out of Portsmouth. And for years I'd relied on her, even after her death, for comfort and direction.

I rarely spoke to Beverly the way I had when I was younger anymore, but I'd done it after returning from my Chatham interview.

Beverly, we did it! I yelled inside my head.

There was no reply, but I knew she was happy for me. She was a part of me and always would be. And I knew if I needed her voice, it would return to comfort me.

Graduation was in May of 1970. In attendance were my parents, Cubby Lee, my great-aunt, my two great-grandmothers, and Grandpop.

As I crossed the stage, I thought of college and my body hummed with excitement. Never in my wildest imagination could I have believed that Chatham would become part of my escape plan. How had I had the great fortune to find it?

I'd ask myself this same question countless times in the years that followed and never come up with an answer. Some might say that it was because of my determination and tenacity and the fact that I was quite intelligent. All I know is that a series of events led me to this end. Some were good, some bad—but they all pushed me forward. When one door shut, another one opened.

Anyway, there was no time to dwell on the why. I marveled at the progress of my escape plan. I was going to college! I looked forward to my next four years. And the four years after that! I tried to not think so far in advance, but I couldn't help it.

Soon enough, I would leave home—and never come back.

The rest of the summer after graduation was a blur. The only memory I'd carry forward was the envelope I received from Chatham. Inside was a questionnaire in which one specific question stood out: *Would you be willing to room with a classmate not of your race?*

Without hesitation, I checked the *YES* box.

Part III

The Escape

Chapter 18
Far from Home

FOR MY ONE-WAY trip to Chatham, Mama bought me a foot-locker from an army-navy surplus store. I placed in it all my worldly possessions and shipped it to the college so it would be there by the time I arrived. My plan was to never return home. I was done with Portsmouth. I wanted to sever all ties to those who had tried to hold me back.

Mama and Mr. Epps took me to the bus terminal.

There were no tears. There were no hugs. Mr. Epps told me to enjoy college and Mama told me to behave myself.

"Don't you bring me back nuthin' to raise!" she said as I stepped onto the bus.

Her response startled me. I paused on the top step before entering the bus.

What does she mean by that?

A week earlier, I had received another letter from Chatham informing me that Fickes would be my dorm and that my room-mate would be Catherine Cusack from Mt. Lebanon, Pennsylvania. I guessed that Catherine would be like so many of the incoming students I'd met during my visit, who wanted to be on campus but still close to home.

Close to home? Not me!

I was picked up by two campus security personnel upon my

arrival in Pittsburgh. The car they came in had CHATHAM COLLEGE printed on its doors.

"We're here to take you to your dorm, Miss Charity," they informed me.

"Thank you," I replied, eyes wide. I hadn't thought anyone would be picking me up this time, and I was pleasantly surprised that the school had sent out not one but *two* security guards to fetch me from the station. It made me feel special and safe.

Sitting in the back seat, I was filled with admiration for myself. *I did it! I'm on my way!*

Nothing was going to stand in my way now. I grinned a good ole Cheshire Cat grin.

When we arrived at Fickes, I got out of the car, thanked the two men, and started walking up the dormitory stairs.

"Your roommate is probably waiting for you in the foyer," the one in the passenger seat called out the window of the car. "Dinner is around 5:00 p.m. up at Woodland Hall."

With that announcement, they drove away.

Sitting on the steps leading to the second-floor dorm rooms was a diminutive young woman with short blond hair and the deepest dimples I'd ever seen. She smiled at me as I came through the door.

"Hi, I'm Cathy," she announced, standing up to greet me.

My new roommate had obviously checked the *YES* box too! I was once again pleasantly surprised. The world was still in black and white, and even though I was attending an integrated women's college, that didn't mean that a white classmate would want to room with me.

"Hi, I'm Lynette." I instinctively held out my right hand, but

Cathy leaned in to hug me instead. The top of her head hit me just below my chin.

"Glad you made it! I didn't want to go to dinner without my roommate!" She smiled with those dimples and I immediately felt at ease with her.

Cathy and I would soon learn that we had been the only two students to check that *YES* box.

"Let me show you to our room," Cathy said. "We're on the second floor. There's also a third floor of rooms. Our room is not too far from the bathroom, which is nice. It's pretty big, with lots of showers and toilets and sinks."

OUR room. Seeing her exuberance, I decided not to tell Cathy that I'd stayed in Fickes during my interview weekend and already knew the layout. Why spoil the moment for her?

"So, Lynette, I decided to make your bed using my sheets," she announced as we climbed the stairs to the second floor. I hope you don't mind. Your footlocker is in the room, but it's locked, and I thought it would be nice for you to be able to go to sleep and change things in the morning."

I was touched. "Thanks," I said. "That's so nice of you."

We reached our door and went inside.

Our twin beds were pushed up against opposite walls, Cathy's bed to the left and my bed to the right. Our desks, back-to-back, were set under the single window in the room. Our chests of drawers were on the wall closest to the door, next to two tiny closets. My footlocker was at the foot of the bed Cathy had chosen for me.

We sat on our beds and the conversation flowed easily.

"Where are you from again?" Cathy said.

"Virginia, from a small city called Portsmouth," I said. "The downtown is nothing like here. The buildings are nothing like here. Where I live, in Victory Park, is nothing like here. What about you?"

"I live in Mt. Lebanon, which is only thirty to forty minutes by car from here," she said.

I asked her why she'd chosen Chatham and she explained that a neighbor lady had told her parents about the school and they had convinced Cathy to apply. "So I did, and I got accepted," she said simply. "What's your major?"

I wanted to know why Cathy wanted to stay so close to home. I imagined it was because she had a perfect home life, perfect parents, and wonderful siblings. Her home life was probably more like what I saw on TV; maybe her parents were like the Cleavers from *Leave It to Beaver*. Parents who obviously loved each other and provided love and support for their children. Not like my parents, who I'd never felt gave a shit about me.

"Oh, I'm going to be a science major," I confided. "I want to go to medical school."

"Wow! Medicine! A doctor!" she exclaimed. "I'm majoring in American studies."

"Great!" I said.

I had no idea what American studies were, but I didn't ask. I didn't want to sound dumb.

We talked a bit about our families, and Cathy informed me that she had six siblings. I was fascinated by this and wanted to hear stories about her large family.

Despite our different career trajectories and backgrounds, Cathy and I quickly established that we both wanted to experience new and challenging ideas. She would be my guide into my new world. Pittsburgh was very different from Portsmouth, and she would be there to navigate the differences with me.

In the coming weeks, Cathy and I would accessorize our room with matching bed covers and a matching window treatment that she sewed herself. Our color scheme was black and white. We had matching black-and-white-checkered bedspreads and curtains in the same pattern. Red was our accent color. We developed a sisterhood that felt so natural. At no point did being the only interracial roommates in the whole damn college seem to cross our minds. I was her *sistah from anuthah muthah*, and that was good with the both of us.

Woodland Hall, the biggest dormitory, housed the cafeteria that fed all students. However, the students at Fickes didn't have to schlep up the hill to get breakfast on weekdays; Fickes had its own kitchen and a cook!

On our first morning, Cathy and I went to breakfast together. There we met Mary, a bubbly, vibrant, older white woman who was greeting all the newbies.

"Hello there," she said, looking at me. "Would you like to try a bagel with lox and cream cheese? Or would you like an omelet?"

I hadn't tried the bagel during my interview weekend, and I wasn't going to try it now. Besides, what was lox?

"I'll have an omelet, please." I'd already seen Mary whisk up some eggs, throw in some grated cheese and something green in a small frying pan, flip it, fold it, and slide it onto a plate for the student ahead of me.

Mary got right to work. "So polite," she commented as she whisked.

I couldn't have imagined speaking any other way. *Please* and *thank you* were requirements where I came from. To not say them in the right situation would mean trouble. Like, *Girl, what do you say to an adult that asks you a question?* or, *Girl! Have you forgot your manners?*

Mary handed me my omelet and I thanked her.

"You welcome," she said sunnily. "The bacon is over there, along with toast."

I got some bacon, a couple of slices of toast, and a prefilled glass of orange juice.

I was so astonished at my great fortune. An awesome new roommate and friend, and Mary, the cook.

I didn't know it yet, but Mary would become a confidante for me that first year. She was always willing to take the time to listen to me—and she *always* complimented me on my manners.

When Cathy ordered the lox bagel, I discovered that lox was smoked salmon. Since I'd never even had salmon, I felt I'd chosen correctly with my omelet.

We chose to sit near some other students, and Cathy, being the bold woman she was— maybe because she'd grown up with six siblings—fell into easy conversation with them.

"Hi, I'm Cathy," she said. "And this is my roommate, Lynette."

When I saw the confused look on our peers' faces, I wondered what was so perplexing to them. Was it really that hard to understand why two young women from different backgrounds might make a bold choice outside of cultural norms? It was the 1970s. After the make-love-not-war, flower-child '60s, what was next? Interracial relationships? Why not?

Maybe they feared judgment from their families, their friends, or other students if they were to hang out with us. All I knew was, they seemed uncomfortable.

"So, you two are roommates?" asked the redheaded, freckled student sitting directly across from me.

I stuffed a big piece of my omelet in my mouth so as not to have to answer her and I allowed Cathy to do all the talking.

"Yes," Cathy said. "Weren't you at dinner? Well, obviously not," she concluded before forging on. "Lynette's from Virginia. She's a science major. She's going to be a doctor."

"Oh, wow!" both students exclaimed simultaneously.

"I'm Heather," the redhead replied.

"I'm Laurie," said the brunette who'd been quiet like me up to that point.

Finally, I spoke. "Isn't this place amazing? And Mary is so nice."

Well, I guess the ice was broken, because after that our new friends no longer seemed to be concerned by the fact that Cathy and I were roommates. We began a conversation about being women at a women's college. It was a great conversation, during which I learned we'd all arrived having come to the same conclusion: Chatham was a good fit for our educational needs.

Once classes began, I saw little of Cathy except for at breakfast, lunch, and dinner, and of course in our room in the evenings. The majority of her classes were in Coolidge Hall, the liberal, artsy building, while all of my classes were in Buhl Hall, the science building. That said, we used our time together to continue to expand our knowledge about each other and about Chatham.

"So, Lynette, you know anything about Hell Night?" she asked me one night.

"All I've heard is that the upper-class women get to play pranks on us," I said, making a face. "Someone said that last year her room got TP'd."

Hell Night was Chatham's rite of passage for first-year women, but I'll call it what it was: hazing. So, Hell Night was upon us. Little did we know that this would be the last one at Chatham—or that Hell Night would end forevermore because of me.

Soon after arriving at Chatham that year—1970—I'd started wearing my hair in an Afro. It was more of a financial statement than a political one. I could not afford to see a beautician every two weeks. I'd arrived at Chatham with straight hair that I curled using sponge rollers, the hairstyle I'd had ever since Mama started taking me to the beautician to get my hair straightened when I was six. Even with the treatments it remained a nappy, kinky, unruly mess. She'd tried to comb and braid my hair best she could for six years. I dreaded it. She and I would sit on the back steps of our place as she did her best to tame my wild mane while I just did a lot of "ow, ow, ow!"

At college, when I noticed my edges getting nappy—what usually signified that it was time for a touch-up—I made the decision: *No more.* I washed my hair, combed and braided it while it was still wet, and the next morning, I picked it out with my brand-new Afro pick.

Voilà! I could have passed for Angela Davis. My 'fro was big.

And it played an important role on Hell Night.

There was excitement in the air that night. Squeals of laughter and downright fun could be heard throughout the dorm. Cathy and I were in our room when the festivities began. We didn't know what to expect.

A knock came on the door; when I opened it, an upper-class woman threw a bucket of water on me.

I rushed out the door to get the culprit, but the floors of the dorm and the dorm rooms were not carpeted and I slipped on the slick floor—falling backward, hitting my head on the hard uncarpeted floor, and knocking myself unconscious.

When I woke up, I was in the hospital.

The doctor who examined me said, "You're a lucky girl. Your hair cushioned your fall."

My hair!

"You have a concussion," he said, "but no long-term damage. No skull fracture."

I did have a pretty good headache, and the back of my head where I'd hit the floor was sore to the touch. But I was otherwise fine.

I returned to Chatham the next day after an overnight observation at the hospital to find Cathy waiting in the foyer of the dorm when I arrived.

She rushed to hug me as soon as I arrived, saying, "Lynette, are you okay? No one would tell me anything!"

She showed me such motherly concern, it was easy to imagine her as the eldest sibling, watching out for everyone else. In fact, she was kinder to me upon my return from the hospital than my own mother would have been in similar circumstances. My guess is that she would have just said, "Lynette's got a hard head. She'll be fine. She shouldn't have been running down a hall in the first place! Yeah, she'll be fine."

I was so fortunate to have Cathy Cusack and her family in my life. They were better than the real deal. I never wanted to go home again.

"I have a headache," I reassured Cathy. "That's all."

I didn't ask her if anyone had called my mother, because I assumed no one had.

But Cathy had other news for me: "The president has officially canceled Hell Night because of your accident!" she said.

Rituals have both positive and negative impacts on us. Religious rituals, for instance, had a negative impact on me growing up Southern Baptist. No matter how hard I tried, according to Reverend Freeman, I was a sinner. So, could we ever *not* be sinners? According to Reverend Freeman, the answer was always *no*.

Then there are ritual rites of passage like Hell Night, where the emotional impact may not be as serious but the likelihood of someone getting physically hurt is high.

At first I felt bad about being "the girl who canceled Hell Night." But the more I thought about it, the less sorry I was that my incident had stopped a tradition that could result in injury. Whose idea was that in the first place? To hell with Hell Night. Good riddance! And I had my hair to thank for saving my life.

Chapter 19
Chatham Girl

EVEN THOUGH CHATHAM College was a liberal arts institution, I had no interest in liberal arts—I was there for the sciences. (Well, I was really there because the college had given me a four-year academic scholarship; their stellar science department with its small class sizes was a bonus.) As a science major, I chose to get degrees in both biology and chemistry. I wanted to stand out when I applied to medical schools, and I thought a double major would help. Maybe there were medical school students who majored in English literature or history, but they still had to do the prerequisites in science. I decided that a double major in biology and chemistry was double the pleasure, double the fun.

Buhl Hall was my place. There, I would take classes in biology, chemistry, organic chemistry, physics, and comparative anatomy—prerequisites to achieve my goal.

It is said that beauty is in the eye of the beholder. Well, I had never really seen beauty where others traditionally did. I'd once seen a picture of *Venus de Milo* in an art book, and all I'd thought was, *This is art? A statue of a naked lady with no arms?*

I loved to read, but screen adaptations of good books were preferable to me than the tomes they'd been made from. I'd seen *Gone with the Wind* at the colored movie theater in downtown Portsmouth when I was in fourth grade. Though it was almost four hours long, none of us had complained about the length. I'd thought it was an amazing movie. When Clark Gable, as Rhett Butler, said, "Frankly, my dear, I don't give a *damn*," a collective "Oooh, he said a bad word" rose from all the mouths of the kids in attendance.

I decided I needed to read the book after that and was pleased to discover a woman, Margaret Mitchell, had written it. I also learned more about the Black actresses in the movie. Hattie McDaniel won the Best Supporting Actress Oscar for her portrayal of Mammy. I later learned that she had not been allowed to attend the premiere of the movie because it had been held in a whites-only theater in Atlanta—and at the Oscars, she'd had to sit at a segregated table at the side of the room.

When Butterfly McQueen, who played the character Prissy, another domestic, said in one scene, "Lord have mercy, I don't know nuthin' 'bout birthin' no babies" in her childlike voice, it amused everyone, us Black kids included. As nine-year-olds, we had no deep understanding of segregation, discrimination, and racism. We were just at the "movin'-picture show," watching a well-told story that kept us engaged for four hours.

That said, I gravitated toward the concreteness of science. I didn't have to *interpret* the ideal gas law $PV = nRT$. Pressure (of a gas) × volume (of the gas) = n (amount of substance of gas) × R (ideal gas constant) × temperature (absolute temp of the gas). Now that, to me, was beautiful!

But Chatham had certain requirements. For instance, all first years were required to visit Fallingwater, a home designed by Frank Lloyd Wright. He'd designed it in 1935 and it had taken three years to build (1936–1939). Not seeing the need for a science major to go look at artsy-fartsy stuff, I tried to get out of it.

The answer was, "You're going!"

It was a ninety-minute bus ride from downtown Pittsburgh. Fallingwater, a three-story home built partly over a waterfall, turned out to be a breathtaking sight for this colored girl from the South! And it was just a weekend home for Liliane and Edgar Kaufmann, who owned Kaufmann's Department Store in Pittsburgh. Fallingwater was 5,330 square feet, with four bedrooms, five bathrooms, and a pool, along with a 1,700-square-foot guest house. I thought about my one-story, one-bathroom, 1,100-square-foot home in Victory Manor and realized it could fit inside the guest house with room to spare.

And did I mention Fallingwater was used only on *weekends*?

At Chatham, the class sizes were small. As a first year, my largest class was Biology 101, and even then there were only twenty-nine other women in it.

Dr. Chilton Knudsen, a down-to-earth woman who would become my mentor, was our professor. I'm not sure how other professors at other schools of higher education relate to their students, but the professors at Chatham, I felt, saw us as part of their family. And they were not afraid to let their hair down. My chemistry professor, Dr. William Beck, for example, acted in our plays—and he was quite good.

Dr. Frances Eldredge, English professor, realized that the science major students were not signing up for daytime English literature classes, so she designed one for us that she taught on Tuesday and Thursday evenings at her home. *English for the Science Major* was the name she gave the course. Learning Shakespeare with her was a treat.

Dr. Paulson, my tall, pale, white-haired, kindhearted organic chemistry professor, once sent out a search party for me when I missed a class. When there are only twelve people in a class, one absence stands out. I was a little embarrassed when two of my science classmates corralled me in the cafeteria at lunch that day.

"Lynette, where were you today? Dr. Paulson asked us to find out why you didn't come to class."

"Uh, I overslept," I confessed.

"Well, you better come up with a better answer than that when you see him," they warned me.

The next class, when Dr. Paulson noted my absence, I had an excuse at the ready: "Sorry, Dr. Paulson. Female trouble."

I think he got even paler!

The tradition of Hell Night did not survive my acceptance to Chatham, but the annual Halloween party, with its Best Costume Contest, remained a glowing success.

This was the 1970s, an era before we understood what it was to be politically incorrect. My frosh year, Dr. Knudsen (who would later become the Reverend Chilton Knudsen) came wrapped in a condom. I, meanwhile, dressed as "an Arab," using just a white sheet with a band holding it on my head and draping the rest around my body, as did two of my classmates; there's even a picture of us in costume in the 1970–71 yearbook (it's a good thing I didn't pursue a career in politics).

The following year I found a very fancy off-white dress with a hoop slip in a hidden room in Benedum, the senior dorm on Chatham's campus. I got a black bolero jacket to complete the look, and my friends and I went to the party as "Snow White and Her Seven Whores." I wore that dress and jacket and carried a wand. The seven women in my entourage came up with fitting names for our theme—Sleazy, Slutty, Seedy, Scuzzy, etc.—and we won the Best Costume contest that year.

So you see, even though Hell Night had been canceled forever because of me, in some ways I redeemed myself at those Halloween parties. No harm, no foul.

There were many students at Chatham who were considered locals. Despite living in the dorms, some would go home on the weekends. That was not possible in my case, but I was lucky to have Cathy, who invited me to her home many times over the course of our first year and beyond.

Cathy's parents, Donald and Elizabeth Cusack, were good Catholics. I had heard growing up that Catholics tended to have a lot of kids, but I hadn't experienced that firsthand until I met the Cusacks and their seven children.

Their home was adapted quite well to the brood. The dining room table was more like a picnic table, with benches instead of chairs. One night when I visited we had lasagna, a new dish for me. This was accompanied by salad and bread. Don sat at one end of the table, while Elizabeth sat at the other end. We kids filled the benches.

Their youngest, Michael, was fascinated by me—in a good way. Let me be honest, there were no colored folk in Mt. Lebanon! So Michael had no one to compare me to. That night, he stared at me and my big 'fro, clearly in awe. He didn't ask to sit beside me at the table. He just pushed his way in between me and one of his brothers. He kept taking a bite of lasagna or salad, tilting his head slightly sideways to catch a quick look, and then turning back and looking down at his food. I laughed every time; he was so cute!

On one visit, I met two of Cathy's cousins, Joan and John. They were eight and five, and just a couple of normal kids from what I saw.

Who knew they would grow up to become movie stars—Joan Cusack and John Cusack.

I must have talked up my visits with Cathy a lot, because one day a classmate who lived on my floor in Fickes, Mildred Morrison, approached me and said, "Lynette, my mom met this couple, the Wellses, and they want to adopt you while you're at Chatham. Would you be interested?"

I just stared at her, astonished. *Adopt me?*

Mildred Morrison was one of the locals. She was also Black. Her mother knew people, and apparently Mildred had told her about the Black girl from Virginia who was at Chatham on scholarship. Apparently, her mother had shared my story with Bob and Anne Wells, a white couple who lived in Mt. Lebanon not too far from the Cusacks, letting them know that I didn't have family nearby and suggesting that I could use some emotional support.

Robert (a.k.a. Bob) Wells worked for Westinghouse, and Anne was a homemaker raising three children: Bob Jr., Heidi, and Jim. They had another son, Charlie, but I don't remember ever seeing him—he was already grown. Bob and Anne became my Pittsburgh family, and when they found out how puny my stipend for school was, they started to supplement my financial aid with an additional $15 a month, telling me I needed a little fun money. They also invited me to visit them a number of times, and I even attended their church on a few occasions.

I was definitely a topic of conversation at the Wellses' church. The congregation was devoid of any people of color, and when the Wellses brought me there, a lot of people had questions. Some churchgoers actually spoke to me, but most just stared and had conversations—more like whisperings—among themselves.

The Wellses did not have to do what they did, and I wondered if any of their neighbors reacted poorly to my visits to their lily-white neighborhood. If they did, I never heard.

When school was out for the summer, I did not go home like the other students. I stayed with friends, the Cusacks, or the Wellses. I also house-sat for professors who traveled during the summer. There was nothing back in Virginia for me, and my goal was to get accepted to medical school and keep moving as far away from that life as possible. I stayed in touch with Mama through an occasional letter, but we never called each other. Phone calls were expensive, and I didn't feel any homesickness or a need to stay in touch with my family—and the lack of interest seemed to be mutual.

The Wellses, however, would remain in my life long after my graduation and eventually become godparents to my children.

During the summer of 1971, between freshman and sophomore year, I decided I wanted to see *Hair* at the Pittsburgh Musical Theater. I had heard that there would be some nudity and that the actor playing the character named Hud, a Black man, was "a real stud." I knew that meant he was good-looking. *And well-endowed.* I wanted to see for myself. So I went. Alone.

I sat in the fifth row of the theater in an aisle seat. The music was so good, with songs like "Aquarius/Let the Sunshine In." But I had come for Hud. When the lights lowered, the cast stood fully clad on stage. When the lights became brighter again, the cast stood naked on the stage. And I mean completely naked!

Hud was in the front row and I couldn't take my eyes off him—or rather, I couldn't take my eyes off his penis! Having only Daddy and my brothers as comparisons, Hud's penis looked different. It started out cylindrical but tapered to a point with the familiar tip—only it was . . . covered?

What's wrong with this guy's penis?

I later learned that I had just witnessed my very first uncircumcised penis. At Chatham, I was getting both a scholarly and a worldly education. It was all good.

In September, Cathy and I moved to Rae dormitory, an upper-class dorm that was a lot nicer than what we were used to.

It was our sophomore year and we needed a third roommate for our new dorm room.

Marilyn Horbaly was from Fairfax, Virginia, about four hours from where I grew up, and her father was a diplomatic attaché. I had to look up what a diplomatic attaché was, but once I did I was fascinated. I read a little about Beirut, Lebanon, where he was posted and where Marilyn had lived for a few years, and I marveled at the fact that she had lived outside the country. I wasn't sure if a ride on the *Maid of the Mist* between the Canadian and US Niagara Falls counted as international travel, but that was all *I* had to boast about.

I was concerned that Marilyn might be too hoity-toity to want to live with us, but she accepted our invitation, and we became a threesome! It was such an easy transition for the three of us, and we loved living in our triple room.

Chatham had mixers where male students from Carnegie Mellon,

Pitt, and Duquesne were invited to mingle with us. Occasionally our brother school, Washington & Jefferson in Washington, Pennsylvania, also sent potential suitors to our functions. There were a lot of Chatham women who married the men of W&J, and those mixers were fun, even though they were chaperoned.

I'm still not sure what possessed Cathy, Marilyn, and me to go out on a blind date one Saturday, eschewing the mixing. We convinced another classmate to join us and off the four of us went to meet four guys, all white and quite the geeks, from Carnegie Mellon. Cathy had a friend who had set up the meet.

It was a movie date and the guys chose *Johnny Got His Gun*, a film in which the lead character is an American soldier hit by an artillery shell during WWI. He lies in a hospital bed—no arms, no legs, no *face!*—conscious and able to reason, but unable to communicate except through Morse code. He drifts in and out between reality and fantasy and wants to die, even tapping out, *Kill me*. Alas, the movie ends with no one granting his wish. What a date night downer!

For some reason, the guys thought this would be a good movie to go see.

They were wrong.

The eight of us left the movie and stayed silent, just looking down at the ground. How do you even comment on such a depressing movie?

Before we even got out of the theater, one of the guys yelled out, "Hey there's an Alfred Hitchcock movie playing at the school. Let's go see it!"

Having a new plan was definitely a mood elevator. And I would take an Alfred Hitchcock suspense thriller over Johnny and his gun any day.

So off to CMU we went.

Charade was a good movie, and I became a fast Hitchcock fan after that night. He was my Waldo—as in, *Where's Waldo?*—before Waldo was a thing, and I enjoyed trying to spot his cameos.

At the end of the movie, we left our dates and headed back to campus. The night turned out to be okay, but we four girls vowed never to go on a blind date again—and we in fact kept that promise to each other all throughout our time at Chatham.

Chapter 20
Walter

"Relax, relax," he cooed. "You're going to feel so good in a moment."

"Walter, stop." I looked into his eyes. They were so reassuring. "Walter, please stop."

It was all happening so fast. A kiss, a hand down my pants, then my pants and panties pulled down to my knees and his penis shoved inside of me! It hurt more and more as he pushed deeper.

"Ow, ow! Stop."

I tried to push him away but he was in some sort of trance—eyes closed, gyrating and making guttural noises. The weight of his body on top of me was suffocating. It was of no use. He wasn't listening. I stopped resisting and just lay there, eyes closed, grimacing. This was not how I had planned my first sexual encounter. I had read *Our Bodies, Ourselves.*

Let it stop!

Suddenly his back arched and he thrust deeper into me; then he let out a deep, long moan and collapsed on top of me. I turned my head to one side and gasped for air. He adjusted himself slightly but did not get off of me.

"Oh, that was so good," he said in a tone of happy bliss. "I liked being inside of you. It's been a while. That was so good. Once I got started, I couldn't stop. It was good for you too, right?"

I was speechless.

He rolled off of me and onto the floor, his pants down around his ankles. He stood and tucked his penis, now short, limp, and covered with semen, back into his pants. I hadn't even seen it erect, it had all happened so fast.

I lay on my back, scared to get up because of the semen oozing out of my vagina. It felt the way blood felt when it oozed out during my menses and was absorbed by the sanitary napkin I wore. I felt nasty. I felt dirty.

What didn't cross my mind was that what we'd just done might result in pregnancy.

What did you just do, Lynette? I was horrified by what had just transpired, but I didn't let myself get mad at Walter.

Walter kissed me again and again.

"It will get better the more you do it, Lynette, I promise."

He kissed me one last time and left.

I lay there for a brief moment, trying to make sense of what had just happened. He had been in my room. We'd chatted for a while on my twin bed. We'd kissed. What had I done that given him the idea that what had just transpired had been good for me? Hadn't I begged him to stop? Hadn't I conveyed that it hurt? How had he gotten my pants and panties down to my knees?

Why did I let this happen?

Angry at myself more than at Walter, as I should have been, I got up slowly, making sure to not allow the icky mess to get on my bedcover.

Robotically, I collected my bucket of toiletries. I removed all of my clothing and stuffed them into a pillowcase. Walter had drooled on it; I made a mental note to do laundry right away. Then I put on my robe and slippers and used my dirty underwear to wipe the ooze running down my leg before shuffling down to the communal bathroom.

No one was there, and I was grateful for the privacy. I showered, starting at my neck and working my way down. I lingered in my pelvic area, scrubbing and scrubbing and scrubbing. I toweled off, peed, took a roll of toilet paper, and shuffled back to my room. I stuffed wads of the toilet paper up my vagina, put on underwear, placed a sanitary napkin inside, and put on my pajamas.

I got in bed, but I remained awake.

I don't know when my roommates returned, but I feigned sleep until the morning. Once we were up, I told Cathy and Marilyn about what had happened and they tried to comfort me.

"Lynette, you need to tell someone. He had no right to do that!" Cathy said as she sat by me on the bed.

"Yeah, Lynette!" Marilyn chimed in.

"I don't want to get him in trouble," I insisted. "He's a doctor! And maybe he thought it was okay." For some reason I was trying to convince myself that it wasn't his fault.

My roommates and I made a pact to keep my secret. I made a pact to myself to forget.

How did a nineteen-year-old Black female college student meet a twenty-six-year-old Black male anesthesiology resident? you might wonder.

In fact, I'm not sure. That memory is gone or suppressed or perhaps just deemed not important enough to imprint by my brain. I know he was a resident at Magee-Women's Hospital, located not too far from Chatham. Did I perhaps go to the hospital for some reason? Did he see me there? He certainly wouldn't have been at any of our mixers. Or maybe he did attend? No one checked IDs at the dorm, or wondered why he was around. I think we'd gone out at least a time or two before he ended up in my room that night.

However we first came together, I didn't go out with him again after that night—but a couple of weeks later, I missed my period.

Cathy, Marilyn, and I had quickly discovered that our cycles were aligned after we'd been living together for a few months, so when they both got their periods and I did not, it concerned me. Actually, I was frantic!

"Lynette, punch yourself in the stomach!" one dorm mate suggested.

"Lynette, bounce down the stairs on your butt!" was another suggestion.

I tried these *techniques* for inducing menses, and they failed.

I couldn't be pregnant! It was my first time! You can't get pregnant the first time, right?

I called the hospital and asked them to page Walter. When he answered I shouted, "Walter, I missed my period!"

There was a pause and he said nothing for too long. Finally, in a weak voice, he managed, "Lynette, you're okay. Maybe your dates are off. This was your first time, right?"

"Uh-huh," I said stiffly.

"I'll get you an appointment for a pregnancy test here, okay? I'm sure it will be negative."

He sounded calm, but I did not feel reassured.

I got the results the very next day. It was official: I was pregnant! *Congratu-fucking-lations!*

Walter took me over to a corner of the waiting area after I took the test to talk.

"Lynette, I will take care of this," he said quietly. "You can't have this baby. You're planning to go to medical school. You can't do that as an unwed mother. And I can't marry you. I'm already married and expecting my first child soon."

He's married? His wife is pregnant? I'm pregnant? How did I let this happen?

Unable to cope with my situation, I disappeared into a fog of confusion. None of it made sense, and I continued to blame myself.

Walter did take care of everything, just as he promised. He enrolled me in a study at Magee evaluating a new drug for a "chemical" abortion. I guess as a doctor there, he had connections. I became a case number, and being in the study was free.

The only thing I had to figure out was how to sneak out of my dorm and not be missed for a few days. The procedure would have me in the hospital overnight.

We planned the timing so that I'd have the weekend to recover, and Cathy and Marilyn managed to get me out of the dorm without anyone knowing, which to me was nothing short of a miracle. The afternoon I was to enter the hospital, they helped me leave the dorm through a low-set window in the back, then walked with me down to a spot on Woodland Road where Walter picked me up.

This clandestine rendezvous ran like a special op. The timing was precise. It still amazes me that no one noticed a young woman exiting from a window, scampering down a road, and jumping into a car.

When we arrived at Magee, Walter had me enter through a side door. I wasn't admitted until I was lying in a bed on a ward. Walter and another man chatted, and then Walter said, "I've got to go," and left.

The next thing I knew, an IV was inserted and I was alone with the medical staff performing the procedure. I wouldn't see Walter again until it was all over.

While the doctors observed at the foot of my bed, a nurse said,

"Frog legs," and gestured for me to bow my legs out like a frog. When I correctly assumed the position, she pulled up my gown, revealing my pubic area, donned a pair of sterile gloves, used her left hand to spread my labia, and used her right hand to insert a syringe and deposit some sort of liquid deep inside my vagina.

"Now straighten out your legs but lie on your back until we tell you can move," she instructed me as she placed a pillow under my knees.

As I lay in my hospital bed surrounded on three sides by a pull-around curtain, the cramping started.

The cramping, which continued through the night, was much worse than any menstrual cramps I had ever experienced. I clenched my teeth and tried not to cry. I was all alone—no one to hold my hand or comfort me. I didn't sleep that night.

I finally got up in the morning because I had to pee. There was a "catcher" contraption in the portable toilet by my bed. I sat on the toilet and just before I peed, a clump of something—blood?—came out. I held my pee and cried out, "Nurse! Nurse!"

A nurse came quickly and looked into the toilet. She removed the catcher and, holding it so I could see inside, she pointed to the bloody glob. "This is called products of conception," she explained. "You are no longer pregnant."

And with that *statement of fact*, she walked away.

Stunned, I peed and got back in bed.

Later that day, I was examined by a doctor I had not seen before.

He put on a glove and stuck his right hand way up my vagina

while pressing on my abdomen with his left hand. When he removed his gloved hand, it was covered in blood.

"Most of the products of conception were expunged successfully, but you're still bleeding," he explained. "This means there's some tissue left inside your uterus. We need to do a D&C." He turned to the attending nurse and told her to make me NPO.

He didn't tell me what that meant, but I soon found out that NPO meant I couldn't eat or drink for a while.

As they explained it to me, a D&C was a procedure that involved sticking some instrument up my vagina and into my uterus to scrape away any remaining "products of conception." This would require going into the operating room and having anesthesia administered.

I would have to spend another night in the hospital.

An orderly picked me up from the ward the next day. "I'm here to take you to the operating room," he said.

I transferred from my bed to the stretcher for transport. He wheeled me through the hallway to an elevator. I can't remember if we went up or down. When the doors opened, the orderly handed me off to a nurse dressed in scrubs, just like the ones I'd seen on the TV medical shows. She wheeled me into a room and I transferred to an operating room table. A person wearing a mask and scrubs at the head of the table said something to me as he put EKG leads on my chest and a blood pressure cuff on my right arm. An IV bottle with tubing had been connected to the IV in my left arm.

I was numb. I was compliant. I was a robot, unfeeling. Why question any of this? It was all my fault.

"Scoot down and put your legs in the stirrups," he directed.

I did what he asked. And then everything went dark.

* * *

When I awoke, I was in the recovery room. I was informed that the "products of conception" had been removed entirely.

I was discharged later that day and Walter came to get me. He said nothing until we got into his car.

"How are you feeling, Lynette?" he finally asked as he started the car.

"Okay," I said robotically.

"I got in touch with your roommates. I'll drop you at the bottom of your dorm."

The special ops in reverse went as smoothly as the original mission. I reentered the dorm through the low-hanging window and made it safely back to my room.

I continued cramping for a couple of days—which, fortunately, were a Saturday and Sunday—and then I was back in class.

Was it two weeks before Walter called to check on me, or longer? I thought very little of him once I returned to Chatham from the hospital. I was trying to recover from the event but also wanted to forget it all.

On the phone, he sounded quite sincere, although it felt as though he was doing a checkup on a patient.

"Have you had a period since the D&C?" he asked.

"Yes."

"That's good." There was a pause. "Listen, I want to take you out. You've been through so much and you had to do it all alone. Let's just go have some dinner together."

For some reason, I agreed.

* * *

He picked me up a couple of days later for what I thought was going to be a dinner for two. Instead, he took me to a party in an apartment where there were lots of adults, everyone drinking. When we arrived, he walked me over to a woman holding a baby. "Lynette, this is my wife and our baby!"

His wife frowned. "So you're the one? Walter told me all about you and I wanted to see the woman who tried to take my husband."

Whaat?

I turned to Walter. "Please take me back to the dorm now," I begged, my eyes welling up. I couldn't believe how insensitive he was to bring me here, or that his wife even knew about me.

"In a minute, Lynette," he said, putting me off.

Take her husband? I mulled over those words. I hadn't even known she existed.

Now, finally, I was starting to feel angry at Walter. We'd had a few dinners together. We'd kissed a few times. We had one sexual encounter where not only had he taken my virginity without permission, he'd also gotten me pregnant. Then, not knowing what to do, I'd had an abortion. I was the one struggling—and now they were here acting like I was trying to come between their marriage. He'd cheated on her, and she was mad at *me*!

I sat in a corner of the apartment, looking at but not seeing all the partying people and wondering where I was. Could I walk back to school? And why had he brought me here? To clear his conscience?

Finally, Walter took me back to the dorm. I got out of the car without a word and walked into the dorm without a glance backward.

Only years later, when someone told me I was raped, would I even consider that possibility. It never entered my mind. Instead I blamed myself for putting myself in a situation where sex could happen. Even though I didn't want it, he made it seem as if it were just a matter of time before it would be as good for me as it was for him. Once I found out I was pregnant, I made the best decision for me. He was there to help, and so in a small way I was grateful to him for fixing the problem he'd caused. But I know now that I never should have been in that position in the first place.

Wrapping your head around a decision that will affect you for a lifetime can be hard to live with. But somehow you must try—and try I did. After having a pity party with myself for a few days after returning from that encounter with Walter's wife and child, I regained my focus and forged ahead.

But I never forgot.

Chapter 21
Pouissant vs. Pinn

MY JUNIOR YEAR at Chatham started in the fall of 1973. I had gotten pregnant, had an abortion, and undergone a surgical procedure the previous school year with no one the wiser. As the new semester started, I continued to have what-if thoughts about my pregnancy, even as I kept my eye on the prize and started looking at medical schools.

First order of business was the MCAT, the Medical College Admission Test. The MCAT was the standardized, multiple-choice exam created to help medical school admissions determine whether I was doctor material or not. There were questions about basic biology, organic chemistry, inorganic chemistry, physics, psychology, sociology, and more—much, much more.

I aced it. With an above-average MCAT score, along with glowing recommendations from my different jobs—in laboratories, as a medical secretary in an ICU, and at a home for disabled children—I applied to four schools.

The University of Virginia and Medical College of Virginia were my third and fourth choices. Being accepted to medical school superseded my disdain for my home state. Harvard Medical School and Tufts University School of Medicine, both in Boston, were my first and second choices.

The final part of the application process was an interview request.

I was elated to receive my first interview request from Tufts. After that, I got up the confidence to contact Harvard and politely request an interview, stating that it would be a financial hardship to have to make two trips to Boston. Couldn't hurt to ask!

To my surprise and delight, Harvard granted me an interview.

I flew to Boston and stayed in a hotel close to both schools. My Harvard interview was first. I took the Boston transit called the T to the medical school at 25 Shattuck Street.

I walked into the reception area and walked straight to the receptionist's desk.

"I'm here for an interview," I told her.

She directed me to a waiting area.

I was meeting with two professors at the school. When I walked in for the first interview, my thoughts started to spin. Dr. Alvin Pouissant was Black!

When I entered his office, he shook my hand and directed me to sit in a chair in front of his desk. Then, to my dismay, he chided me for not going through *proper channels* for the interview. He seemed perturbed by my presence.

Seemingly done lecturing me, he launched into his interview. "So, Miss Charity, you are a junior at Chatham College, correct?"

"Yes, sir," I said.

"Where is that exactly?"

"It's in Pittsburgh, Pennsylvania," I replied.

"It's a women's college, correct?" He sighed as he took off his glasses.

"Yes, a very exceptional women's college, sir," I replied with pride.

"Ms. Charity, here at Harvard we only accept the cream of the crop from the best schools." When he said Harvard, he dragged out the syllables as many New Englanders have a tendency to do. It wasn't *Har-vard*, but more like *Haaar-vaard*. He leaned back in his high-back leather chair. "So, as a Black woman coming from a small liberal arts women's college, what could you possibly offer a prestigious medical school such as Haaar-vaard?" The *you're not worthy* tone in his voice was all too familiar to me.

What the hell! I thought, fighting to keep a neutral expression. *Who does he think he is?*

A wonderful aspect of attending a women's college was that I had been encouraged to express myself over these three years. There was no reason for women, especially, to dumb ourselves down because we didn't want to outshine the men in our classes, or to worry about professors ignoring us when we raised our hands, because there were no male students at Chatham! And this no-makeup, occasionally no-bra-wearing, Afroed Black woman was not afraid to speak her mind. I was confident, and I was not going to allow this pompous man to put me *or* my school down! I simply wasn't going to tolerate it.

"Dr. Pouissant," I said with confidence, "I am an exceptional candidate for Harvard. Being Black, being a woman, is irrelevant. I'm a biology-chemistry double major who will graduate with honors. I scored well on the MCATs. I plan to do research on sickle cell anemia as my senior year tutorial. I presently work at a care facility for disabled children. I've dedicated myself to doing what it takes to go after my dream. Becoming a doctor is very important to me, and attending Harvard Medical school will get me there."

"Thank you for your candor," he said. "Your next interview is soon. Please wait in the adjoining room."

My eyes widened. *What? We're done?*

Now, I knew nothing about either of the men I'd be interviewing with that day, but I'd learned a lot about Dr. Pouissant in my short two minutes with him. He was dismissive and pompous. I was shocked when I later found out that he was a professor of psychiatry at Harvard Medical School! The man clearly had some work to do on himself.

The next interview was very different. The professor stood out simply for being nice to me. He was soft-spoken and seemed to enjoy listening to me talk about my experiences at Chatham. But it was clear to me that his interview wouldn't carry as much weight as that of Dr. Pouissant's.

I left knowing, but not really caring, that I had blown it.

Later, when I shared my story, someone suggested that Dr. Pouissant was trying to psychoanalyze me. Perhaps after my response to his question, he decided that I suffered from grandiosity. But certainly he did too! I imagined he had an inferiority complex. I could almost hear the wheels turning while he stared me down that day: *Who are you to think that you could weasel your way into "Man's Best Medical School"?*

Their loss. Tufts's gain.

The following day was my interview at Tufts. But instead of meeting at the school, Dr. Vivian Pinn and Dr. James Morehead, my interviewees, took me to lunch at a nice restaurant in downtown Boston.

After we ordered food—what kind doesn't matter, except that it was fancy and expensive and I was happy to take advantage of getting a free meal; between airfare, meals, and hotel, traveling to Boston for the two interviews had used up much of my savings, despite the additional help from the Welles to get myself there—Dr. Pinn spoke.

"So, Lynette, your MCAT scores are good. You have completed all the prereqs. We like what we read in your application."

Dr. Morehead nodded in agreement.

Dr. Pinn leaned forward. "So, where is Tufts on your list?"

Dr. Vivian Pinn—Black, beautiful, and a pathologist at Tufts University School of Medicine—looked at me inquisitively as she waited for me to answer.

I found myself hesitant, especially after what had happened with Dr. Pouissant the day before. Be assertive? Not be assertive? How should I answer this question?

"Tufts is number one on my list," I lied. Why share my disastrous experience at Harvard?

It was a wonderful, relaxing interview. I learned about the school, and they learned about me. There was not a single mention of my race or my gender, outside of Dr. Pinn introducing herself as assistant dean of Student and Minority Affairs and letting me know that she had a strong desire to find qualified minority applicants.

Okay, I'll say it: as a Black woman medical school candidate, I qualified!

After lunch, Dr. Pinn assured me that I'd hear from Tufts "pretty soon." I realized I would have to be patient, but I felt confident that my interview had gone well. Now I needed to return to Chatham and stay focused. No matter the outcome, I still had my senior year to complete.

A week, or maybe two, later, I received a letter from Harvard. It was terse and to the point. I don't remember the exact wording, but to my mind it read something to the effect of *You pissed off Dr. Pouissant, and as a Black woman at a small liberal arts women's college, we don't see that you have anything to offer Harvard. Thank you for wasting our time.*

Harvard was out, but that was expected. Now Tufts really was my number one choice. My third and fourth choices had my applications, but no interviews had been offered as yet.

I had no plan B. It hit me that if I did not go to medical school, I would be lost. Could I be a science teacher? Maybe continue my research in sickle cell anemia without going to med school? Maybe get a PhD in something? But what?

I was in a quandary.

What was I going to do if I didn't get into medical school? It hadn't occurred to me that I'd need to consider more than four medical schools, and I went to sleep the night of getting the rejection from Harvard tossing and turning, worrying for my future for the first time since I'd arrived at Chatham.

I received my letter from Tufts the next day. This was not a terse letter; it was an offer. I'd been accepted—and the letter was signed my Dr. Pinn herself.

And that was it! I couldn't believe the contrast in my feelings from the previous day. Yesterday, I'd been in darkness, deflated and dejected. Even after I had finally gone to sleep the previous night, it had not been a restful one. And when I'd awoken that morning, I'd found myself unable to see any silver lining. My escape plan had one route, and I just couldn't see any clear detour.

And then the letter from Dr. Pinn. I held that letter close to my chest, let out an audible whoop, and did my version of a jig, skipping around the mail room. I stopped and slowly took in a breath and exhaled. I think I was trying to rid myself of the negativity that had engulfed me for the previous twenty-four hours.

It felt so right! I was going to become a member of Tufts University School of Medicine's Class of 1978. I couldn't stop grinning.

"A goal without a plan is only a dream," says motivational speaker and author Brian Tracy. My dream of becoming a medical doctor was a dream that I'd turned into a concrete plan—and now that plan was coming to fruition. Mission accomplished.

There had been many obstacles along the way. I'd been up against the odds—stymied by folks who didn't want me, didn't think I was exceptional enough, and by my own dysfunctional family life and where I'd come from. And, of course, I'd made some personal missteps here and there. And yet the number of blessings I'd received on my path to this moment had far outweighed the challenges. My acceptance to Cradock High School had been a win, despite the difficulties I faced there. It put my escape plan in motion. And then there was my father's acknowledgement—"Lynette don't need to cheat. She smart." Would I have been expelled or at the very least received an F in my government class if not for his defense of me? Then there was Peggy Donaldson, who facilitated my admission to Chatham—such an unexpected win after my guidance counselor refused to help me. Phew! And once I got to Chatham, my classmates and roommates were so essential to my success. My escape plan would certainly have been derailed if not for them.

And now there was Dr. Pinn. Wow!

I'd made it. My dream was unfolding in real time. What had gotten me here, in the end? Was it perseverance? Resilience? Or just plain damn luck?

Chapter 22
Graduation

I STARTED MY SENIOR year of college in the fall of 1973 knowing that I had been accepted to Tufts University School of Medicine. I was almost to the finish line, ready to start a new beginning. My escape plan was really coming together.

My senior year at Chatham saw me without roommates for the first time. Cathy and Marilyn graduated a semester early and decided to move to Virginia, where they got a place together. Left on my own, I moved back into Fickes and got a treasured senior single on a floor called "two and a half," which was out the back hall of the second floor and had access to its own bathroom. It was quiet and private, ideal for a senior working on her tutorial.

I'd chosen my senior project at the suggestion of my mentor and tutorial advisor Dr. Knudsen. Hemoglobinopathies are a group of blood disorders and diseases that affect red blood cells. Sickle cell disease is one of these, and it's a blood disorder that disproportionately affects Blacks, causing symptoms including stunted growth, anemia, and pain. Sickle cell anemia is inherited and gets its name because the unhealthy red blood cells become misshapen and break down. These *sickle-shaped* cells can block blood flow and cause pain, which is called a sickle cell crisis. The life expectancy of people born with sickle cell disease is less than twenty years of age.

Dr. Knudsen had a connection at the University of Pittsburgh who allowed me to work in their sickle cell anemia lab under the tutelage of their primary lab technician, Worth Scott. Working with Mr. Scott taught me so much about research. I also learned how to take blood from patients and how to prepare slides and review those slides under a microscope. When I presented my research—my paper was titled "Hemoglobinopathies: Blood Dyscrasias"—before the tutorial board at the conclusion of my time at the lab, which came at the close of first semester of senior year, Dr. Knudsen and the other professors marveled at my research; in fact, they told me that what I'd done was PhD-level work! What a compliment.

Working with Worth Scott, I had learned how to draw blood, centrifuge the blood, make slides of blood cells, and do statistical analysis. My tutorial was extensive and well thought out. I didn't invent a cure, but I did further my knowledge, as well as the knowledge of those who heard my dissertation, of sickle cell anemia.

Worth Scott and I were featured in the *Pittsburgh Post-Gazette* for our work, which led to an invitation to a dinner hosted by the Sickle Cell Anemia Foundation. At that soiree, I met Terry Bradshaw, Franco Harris, and Frenchy Fuqua, members of the Pittsburgh Steelers. These were *big*, athletic men—and nice guys. I carried on a pretty good football conversation with them, but mostly I was thankful for their contribution to the foundation. I was happy to learn one year later, in January 1975, that they won that year's Super Bowl. What an unexpected highlight of my work in a sickle cell anemia lab!

As a senior on scholarship, there was no reason to graduate early in spite of my acceptance to medical school. Where would I go? Room and board were paid for at Chatham, and I was biding my time, waiting for Tufts and the next chapter of my life. That spring, I registered for the most outlandish classes Chatham had to offer—including ceramics and basket-weaving—in an attempt to get in touch with my creative side. I continued to work at a children's home for the disabled. I babysat ($2 an hour for one child, $2.50 for more than one child). I house-sat for my professors.

At graduation in May, Cathy, Marilyn, and I reunited. We squealed and jumped up and down when we reconnected, the three of us talking all at once, and threw our arms around one another in a triple-person hug. It had been six months!

Their parents met my mother and great-aunt at the graduation luncheon on the quad that day. The Cusacks later invited us to dinner.

Mama had flown to Pittsburgh. Granny, now in her eighties, was too fragile to travel. Hunter Sue had planned to fly with Mama, but Grandpop, who had never flown, had outright refused to take his first airplane trip into the friendly skies on Allegheny Airlines—or any other airline, for that matter. Frustrated, Hunter Sue had purchased Mama a round-trip plane ticket and agreed to travel with Grandpop on a Greyhound bus.

Hunter Sue loved her brother, but she often called him "backwards"—a fair characterization. He had never set foot outside of the Tidewater area of Virginia. He was a great driver but refused to drive on any of the interstates—even after the state built a two-lane Interstate 264 connecting Norfolk to Portsmouth, which included a tunnel that traveled *under* the Elizabeth River, in 1960. When we moved to Portsmouth in 1961, everyone knew the interstate was a quicker route from Norfolk to Portsmouth, but Grandpop, eschewing change, continued to take the longer, more circuitous route across a rickety bridge *over* the Elizabeth River.

Hunter Sue, on the other hand, was a world traveler. She'd visited London, Rio de Janeiro, Rome, Mexico, and many other places in her lifetime. And yet she boarded that bus and traveled the twenty hours to my graduation because her brother refused to fly.

I had moved out of my dorm and was staying in an attic bedroom in the home of my physics professor. Hunter Sue and Grandpop stayed in a hotel room near campus; Mama stayed with me.

My brother Steve, now twenty-five and looking very much like Isaac Hayes—bald-headed and sporting a goatee—attended my graduation ceremony with a friend. He looked dapper in his plaid bell-bottom pants, blue shirt, and platform shoes. Butch, now a drill sergeant stationed at Fort Irwin in California, was unable to get away; Kevin, just fifteen years old, stayed at home with Granny; and my father was in the hospital, being treated for esophageal cancer.

After the graduation, Steve and his friend left, and I introduced Mama and Hunter Sue to the Cusacks and the Horbalys. We would have dinner at the Cusacks' that night.

Dinner at the Cusacks' was an affair to remember. They served lasagna with a salad and dinner rolls, a meal I had eaten with them on several occasions at their home. Mama had never eaten lasagna.

"It's a twist on spaghetti and meatballs, Mama," I told her, and encouraged her to try it.

But when a serving was placed on her plate, she made a face. And for the rest of the meal, she picked at it, eating only the meat in between the layers of pasta. She barely even touched the delicious salad Mrs. Cusack had made.

Mama didn't say a word, but I felt she was expressing her disdain for new culinary experiences. She wasn't going to try anything new or unfamiliar.

I was annoyed. This was a woman who ate pigs' intestines, as well as their feet, ears, and tails! Why couldn't she be more gracious?

Lasagna was nothing compared to eating a pickled pig's foot, in my opinion, or eating chitlins!

On the second night, the Wellses drove us (minus Grandpop, who stayed at the hotel both nights, which I didn't mind; I knew it had taken him great effort for him to come to my graduation, and I wasn't going to force him to do anything that made him feel uncomfortable, such as be around a lot of white folks) to their home in Mt. Lebanon and treated us to a lovely dinner that did not include lasagna.

During dinner, Mrs. Wells told Mama how proud she was of me and said how wonderful it was that I was going to medical school.

It was complicated to have Mama and Hunter Sue in the environment where I'd thrived these past four years. Whereas Hunter Sue took it all in stride—eating the damn lasagna and salad and even asking for more—Mama had a fear of the unknown. She could have lived in New York with her mother, but after one visit and attending one of the PS Schools, she'd begged her mother to send her back to Virginia. She'd briefly attended a boarding school for colored girls but had also begged to come home after just a few weeks. This is a woman who'd graduated from high school at sixteen and attended college for two years and then given it up to marry a man she'd met at a party.

She'd never had an escape plan, because she'd always planned to just stay put.

That night, Mr. Wells asked me about my summer plans.

"I'm staying with Dr. Adler and his wife until I leave for Boston in August," I told him.

"That's where we're staying right now," Mama chimed in. "Do you know they don't have any curtains on their windows in the living room? People walk by and can see right into the house."

I wished Mama would quit talking, but she wasn't done.

"They're letting Lynette stay in their attic bedroom for the whole summer!" she announced. "She's gonna babysit their baby girl, Zoe, when she's not working her job taking care of the disabled kids. She borrowed some furniture from the school. She has to return it before she leaves. President Eddy let her use it. Isn't that nice?"

I felt Mama had told Mr. Wells much more than he'd asked for.

Now he looked intrigued. "How did you get the president to loan you furniture, Lynette?" he asked.

I cleared my throat. "Well, I walked up to Gregg House," I explained, referring to the campus home for presidents of the school. "I knocked on the door, and when Mrs. Eddy answered, I asked to speak to President Eddy. I told him I was staying in Pittsburgh for the summer and had found a place to stay but needed a bed, dresser, desk, and chair. I added that the dorm furniture went unused during the summer, so no one would miss it. I told him I would return everything before I left. President Eddy smiled and then said yes."

I'm not sure what I expected going up to that house, but I did feel I'd stated my case in a cogent manner. How could he have said no? I wondered if he remembered me as the girl who'd gotten Hell Night canceled, but I didn't remind him.

"Well, that's something, Lynette," Mr. Wells said, smiling. "I betcha that was a first for him."

After dessert, we said our goodbyes and Mr. Wells took Hunter Sue to her hotel. When Mr. Wells dropped me and Mama off at the Adlers', I gave him a big hug.

"Thanks, Mr. Wells, for everything," I said sincerely. "I will stay in touch."

I think he wanted to give Mama a hug, but she just shook his hand and said thanks.

Mama had arrived the Thursday before graduation and she left the following Wednesday. During the rest of her visit, we walked around the Shadyside neighborhood where the Adlers lived. I also introduced her to Reuben sandwiches and pizza at the local eateries that lined Walnut Street, the main drag. (She didn't particularly like either.)

I told her that before I left for Boston, the Adlers were taking me with them to Martha's Vineyard for two weeks in August as Zoe's nanny.

"Where's Martha's Vineyard?" she asked.

"It's an island off the coast of Massachusetts, Mama."

"An island! How you gonna get there?"

"We're gonna take a ferry. David's going to take his car. He's rented a house there."

"My, my! Fancy!"

My mother had a way of denigrating me without others being in on the criticism. For that one week, she had come into my world, but rather than coming with an open mind she'd chosen to turn up her nose and express, albeit subtly, her views—which, for me, were "backwards." Why couldn't she try pizza or eat lasagna? Yes, these dishes were different from soul food, but they were quite tasty. Why play with your food and never even try it? As for Martha's Vineyard— many people rented vacation homes and traveled if they could afford to, didn't they?

I didn't expect my mother to change her stripes completely, but

I wished she had acted more like Hunter Sue, who'd refrained from making any sly comments, on this trip. At least the Adlers—I now thought of them as David and Nikki, as they insisted I refer to them by their first names—had not seemed to make any note of Mama's negative comments. Still, I felt they were in poor taste, especially since we were both staying in their home!

I was relieved when Mama boarded her plane the next day and Grandpop and Hunter Sue went to the Greyhound station. It had been nice having them there, but their world was no longer my world. I was not embarrassed by them, but I felt I had—dare I say it?—outgrown them.

Chapter 23
An Extraordinary Summer

AT THE BEGINNING of August, David, Nikki, and I packed up the car, strapped Zoe into her car seat, and drove to Massachusetts.

When we arrived at the ferry, David maneuvered his car up the ramp and was directed where to park. We then left the car and headed to the open deck—and once all cars and passengers were on board, off we went.

It was a hot summer day, and the breeze was refreshing. I held Zoe's hand as she peered through the railing at her level—after all, she was only two. As we stood there, I noticed people looking at us. I imagined that seeing a tall, Afro-wearing young Black woman with a beautiful little white girl was not commonplace around these parts.

I picked Zoe up. "Are you excited to be on the boat?" I asked her.

"Boat!" she yelled.

I pointed toward Martha's Vineyard. "I've never been on such a boat, and I can't wait to get over there so that we can have lots of fun together. Being your nanny is the best job ever!" I gave her a big squeeze, and she giggled.

Zoe was a sweet little girl, and I enjoyed her parents, too. I appreciated being included in these summer plans.

Until the "starefest" on the ferry, I had no thoughts about what kind of reception I would receive on this trip. I was just thrilled to be going to Martha's Vineyard, a resort for the rich and famous! When we arrived and drove off the ferry, I felt so fortunate to have met the Adlers.

As David drove, I surveyed the land. This was going to be a summer vacation that I would never forget—I just knew it.

We settled in at the rental house, which was huge! It reminded me of the summer homes of the elite of Pittsburgh that were now used as dormitories at Chatham.

I took Zoe out to the beach. We sat in the sand with our plastic pails, which we filled with sand and dumped out repeatedly.

I noticed a woman in the house next to ours staring from her deck.

"Hi there," I said, waving.

"Who are you?" she asked.

"I'm Lynette and this is Zoe. We're here on vacation."

"Vacation?"

She seemed tense; I quickly realized what she woman really wanted to know, so I just told her: "Yes," I said. "I'm here with the Adlers and I'm Zoe's nanny. This is an amazing place!"

The worry lines eased and she appeared calmer. I was sure she'd pass on the word: *Hey, everyone, we have one of* them *on the island, but she's here as a nanny, so don't get agitated. She won't be staying too long.*

After that I did get less stares, so maybe the neighbor did share the news—or maybe my friendliness had its intended effect. I didn't care. I wasn't going to let the neighbors or the regulars spoil my summer. I imagined they felt safer knowing that I knew my place. They probably told themselves, *What harm can she do? It's just her, not a whole army of* them!

After our first couple of days there, they paid me no nevermind.

I spent the days with Zoe building sandcastles and playing make-believe with her dolls. Despite my day-to-day duties of keeping Zoe entertained while the Adlers relaxed, I found that I still had lots of time to explore on my own. Over time, I realized that the Adlers had brought me with them more as a guest than as hired help.

Being including felt good, but I would have been okay if they had treated me as just the nanny. I was not out to want people to like me. I just wanted people to be nice.

Soon after we arrived, Nixon resigned. Watergate had done him in. Faced with the choice of being impeached or resigning, he chose the latter.

There was no TV in our rented house, so I sat in the car and listened to the radio. I knew nothing of Gerald Ford, but he was appointed the thirty-eighth president of the United States while we were on Martha's Vineyard. I learned that he had first been appointed vice president after Spiro T. Agnew resigned due to allegations that he avoided paying taxes while governor of Maryland.

There was little talk about Nixon on the island. Maybe it was because people were desperate to be away from the real world for the summer, or maybe it was because there were so many other things going on to distract us.

For me, one of the most exciting events that occurred there was the Woody Allen Film Festival. I'd been a big fan of his since seeing his film *Bananas*. (I could not have foretold as a twenty-two-year-old that Woody Allen would fall from grace all those years later, of course, so I stand by my enjoyment of all things Woody Allen at that particular moment in time.)

By this point I'd seen a number of Woody Allen's movies and considered myself an authority on his work. He was a master at slap-stick humor, and I looked forward to rewatching many of his movies I'd already seen, along with *What's New Pussycat?*, *What's Up, Tiger Lily?*, and *Play It Again, Sam*, over the course of the two-day festival.

I arrived at the local theater house in Oak Bluffs and stood in line to purchase my ticket. As I looked at all the people milling around, I saw a couple that looked familiar. I recognized him first—after all, I'd bought his 45 "Fire and Rain" in 1970 and "You've Got a Friend" in 1971. Albums were expensive, so I was selective. I had heard he'd married Carly Simon in 1972, and I had some of her music too. I liked her songs "Anticipation" and "You're So Vain."

I couldn't believe that James Taylor and Carly Simon were standing right in front of me!

I was a bold, young college grad, fearless in the world. I walked right up to them and introduced myself.

"Hi," I said. "You're James Taylor"—I pointed to him—"and you're Carly Simon!" I exclaimed, swiveling my finger in her direction. "My name is Lynette Charity. You like Woody Allen?"

"Yes, I do," James replied.

"Me too," Carly agreed.

We struck up a conversation. James gave me some background about the island and explained that his family had a home nearby. I explained why I was there, and that I was starting medical school the next month. Both appeared impressed with this information. As we got closer to the entrance to the theater, James said, "Sit with us, okay?"

"Sure!" I said, and into the theater we went.

We had a great time eating popcorn and laughing.

* * *

It turned out to be my summer to meet celebrities. Unbeknownst to me, there was a big production crew on the island that summer, film-ing a movie about a shark that would later become one of the most famous movies of all time.

When I found out more about *Jaws* and who was starring in the film, I was fascinated. I tried to figure out a way to get to the beach to catch a glimpse of somebody famous. On one of my days off, I was sitting in the local ice cream shop, having a double scoop of butter pecan, when three men walked in. One was much shorter than the other two. They were loud, but not loud enough to get a rise out of anyone in the shop. No one appeared to recognize them. No one was oohing and aahing over them.

I looked up, and the short one met my gaze. I smiled. He came over.

"Hi," he said, "I'm Richard. Those are my two friends. That guy with the funny accent, his name is Robert, and the other guy is Roy. We're the three *R*'s. So, we're making this movie called *Jaws*. Have you heard about it?"

If I had been a local or even a blond female tourist, they might have paid me no nevermind. But I was a young Black woman with an impressive Afro, out of place. There was no way, at first glance, anyone would not do a double-take or be compelled to have an inquiring mind. This happened in every situation where I was "the only." It had happened in Mt. Lebanon with Cathy's younger brother and with the Wellses at their church. I was pretty used to it by now. And I certainly wasn't going to shy away from this close encounter with celebrities.

"I just did," I said, "and I was trying to figure out a way to get over there to meet somebody famous!"

"Well, we're famous! We're the stars!" Richard said.

He motioned for Robert (Shaw) and Roy (Schneider) to come over.

"This is . . . uh, what's your name?" Richard asked.

"My name is Lynette Charity," I said. "Nice to meet you."

"What brings you to the island, Lynette?" Robert asked me after we shook hands. I noted his English accent.

Just like I had a few days earlier with James and Carly, I explained that I was there as a nanny for the summer before going to Boston to start medical school.

"Medical school? Wow!" Roy said.

Richard (Dreyfuss) seemed impressed also.

Robert was too busy undressing me with his eyes to voice his thoughts. It seemed that he saw something that he liked. While Roy and Richard chatted with me, Robert just ogled. Still, I was young and impressed with them—so I was over the moon.

Thus I had a trifecta of extraordinary events occur in the span of two weeks: a US president's resignation, having James Taylor and Carly Simon as movie buddies, and meeting the main three stars of *Jaws*. I would leave Martha's Vineyard with an appreciation that all things are possible—or at least that there's something to be said about being in the right place at the right time.

Upon returning to Pittsburgh with the Adlers after our stay on the island, it took me one week to get myself ready for Tufts. I returned the furniture to Chatham—I made sure to thank President Eddy once again—sent off my things to my new apartment in Boston, and boarded a flight from Pittsburgh International Airport to Logan Airport.

Tufts University School of Medicine awaited me. I was ready.
Or was I?

Chapter 24
Imposter Syndrome

I BEGAN MEDICAL SCHOOL on September 4, 1974. This was it! I'd made it!

I walked up the steps of the main building and entered to hear someone shout, "Orientation is in Patten B!"

Patten B was a large auditorium, and when I entered, I was overwhelmed by the crowd of people gathered there. Some appeared to know each other. Others were having get-to-know-you chats. I heard questions rising above the noise like, "Where did you go to college?" and "What's California like?" Many of my peers were just looking around in confusion, like me.

"Name?" a woman asked me.

It was 10:00 a.m. on the nose—time to distribute our orientation packets. Several people weaved through the crowd, asking for names and handing out packets.

"Uh, Lynette Charity. Last name spelled *C-H-A-R-I-T-Y*." This was a habitual response due to how often my name was misspelled as *Chairdy* or *Chairty*.

"Here's your orientation packet." As she handed it over, she explained that it contained my course schedule for first and second year. "Later today, around 1:00 p.m., you'll be getting your picture taken for your ID. That will be in the Arnold Building—and don't worry, we'll make sure you get to where you need to be."

"Thank you," I said.

I took the packet, found a seat close to the door, and observed as the other members of the Tufts University School of Medicine Class of 1978 received their packets and mingled.

At 10:15 a.m., once all packets had been distributed, a brief presentation was made on financial aid. I listened intently, since I would be receiving said financial aid in the form of a student loan, along with scholarship funds and a work-study job. First-year tuition was going to be about $3,300! To cover expenses for the three years to come, I joined the Public Health Service. In return for enlisting for three years post medical school, the PHS would cover my tuition and apartment expenses, as well as provide a food allowance.

When the financial aid briefing was completed, we were introduced to the who's who of Tufts Med from the auditorium stage: Dr. Lauro Cavazos, the acting dean; Dr. Lon Curtis, the associate dean for student affairs; and several others who would play important roles in my life over the next few years. After a greeting from the president of the Medical Student Council, we all grouped up for a hospital tour. Tufts-New England Medical Center was across the street from the medical school.

I felt an elation that was hard to describe. I was a medical student at Tufts University School of Medicine! I had chosen "to be" rather than "not to be." I had suffered the slings and arrows of outrageous fortune and survived! I had been tenacious! Chatham had laid the groundwork for me to "assimilate" into the white world, and now I believed that completing that mission was within my reach. I anticipated a sense of equality. A sense of respect. I truly believed that my chosen career would be colorblind.

"Hey, can I talk to you for a sec?" a new classmate asked.

"Sure," I said, and rose to follow him.

He held his packet in his left hand as he guided me to a corner of the auditorium with his right. He was white, dark-haired, and wore glasses.

Once he had me where he wanted me, he pointed a finger in my face. "You're only here because of Affirmative Action," he snarled. "Did you know that? My friend wasn't accepted because of you and the others. You all got accepted because Tufts had to meet its quota! And they got a two-fer with you, Black and female!"

I was too stunned to even respond. *A quota? A racial quota? A gender quota? Affirmative Action? Me?* I still couldn't find my words, but I was incensed. I didn't need no stinkin' Affirmative Action to get into medical school! I had strong MCAT scores and great grades from college. I'd worked my butt off for four years at Chatham. I'd earned my spot!

Or did I?

"You're gonna flunk out! Wait and see." He glared at me over his glasses.

Then, before I could regain my voice, he left, blending into the crowd on their way to the hospital for their tours.

I stood there for a moment, caught up in my thoughts.

I felt fear. Not a fear from him, but from his words! It was a fear I had never experienced before. A fear that I hadn't earned my dream— that somehow I was here only because of my sex and the color of my skin.

It was accurate that I was where I was as a result of *Brown v. Board of Education*, and perhaps whatever Affirmative Action policy was in place that had helped Peggy Donaldson find me and accept me to Chatham. But hadn't that been a wrong made right after years of Blacks not being granted access to higher education? And hadn't I done the work? I'd graduated with honors from Cradock and then from Chatham. In addition to my good MCAT scores, I had racked up extracurricular activities that showed my motivation to become a doctor. I was a great candidate, a deserving candidate. Didn't being Black and female push me into the *exceptional* candidate category?

I wanted to believe this, but my classmate's words were hard to shake.

"Hey! Are you going on a tour of the hospital?" another classmate asked, breaking my fugue state. This guy was tall and Black and sported a large 'fro and beard.

"Yes," I replied, trying to shake off the experience I'd just been subjected to.

"I'm Reggie," he said. "I'll be living in Posner Hall."

"Hi, Reggie." I smiled. "I'll be sharing a two-bedroom/two-bathroom apartment with a student attending Northeastern University. Someone at Tufts gave her my name and she contacted me. I know Posner Hall is right next door, but I didn't want to live in a dorm again. I think I was spoiled at my college my senior year. I was in a single and I loved having my own bathroom."

I realized that this was probably more information than he needed on our first encounter, but I think it was a vain attempt to expunge that white guy's words from my head.

Affirmative Action. Quota. Two-fer.

Denise Saddler, a Black senior student at Northeastern University, was the one who had put out a flyer at Tufts looking for a roommate for her two-bedroom/two-bathroom apartment in Longwood Apartments. The rent would be $100 a month plus utilities. I'd taken the room sight unseen! It was an easy transit ride from 75 Alphonsus Street to the medical school—and luckily, upon arrival that week I'd found that it was good enough.-

"Let me introduce you to the others," Reggie said.

By "the others," he meant the Black medical students. There were 18 of us, counting me—11 men and 7 women out of a class of 151.

I met Elsie, Ed, Steve, Lloyd, John, Dottie, and others. They had come to Boston from many different states. Ed was from Pittsburgh and knew of Chatham College. By the time we were finished with the hospital tour, I had met all of my fellow Black classmates.

It was nice to have some new friends. But as the day progressed, I was haunted by my white classmate's accusations.

It didn't help that my ID picture could easily have passed for a mugshot!

Be on the lookout for this woman. Black. Height five feet eight inches. Large Afro. Squinty eyes. Last seen in the company of several others of her kind. Caution: Doesn't smile when taking a picture. Oh, and she's only at Tufts Medical because of Affirmative Action.

That afternoon, we attended a beer party hosted by the second years. The food and alcohol were free, and I had the opportunity to introduce myself to many non-Black classmates—white, Asian, male and female—as I scoured the crowd for Mr. Affirmative Action. I didn't find him, and I willed myself to have a good time and remain open.

That night I crashed into my bed at my new apartment. My first day of medical school had had its moments—and there would be more to come. The real work would start tomorrow.

I took the Green Line to school on day two. I was already thinking about that Friday's Gross Anatomy Lab, where we'd be dissecting cadavers. The closest I'd ever come to dissecting anything was in Comparative Anatomy with Dr. Chilton Knudsen at Chatham. Somehow, I felt that dissecting a frog and a baby shark would pale in comparison to what lay ahead for me: cutting into a human body that once had a beating heart and a thinking brain.

As I walked to Longwood from the stop, a nagging thought ate at me: *I'm part of a quota? I'm here only because of a quota? I'm better than a quota! I'll prove it!*

I don't remember much about that day except getting a locker, receiving a box of histology slides, and swearing on a stack of Bibles that I would donate a kidney to the school if I dropped any of them! There was a fee if any slides were missing at the end of the course.

I also attended a lecture that day on something called "sweaty sock syndrome," which was explained as a condition where the skin on the soles of the feet of children and young teenagers becomes scaly and red. The cause was unknown, but after hearing about it, I knew I had it! (As time continued, I would also decide I had maple syrup urine disease, too, which causes one's urine to smell like maple syrup, and Tay-Sachs disease, a malady of children of Jewish descent.) It would turn out I had something even more common: medical students' disease, a condition where medical students become convinced that they are experiencing the symptoms of a disease that they are studying. It usually presents in the second year of medical school. I developed it early.

On day three, I met Dr. Pai, our anatomy professor. Dr. Pai was a native of India. He looked very young in his long white professor's coat—a coat I wouldn't be sporting for another eight years. Medical school and residency had to be completed first.

Dr. Pai had a thick mustache above his ever-present smile, which revealed nice white teeth, and the hair on his head was thick and wavy. I knew nothing about his medical background, but I soon learned that he was skilled in the art of dissection. He was so unlike many of my other professors, who were mostly middle-aged white men, with a smattering of white women. The non-whites—like him, and like Dr. Vivian Pinn, the one and only Black woman physician and professor at Tufts—stood out.

I learned that Dr. Pinn had joined the Department of Pathology at Tufts in 1970 at the age of twenty-nine. Now age thirty-three and vice president of Minority Student Affairs, she was tasked with finding the best minority students for Tufts. She exuded an indescribable sageness with a young-body vibe. Dr. Pai and Dr. Pinn quickly became my favorite professors at Tufts.

The Gross Anatomy Lab emanated a gut-wrenching, nausea-provoking odor. Dr. Pai, all smiles, passed around spirits of peppermint to put on our upper lips. This was to mask the pungent, puke-inducing vapors that slammed into our nostrils, making our eyes water. The peppermint helped.

We all knew that the bodies were preserved through a combination of embalming fluid and refrigeration. They needed the bodies to not decompose for at least the time it took to get them dissected to the satisfaction of Dr. Pai.

My association with the smell of the embalming fluid was from the day I leaned over the pink coffin and kissed my sister goodbye.

The memory of Beverly in her coffin was a jolt out of nowhere. When was the last time I'd thought of her? Maybe when I first met Cathy at Chatham? That day, when she mentioned all of her sisters, I declined to mention that my one and only sister had died.

Had it really been that long? Four years? Or had I thought of her to soothe me during my abortion? Maybe. I wasn't sure. I'd needed her to get through high school, but at Chatham I'd had more support. I'd been in my element, learning and preparing for my escape, and her voice had receded into a place in my brain that stored such things.

Now, the unctuous odor of the Gross Anatomy Lab had brought back her memory.

I was glad to be thinking about her, but I also needed to get focused on the task at hand.

"Hello, everyone," Dr. Pai said with a big smile. "Please go to your assigned table, where you will meet the person you will learn from during this class."

By my quick count of the dissecting tables, there were at least twenty-five bodies in this formaldehyde-drenched room. Our names were in dark bold letters at the foot of each table.

I moved through the rows of tables, looking for my name. When I finally saw it, I moved to the head of the table. The person I would learn from was a deceased white male of indeterminate age. His whole head was shrouded in an opaque covering. My first thought was, *Is this a way to not scare us? A faceless corpse?*

Slowly, one after another, my lab partners arrived at the table. In total, there were six. All males. All white.

"You will notice that your cadaver's head is covered. We share bodies with the Dental School, so head and neck dissections go to the dental students first." Dr Pai explained without anyone asking—and as he explained, he smiled and then let out a chuckle.

It seemed he found what he had just said quite funny. None of us joined in. But I appreciated how much he loved his job.

"Today, we will start with a simple dissection. It's the dissection of the femoral triangle, located in the groin."

We listened intently.

He moved to one of the tables, followed by his assistants, and continued, "The initial skin incision has been made and some fatty tissue has been removed to enable you to better dissect out the major components of this triangle."

I looked down at the groin area of our cadaver. I wondered if an autopsy had been performed on Beverly's little body after she died. I never knew. She was hit by a moving car, run over and killed. What would the point have been? I regained my focus.

"You will dissect out the femoral nerve, the femoral artery, the femoral vein, and the lymphatic system," Dr. Pai instructed. "Lateral to medial, the mnemonic for this is NAVL: nerve, artery, vein, lymphatic. This will help you remember when you take your exams."

"Lynette, you go first," one of my lab mates suggested.

I wasn't sure if he was being polite or if maybe he didn't want to be the one to start, but I picked up the scalpel and, aided by the soothing voice of Dr. Pai and the guidance of his lab assistants, I slowly, methodically, dissected through the tissues in the cadaver's groin.

I couldn't imagine ever doing this on a real, live patient. The dissecting didn't bother me; even making a mistake on this cadaver didn't feel upsetting. It was part of the learning process. But doing an operation on a patient under anesthesia wasn't my area of interest. I could not see myself as a surgeon. I wondered how those in our class who were leaning toward becoming surgeons would have the gumption to do this on living flesh.

"Make sure everyone gets a chance to get the feel of the scalpel on the tissue." Dr. Pai coached. He was so patient.

That first Gross Anatomy class took a while to finish, especially since all seven of us had to use the scalpel, but the dissection went well. Nerve, check! Artery, check! Vein and lymphatics, check!

Eventually, it was time to wash up and go home.

On my way to the sink, I saw a notice, handwritten in black marker, that said, *Use buckets under tables for dissected material ONLY. Not paper towels or gloves.* My lab mates had gone to the sink before me. While washing my hands, I looked down at the bucket. I didn't know which of my classmates had disregarded the sign, but I leaned over and removed the paper towels and pair of gloves someone had dropped into the bucket, wondering who in our group didn't know how to read, or whose mother always picked up after them. I made a mental note to emphasize the instruction during our next visit to the lab. Why leave more work for the assistants to do?

Back at my apartment that first day, I learned a little more about the people of Boston. It was 1974, and even though the Irish were the predominant ethnic group, the city teemed with people from Canada, Italy, Portugal, China, Armenia, Haiti, and Vietnam, to name a few. That said, there was no love lost between those groups, especially the Blacks and whites, and integration through school busing during this time made for many tense situations. I was surprised that this was still an issue in the north, where people were supposedly more tolerant. *Didn't we go through all that shit in 1966?*

The racial hatred in Boston was palpable. Lines between communities were cut in stone and not to be crossed. Being in the wrong neighborhood at the wrong time could put your life in peril. I couldn't believe how much unrest there was over busing. There were death threats aimed at judges who were for busing. There were protests around city hall. White neighborhoods and Black neighborhoods clashed. An anti-busing group called Restore Our Alienated Rights (ROAR), comprised of mainly women, staged sit-ins and prayer sessions and intimidated Black students, hurling racial epithets at them. They even burned a wooden school bus in effigy. Bused students were jeered at and periodically attacked. It felt as though the Little Rock,

Arkansas, situation was repeating itself after twenty years, but with more violence.

Two years later, in 1976, a photographer would win the Pulitzer Prize for his picture of a white protester attacking a Black lawyer at city hall. The title: *The Soiling of Old Glory*.

I couldn't allow all this uproar to sway my resolve. I had survived similar situations and more growing up, and I would do it again. I had to. My priority was to become a medical doctor. Despite the turmoil, the people of the city knew that with three medical schools in their midst—Harvard, Tufts, and Boston University School of Medicine— there were bound to be formaldehyde-covered first years of all races and genders there regardless of what was happening around them, and because of that we were perhaps tolerated more than most.

In the first days of my arrival to Boston, I was ignored or tolerated while waiting at my Green Line stop. I still sported a large Afro, but with my short white coat, books, and Littmann stethoscope, it was clear I was a medical student, or at least impersonating one. I could sit where I wanted to sit. But all that changed after my first day in Gross Anatomy Lab. A cough here, a sniff there, and a distancing of avoidance became the norm. Before, people pushed past me to get on the T. Now, I was allowed to get on first! I felt like Moses parting the Red Sea each time a path opened up for me to navigate to the back of the car. This gave a new meaning to "Go to the back of the bus!" Now it was not because I was Black but because I smelled awful.

I accepted my new routine, and my new fragrance. "Eau de Formaldehyde" was to linger for a while, partly because my work-study job was as a diener, a morgue attendant. (The word *diener* is derived from the German word *Leichendiener*, which literally means "corpse servant.") I was given this job just a couple of weeks into my first year. I saw it as another learning experience. I was paid $25 an hour to handle, clean, and prepare the deceased for autopsy.

Not all bodies in the morgue required an autopsy. I assisted mostly on people who had died of "suspicious" circumstances— maybe a fatal accident or a gunshot wound or just an unexplained death where an autopsy was requested by a family member. There were plenty of other deceased individuals in the morgue that were simply awaiting transport to a funeral home for embalming and subsequent internment.

On occasion, during an autopsy, I was allowed to make the classic "Y" incision to open up the chest cavity. With a scalpel, facing the body, I would start near the right shoulder and make an angled incision to the sternum, the breastbone. I would then do the same coming from the left shoulder. Where they met, I would then incise straight down past the navel. This incision allowed for an in-depth view of the chest cavity, particularly the heart, trachea, lungs, and diaphragm, after the sternum or breast plate was removed. The longitudinal incision from sternum to pubis revealed the contents of the abdomen, stomach, intestines, liver, gallbladder, and more. Examination of the brain required cutting through the skull in a circular manner with a bone saw. When properly done, this allowed for a piece of the skull to be removed, exposing the entire brain. It took me a while to master that saw.

Once the autopsies were completed, I was given the opportunity, if time permitted, to sew up the incisions. I thanked each person I worked on for allowing me to use them as teaching tools, helping me better take care of living people—and helping me prove to others that I was not just an Affirmative-Action-two-fer-part-of-a-quota kinda girl! At least I hoped so.

I must admit that I was stressed during the first trimester

because of the nagging issue of whether I belonged. I often felt out of sorts. But looking back, I accomplished a lot in those early months: I assimilated into a new city with new challenges, managed to do the work required of me in medical school, got a job, and made friends. I was on my way to fulfilling my dream and successfully and officially escaping my past.

If Mrs. Pollard could see me now! This colored girl had gotten into medical school, and she planned to graduate!

I made it through the exams of the first trimester and passed everything, including Gross Anatomy. The holidays were upon us. My roommate left for Christmas. I didn't want to go home, but my mother begged me to come and my father had metastatic esophageal cancer, so it might be the last time I ever saw him.

I wasn't convinced that I needed to see him one last time, but I went.

I read up on his condition: *Squamous cell esophageal cancer, which is relatively rare overall, is far more common in Black men with a history of alcohol and tobacco use.*

My father, the wife beater and man who'd wished I'd died instead of Beverly, had smoked three to four packs of Camel unfiltered cigarettes per day for about thirty years. He also loved beer, whiskey, scotch, and bourbon. Oh, and he was Black! *Ding, ding, ding!*

I was ambivalent about my father's impending death. We had never been close, and I couldn't access any empathy for him after all we'd been through. Yes, he'd provided for his family—but at what cost? I had always seen him as a drunk. My great-grandmother Annie Holloway—who, in her own way, had taught me much—had died my senior year of high school. I'd felt her loss. I'd cried. But when I left home for college, with the plan of severing all ties, I'd known I would miss no one.

Perhaps all the violence I had seen in my family had made me callous; perhaps that's why I had almost no ability to feel anything toward them. Whatever the reason, I knew I wouldn't be able to fabricate any positive feelings on this visit.

It didn't help that I was having my own gastrointestinal issues.

The vague abdominal pains, cramps, and spasms had begun a month or two after starting classes. I had begun avoiding spicy foods and lowered my alcohol intake. I had also started drinking a lot of whole milk. When I was diagnosed with the stomach ulcer as a child, whole milk had soothed the pain. It was also working on whatever this was. I didn't think it was a recurrence of my ulcer, but I treated the pain as if it were.

In the end, I went home more for my mother than for my father. At least I felt *something* toward her.

By the time I arrived in Virginia, my father been readmitted to Maryview, a hospital close to our home. At his first hospitalization, they'd tried a brand-spanking-new procedure on him: a colonic interposition. This involved removing his cancerous esophagus and replacing it with his upper intestines.

When Mama told me that, I took in the information as if I was listening to a bedside evaluation: as if I had no connection with the patient and had no real opinion. It had been done and could not be undone even if I had made a fuss. And what did I know? I was a first-year medical student, and my mother had not included me in the decision-making process. So what did she want me to do now? And besides, the procedure was a Hail Mary, in my opinion. He was dying; what did he have to lose? If it was successful, it might buy him a few more months.

During the procedure, the doctors had discovered that the cancer had metastasized to his lungs and liver. So removing his diseased esophagus had turned out not be helpful at all. And now, having suffered every complication in the book from the surgery—bleeding, infection, low blood pressure—it appeared my father would die sooner rather than later. He was not able to eat, so had to be fed through a tube in his neck. It hadn't been too long after his discharge from the hospital following the colonic interposition that my mom had called the ambulance and he'd been readmitted for what would come to be end-of-life care. He would not die at home as planned.

When my mother picked me up at the airport a few days before Christmas, she warned me, "Now, Lynette, he's gonna look real different when you see him, okay? He's lost a lot of weight."

"Okay," I replied, not interested in putting too much emotion into my response. I imagined he'd look like an emaciated corpse, and I was used to seeing dead bodies. He was just one that was still breathing for the time being.

Besides, we weren't even going to see him until tomorrow.

After an unrestful night back in my childhood home, we got ready to go to the hospital. I declined breakfast and just had a big glass of milk.

"That's all you're gonna have?" my mother asked.

"Yeah, Mom," was all I said. Why give her any additional worries? I continued to have insomnia from the shenanigans at school, and now, despite my detached feelings about my father, I was very concerned about how I would react to seeing him in his present condition.

And my stomach hurt. It felt on fire—a constant persistent, nagging, burning sensation, sometimes made better with milk, but not always. This hurt felt worse than the one I'd experienced when I was nine. And I didn't want to get it checked out. What if it meant I had to leave medical school? What if I had to return home? What if I had cancer?

Stop thinking that way, Lynette! I berated myself.

We drove to the hospital and entered his hospital ward. There he lay in his bed—a defeated man, gaunt and on death's door. His skin hung on a skeleton frame, so dry and ashy that he appeared a few shades lighter than his normal coloring. My father had once been a dark-skinned Black man, but now he appeared to be gray.

There was a tube coming out of his neck and his side. His glass IV bottle, with a clear liquid inside, was attached via tubing to a vein in his arm. It said LACTATED RINGERS in big bold black letters on its label. I knew that it was being used to replace the electrolytes he was losing.

It was shocking to think that this man had once used his wife as a punching bag. Instead of smelling like stale cigarettes and liquor, he now smelled of dried blood, bad breath, and aftershave. Mom shaved him every day and tried to cover up the odor of his decomposition with Aqua Velva.

"Mrs. Charity," a female voice chirped, "Mr. Charity weighs eighty pounds today! He's up a pound!"

I turned to look at the candy striper delivering this information to my mother. I had nothing but disdain for her naive exuberance.

She didn't have a clue. This man was dying of starvation. He couldn't eat because he no longer had his cancer-ridden esophagus and his intestines hadn't figured out their new job description.

I said nothing to the candy striper. I turned back around and looked at my father with uncaring eyes. I was angry at him for putting Mom through this dragged-out end-of-life saga. Why was he still alive?

He looked at me, perhaps trying to evoke some sympathy, but I wasn't having any of it.

"Hey, Lynette, how ya doin'?" he rasped.

"I'm okay," I said stiffly.

"I'm sorry you have to see me like this," he said. "I'm so weak. I'm in so much pain. The doctors tell me there's nothing else they can do for me."

Tears welled up in his eyes, but that only made me angrier.

"Listen, Dad, sit up!" I snapped. "Stop slouching! Stop crying! You brought this on yourself!"

"I'm so sorry for what I did to you. But can you help me? Can you help me, Lynette?" he begged.

"There's nothing I can do," I said with stony resolution.

He wanted absolution on his deathbed for everything he'd done to us, and I was having none of it. Here was a man who'd been physically strong his whole life. He'd never shown vulnerability. He'd beat on my mother and ignored his children. The only time he'd truly interacted with us was when he was drunk.

When Beverly was alive, I had seen a glimpse of what a loving father could be. The last time we'd gone to the colored beach, a couple of Saturdays before Beverly died, Daddy had come over while she and I were playing in the sand, picked her up, and put her on his shoulders. He'd then waded into the water with her squealing in delight. Daddy had smiled and showed such tenderness toward her. But when he was done, he had not offered me the same joy ride. She'd been his favorite, and as much as I could understand that, I couldn't now act as if all that had happened between us was water under the bridge.

"Lynette, why you being so mean to him?" my mother whispered. "He's dying." She had tears in her eyes too.

But I couldn't access anything but my anger. I was angry at my father, but I was angry at my mother, too, for taking care of him after everything he'd done to her.

There's birth and there's death, I thought. *There are some that were taken from this earth too soon and those who stayed too long. Beverly should be alive, and you, Daddy, should have died years ago.*

"Well, Chairdy, let me shave you and clean you up a bit," Mom said, and she started her hygiene ritual for my father.

My father had stopped using my mother as a punching bag when my brothers got old enough to physically pick him up. One night, he'd gotten drunk as usual; he was just about to hit my mom when my brothers grabbed him.

"You not hitting our Mama no more!" Butch told him.

"Yeah, no more!" Steve joined in.

And with that acknowledgment, they effortlessly threw him.

Daddy hit the organ bench and the keys hard. He was startled. After he picked himself up, he just went into the bedroom without saying a word and closed the door. And he didn't hit her again.

This did not make up for the years of abuse my mother endured. I was not about to forgive him just because he was dying. My mother, however, had already forgiven him—maybe had made a lifelong practice of forgiving him over and over again. Ever the dutiful wife.

I left for Boston the day after Christmas. I'd had my fill of a dying dad, a crying mom, and the stagnation of life in my old neighborhood. I wanted no part of that world. I had escaped, but feared that each trip back would suck me in. I needed to return to school.

After the holiday break there would be Pathology, Immunology, and Molecular Biology, as well as Genetics, Infectious Disease, and Hematology to tackle. I craved the distraction. I needed not to care about my father wasting away in a hospital bed; I needed not to care about my mother and her determination to care for my father until the end; and I needed not to care about my gut!

Focus, Lynette, I kept telling myself.

First year was going pretty well except for the continued nagging feeling of being an imposter, not really belonging. And my gut pain, of course. But I just had to push through it all. I could not dwell on anything that didn't keep me moving forward. Maybe I was depressed, but I hadn't done that class yet.

Later on, I realized that that was exactly what I was. Staying focused on the tasks at hand is likely the only thing that kept me from spiraling down into a darkness that I might not have emerged from. The constant ruminations and fear that someone would approach me and say, *You know, Lynette, you appear to be doing well here, but we still think we made a mistake, so sayonara!* kept me in a heightened state of stress. To combat it, I studied, studied, and studied some more. I blew off opportunities to go out and have a good time. There were no grades at Tufts, just pass/fail, and I was passing all of my courses. I had to make sure it stayed that way.

Please, oh please, let me escape!

Chapter 25
The Collapse

A<small>S MY FIRST</small> year was winding down with only a few weeks and final exams to go, I continued to be completely stressed out. My abdominal pains intensified to the point that I could no longer eat full meals; I could take no more than a bite or two of something, and that was it. And the spasms sometimes made me double over in pain.

I kept my secret quite well, avoiding eating out with classmates. During lunch breaks, I would disappear to the library to study and not eat. I would sometimes doze in the quiet, too. Getting a good night's sleep had become a problem. My mind would keep me up going over a lesson I just learned or thinking about being kicked out for being a fraud. And trying to ignore what was going on in my body. After all, what good would it do me to get evaluated? Getting a workup would take time. Time that I didn't have. I was on a schedule: four years of medical school, get my MD degree, and move forward with internship and residency. I was locked in. There was no room for a break to figure out my health.

Keep going, Lynette. Keep going. Think about your escape plan. Don't falter. Keep going.

And then one day, I collapsed. A gut spasm caught me off guard. Maybe it was a vasovagal swoon—the pain of the spasm getting so intense that it led to a slowing of my heart rate and a drop in my blood pressure. Whether that was it or not, I fainted, and the next thing I knew, I was on a stretcher, surrounded by paramedics.

I felt embarrassed to have caused such a fuss. My classmates were all around me—and the hospital was across the street from the medical school. Calling an ambulance seemed like overkill. With the help of a couple of classmates, I could have easily managed to get down the stairs of the school, looked both ways, and crossed the street.

Fortunately, the paramedics did decide that putting me into the back of an ambulance was a waste of time, so they just pushed the stretcher across the street and into the ER.

I closed my eyes so I didn't have to see what was occurring on Harrison Avenue. There were some gasps and some horn-honking, but we arrived safely.

Once in the ER, several people descended upon me. An IV was started. EKG leads placed. My clothes were removed and replaced with a hospital gown. My vitals were taken. Some of the faces I recognized, because they were my fellow medical students! I couldn't believe I'd fainted; I reprimanded myself for losing control.

A young male in a white coat spoke. "This is a twenty-two-year-old Black female Tufts medical student who collapsed today while attending a class at the school. No apparent cause. No evidence of head trauma. Upon admission, she was semiconscious."

No, I wasn't! I was faking out of embarrassment.

"Blood pressure was 82/50, heart rate was 72, respiratory rate was 16. Skin was warm to the touch. No height or weight. Auscultation of the heart and lungs were unremarkable. Labs have been drawn and further workup, along with more history from the patient, will reveal what other tests need to be performed."

I soon learned he'd graduated from Tufts medical school and was the intern on my case.

Later that day, with the help of a nurse, I stood on a scale.

She first took my height. "Height 68 inches," she shared with me. Then she looked at the scale. "Weight 80 pounds." Her brow furrowed with concern. "How much do you usually weigh, Lynette?"

"One-ten," I replied.

"Where did those thirty pounds go?" she asked.

I shrugged.

How should I know? Last time I weighed myself, I'd weighed 110 pounds. When was that? It dawned on me that I had not weighed myself at all since college. But what scared me the most was that I hadn't noticed my weight loss, and neither had my roommate or my classmates. Every first-year medical student was in study mode and stressed out for various reasons. Other people's weight or hygiene or latest sex partners just didn't register.

Because of my weight loss and symptoms, I was scheduled for a barium swallow and a colonoscopy. I knew all too well about a barium swallow from when I was nine. That's when I'd been diagnosed with a stomach ulcer. Thirteen years later, as I prepared to drink barium for the second time in my life—this time armed with knowledge gained from studying medicine—I well understood that my childhood ulcer had been the result of psychological stress. Seeing your one and only sister, the person you love more than anything else in the whole wide world, get run over and die definitely qualifies as a psychologically stressful situation. Not to mention how my father treated my mother. That day he hit her so hard I thought he'd killed her had left me feeling like I'd be alone in the world. No sister, and then no mother.

Did I have an ulcer again?

A barium swallow and colonoscopy revealed a diagnosis of something called *regional enteritis*. I had to look it up. When I did, I discovered that I definitely had some of the symptoms—namely, stomach cramps and weight loss. But saddled as I was with too much knowledge, my dad dying, and medical student disease, I was convinced I had cancer.

A nurse informed me that the school had called my mother, but she didn't call me for three days. On the fourth day of my hospitalization, the phone by my bed rang.

"Hey, Lynette," she said. "I hope you're okay. I just wanted to let you know that your daddy died. We're making preparations for his funeral next week. I spoke with Dr. Pinn, and she said she'll get you on a plane to come home. Okay?"

"Okay." That was all I said, and then we hung up.

Only after I got off the phone did I actually feel anything—and that feeling was anger. *No! Not okay.* I probably had cancer. I *definitely* was suffering from stress! I didn't want to go. Why did I have to? He was dead and I didn't want to see him dead. I was caught up in my memories of Beverly's funeral. I never wanted to see another dead relative, *ever*! And I certainly didn't want to be forced to kiss my dead father inside his coffin.

Not again! I can't!

My father died on April 6, a Sunday. I was discharged from the hospital on the following Tuesday, five days after my collapse. Dr. Pinn and others felt it would be *appropriate* for me to attend my father's funeral. I disagreed, but two days later, Thursday, April 10, there I was boarding an Allegheny Airlines flight from Boston to Norfolk.

I was barely able to walk onto the plane. My outfit had room for a second person.

I eased myself into my window seat and closed my eyes. Why was I continually being drawn back to the very place I had hoped to leave and never return to?

"Are you okay, miss?" the stewardess asked.

"Yes," I lied. I was in agony, physically and mentally. I wanted no part of the funeral ritual that was about to take place. I wanted to just die aboard that plane.

Upon arrival in Virginia, I imagined the stewardess would find my mother and tell her, "Mrs. Charity, we are sorry to inform you that your daughter died en route. She closed her eyes when we took off. We thought she was sleeping. However, when we landed, we determined she was not asleep, but dead."

Dying would be a good excuse to skip the open-casket ceremony.

At the funeral, someone, maybe Reverend Freeman, would say, "Lynette, Clarence Charity's daughter, is not in attendance. It seems she died on the way here."

I couldn't imagine anyone who would be in attendance at the funeral would know what it was like for me to have to see an open casket again. Whatever was in that coffin for all to see would not be my father.

Before I knew it, we were beginning our descent. Since I hadn't died on the plane, I made a mental note: *My dying wish is to be cremated! No open casket for me!*

When we landed safely at Norfolk International Airport, I forced myself off the plane. Mom met me at the gate, along with one of Dad's brothers (I didn't even know my uncle's name, that's how little I knew about my father's family).

They took me to our house at 512 Taft Drive. Too many bad memories flooded my head as soon I entered. I sat down on the couch and lost consciousness.

I awoke in the very hospital where my dad had taken his last breath. I had an IV drip in my left arm. Turned out I would miss the funeral after all.

The funeral was on Saturday, April 12. Mom visited me after the service. There were no tears this time. She regurgitated the events of the day in one long run-on sentence: "Your Uncle Linwood picked me and Kevin up and took us to the funeral home your dad looked nice in his suit Graves did a good job just like they did with Beverly it was a nice service I'm glad he bought all those plots out at Roosevelt Memorial Cemetery when he did I wished we could've moved Beverly but they said there's nothing there to move you know I put her in Calvary Cemetery because they had a children's section and we didn't have the plots in Roosevelt yet yeah it was a good service sorry you got sick again and missed it he looked real good."

I was discharged the next day. All I could think about was how much valuable classroom time and exams I'd missed with these back-to-back hospitalizations.

I moped around the house for another three days, waiting to go back to Boston. I sat on my mother's porch, feeling beaten down. All the work I'd done to reach this point—for what? I was depressed! My escape plan had hit a glitch that I might not recover from. I wanted to disappear. I wanted to die.

I heard the phone ring. Mom answered it as she always did: "Charity residence, Anne Charity speaking."

I couldn't imagine the call had anything to do with me so I tuned her out.

But then there she was, peering through the screen, talking to me. "Lynette, that was Dr. Pinn."

I turned to look at her. "Yeah? What'd she want?" Feeling the weight of my depression and the loss of my dream as I was, it was hard to even speak.

"She asked how you were doing. I told her not so good. I told her that you didn't seem to want to do anything. And you know what she said?" Without giving me any time to play her guessing game, she said, "Dr. Pinn wants you to come back, Lynette! She said, 'If it were anybody but Lynette, I would tell you to keep her home for a year. But it's Lynette, so you send her back to me and I will make sure she gets caught up and moves to second year with her class!'"

I sat on the porch, trying to process what Mom had just said.

Then, finally, I cried.

The tears came on so hard and so fast that they racked my whole body. I hadn't shed a tear about anything in so long, but this revelation evoked a tsunami of tears—tears of gratitude.

Dr. Pinn wanted me back!

I flew back to Boston and my medical school life. I was so thankful to Dr. Pinn. She had saved me. Who knows what would have become of me if I hadn't gone back? My old neighborhood hadn't changed in the five years since I'd graduated from high school and moved away. It had held on to many of its youth, ones I'd known growing up. Now we were adults, but too many of the girls I knew were already mothers. Some even had more than one child with their baby daddies, and one had a gold tooth! It was the threat of a gold tooth, being an unwed mother of twelve, and living out my existence in that neighborhood on welfare that had pushed me to escape. It was not the life I wanted. I would have died an early death there. I probably would have killed myself.

I arrived in Boston and headed to my apartment. I was not miraculously all better, but I was ecstatic to be back. This was my home now.

My roommate was so happy to see me that she made me some soup. It tasted good, and there was no pain when I ate it. I had a second bowl. For the first time in a long time, I was hungry.

I wondered about my diagnosis but didn't dwell upon it. Maybe it would resolve on its own; regardless, I had no time to think about that or what was happening with my family back home. Exams for the first trimester had occurred while I was away. The second trimester had started. I was playing catch-up.

Luckily, I had my classmates to help me.

They came over to my apartment after the last class that Friday, and everyone was so happy to see me. There were hugs and smiles— and then we got down to business. This was going to be a special tutoring session so that I would be prepared for my makeup exams. Passing these exams would put me back into schedule with my cohort.

"Lynette, name the eight bones in the wrist," Reggie fired out from his seat on the living room couch.

There were many mnemonics in medicine to help remember anatomy—like NAVL, the one Dr. Pai had taught us for the femoral triangle. There was a mnemonic for the eight wrist bones, but I didn't like it, so I'd made up my own: How Come Tom Takes So Long To Piss?

"Hamate, capitate, trapezium, trapezoid, scaphoid, lunate, triquetrum, pisiform," I answered.

"That's correct!" Reggie shouted, then smiled.

"What is histoplasmosis?" Terry asked next.

"What are the signs of Parkinson's disease?" Ed asked as soon as I answered Terry.

More questions came from Dottie, John, and Helen. More correct answers were given. What a great group of students. What a great group of friends.

After a weekend of cross-examination by my classmates who had taken the exams and passed them already, I felt confident that I would pass them also.

And just a few days later, I did.

Second trimester had started without me, but only by a few days. It was very easy to catch up. Was it possible that my stomach issues were really all in my head? I hadn't had the psychiatry class yet, so I didn't feel qualified to self-diagnose. Maybe it would shed some light on all of this.

The counselor I saw for a few sessions after my return, at the recommendation of Dr. Pinn, listened intently as I shared my so-called life and then simply said, "Well, looks as though you're handling things much better. If you need to chat more, you know where to find me."

I must admit that the doctors at Tufts-New England Medical Center didn't seem very interested in me or my symptoms after my hospitalization. No one had even suggested that I make a follow-up appointment, despite the diagnosis of regional enteritis. But despite my lingering confusion about my health issues, I felt better, physically and mentally, that trimester. The Affirmative Action issue that seemed to have started my spiral down into severe abdominal pain and emaciation seemed so distant now. And with the death of my father, I felt relieved that my mother would now have a life unencumbered by being a caregiver to her abuser. Secretly, I hoped that she would find a new partner. After all, she was only forty-six!

For my part, I reintroduced food gradually while waking up every day ready to go to work. Second trimester contained classes in pathology, immunology, molecular biology, genetics, infectious disease, and hematology. There was also a blood-drawing lab in which for the first time we practiced on living victims: ourselves! We had to start somewhere.

As it turned out, I was pretty good at drawing blood. I got it right on the first poke each time.

First year came to an end with final exams. Again, my Black classmates and I all passed. We studied as a collective, swearing to leave no one behind.

At the end of the semester, I found my way to the Office of Student Affairs, where Dr. Pinn was sitting at her desk reading what appeared to be a scientific paper. Her head was down, so I gently rapped on the side of the opened door.

She looked up and smiled. "Hi, Lynette. Come on in." She wore the long white coat of a real doctor, monogrammed with her name on the left breast pocket. The wide collar of her blouse was folded over the collar of the coat. Her shoulder-length hair was loosely pulled back into a ponytail. Her small hoop earrings finished off the look. She was so stylish.

I entered and chose to stand rather than plop down in the chair in front of her desk.

"Dr. Pinn, I didn't get to thank you for what you did. As soon as I got back, I had to cram for those make-up exams." I told her about the help I got from Ed, Elsie, Reggie, John, Terry, and Helen. I couldn't have passed those exams without them, or without my professors. "I wouldn't be here right now without you," I said. "My mom told me what you said. Thank you for having confidence in me."

"I knew you were doctor material the first time I met you, Lynette," she said kindly. "I've seen other medical students experience a setback such as an illness or a death in the family and they were not able to bounce back. *You* experienced both! And look at what you've accomplished with the help of your classmates. Your class is a great group."

I agreed. In a world where medical students could be callous—like crabs in a barrel, stepping over each other to get to the top—our small group of minority students had joined together to help each other succeed. We came from different backgrounds and different states, but Dr. Pinn had a keen sense of who belonged at Tufts. We had all become friends and collaborators. Everyone had a specific strength, and by pooling those strengths, we were all able to move forward. And we wanted to make Dr. Pinn proud of her cadre of hand-picked students.

She stood up and walked around her desk toward me. She smiled and approached me with open arms. Her excitement over how things had turned out was palpable. I gave her a big hug, tears streaming down my face.

The ability to cry was new to me. I had lived much of my life to this point abstaining from showing much emotion because I felt that crying was a sign of weakness. I now realized that crying was a part of being human.

"Dr. Pinn, you're the best!" I managed to utter.

She relaxed her hug, grabbed my shoulders, and looked me in the eyes. "And you are going places, Lynette."

Because of her, I could now lay to rest my concerns about whether I belonged at Tufts. My vague stomach pains, regional enteritis or not, were slowly but surely subsiding, and my future looked bright. My escape plan was back on track.

"Have a great summer, Lynette," Dr. Pinn said as I turned to leave her office.

"I will, Dr. Pinn. Thanks again."

Chapter 26
Rotating

DURING THE SUMMER break, I continued to work in the morgue. I was pain-free now and had gained back some of the weight I'd lost. I was looking healthier, more nourished. I had more energy.

I directed that energy toward studying in preparation for my return to the classroom for my second year.

Third- and fourth-year clinical rotations are the times medical students spend as members of a medical team (albeit as the least-qualified members of said team). During that time, students learn what is involved with each medical specialty, such as obstetrics and gynecology, internal medicine, family medicine, pediatrics, psychiatry, neurology, and surgery, and some make decisions on their residencies—the training that comes after medical school—based on these rotations.

As a second-year student, I prepared myself for what would come the next year by signing on for a physical diagnosis rotation. Shadowing actual hospital physicians, I would learn how to take a proper medical history and perform a complete physical exam on a live person. I would call it an "H&P," like they did, and I would actually "lay on the hands" (that was what they called a physical examination, the "laying on of the hands"—so cool!).

Now, having been examined twice in my first year of medical school, as well as during my sophomore year in college, I could say that I had a slight advantage over my classmates. Hell, I was pretty much an expert on the subject! With a Littmann stethoscope around my neck, wearing the short white coat of a pre-doctor, I was determined to be the best "H&P" taker ever.

Medical school was a seven day/week advocation. There were no classes on weekends, but studying did not stop.

Usually.

But one of my classmates, Kathy Brown, changed that one April day.

Denise had graduated and moved away, and Kathy was now my apartment mate. She and I were studying with the rest of our crew when she suddenly said, "Say, guys, wanna go see *The Wiz* in New York?"

The Wiz, advertised as a "Super Soul Musical in the context of contemporary Black culture," was an adaptation of *The Wonderful Wizard of Oz* by L. Frank Baum. *The Wiz* had opened in Baltimore in late 1974 and moved to Broadway's Majestic Theatre in January 1975.

By this point we had been inundated with eight months of almost nonstop medical experiences. We needed a break.

Plus, I loved *The Wizard of Oz*.

"Hell, yeah!" I said.

Five of us ended up going—me, Kathy, Ed, Stanley, and another Black medical student finishing up his first year who'd heard us talking about the trip and begged to come. For the life of me, I can't remember his name, yet I have several pictures of him—of course with no caption, since at the time I did know his name.

Whoever he was, he was fortunate. We'd not had the opportunity to get away like that when we were first years. I think Kathy realized that and that's why she'd allowed him to come. He was the odd man out, but he didn't care.

Ed and I had started dating earlier in the school year. Stanley and Kathy, at six foot two and six feet respectively, made a great-looking couple, but were just very good friends.

Kathy had a sophistication to her that made her stand out just as much as her height did. I don't remember her parents' professions, but I knew that her parents, unlike those of many of us minority students, were upper-middle-class. She was from California and owned an orange Volkswagen beetle—a fact that impressed many of her classmates, including me.

On a Friday after class, with very little of our second year left, we piled five people into Kathy's California car and took off for New York City.

"My friend Aljernon is going to let us crash at his place for the two days we're in New York," Kathy shared as we headed out of Boston.

Wow, I thought, *she has friends in New York City! How cool is that?*

The bug jerked forward and back as she shifted gears, heading toward the highway. Once on the interstate, the ride seemed smoother.

"Thanks so much for planning this!" I said to Kathy as we cruised along. "The last time I was in New York was when I was in eighth grade. We took a bus trip to see Niagara Falls. My grandmother lives in the Bronx, but I've never visited her there. Maybe I will now."

We were so excited to be on the trip that we never complained about being crammed into the backseat while Kathy drove, with Stan as her co-pilot.

Ed sat directly behind Stan, and I was in the middle with our other backseat passenger behind Kathy.

"Hey, Stan, do you feel like a pretzel?" Ed joked.

"Nah, I'm okay," he replied, shooting us a grin.

Despite his revered front-seat position, Stan looked uncomfortable; in order to accommodate the six lower extremities in the backseat, he'd had to bring his seat forward until his knees made an inverted *V* since Kathy, with her long legs, needed leg room to manage the stick shift. I don't think she had ever traveled with so many people in her car, and I'm positive she never again attempted such a feat.

We attended the Saturday night showing of *The Wiz*. It was a magical experience. Black actors and actresses telling a modern interpretation of the classic—incredible!

I had never been to the theater. In fact, except for Kathy, we were all newbies to the experience. I don't know about the others, but watching those Black performers onstage, I felt a sense of possibility. I had chosen medicine after being inspired by a white TV medical doctor. The children in the audience might now be inspired by the characters on stage to pursue theater.

When the show was over, we left the theater and in unison sang "Ease on Down the Road," followed by "Don't Nobody Bring Me No Bad News."

The night couldn't have been more perfect.

Sunday morning, we piled back into the Bug and headed back to Boston.

I was still on a high. Smashed between my two backseat mates, I started singing "Ease on Down the Road" again, and we all laughed. We were in the moment, and even though we were returning to the real world, I think this chance to take a break was the best thing to have happened to us in a while.

Medical school was rewarding. With each new disease we learned, we felt empowered. We all wanted to gain knowledge to better serve patients. But it was hard and stressful too—maybe harder and more stressful than we'd imagined going in. This trip was the tonic we'd needed to keep going.

We'd be entering the final weeks of our second year upon our return to Tufts. I thought about what that actually meant. I would spend the next two years on clinical rotations, solidifying the knowledge I had gained in classes over the previous two years. Just two years to go, and my escape plan would be complete.

I was positive I could do it. Especially after seeing what the future held: a chance to go back to New York!

The summer of 1976, I moved to a studio apartment in Mattapan, a neighborhood in Boston. It was July. I was now receiving funds from the Public Health Service and could afford to have my own place.

My mother had recently purchased herself a used 1975 Buick LeSabre. She hadn't wanted to trade in her old car for her new old car, so she now had two cars: the LeSabre and a 1970 Chevy Nova.

I called her before my move, asking for a favor.

"Without a car, it will be difficult for me to get to my different rotations using just public transportation this year," I told her. "Can I borrow your Nova?"

There was a long period of silence. Before she could gather her thoughts and possibly say no, I shouted into the phone, "Ma! One of my rotations is in Rhode Island!"

"My, oh my," she said. "That sounds far away."

More silence. I waited.

"All right," she said slowly, "but I want my car back after you graduate, okay?"

"Yes, ma'am," I said with a sigh of relief. "Thanks."

I flew home and drove the car back to Mattapan, where I parked it in my residents-only parking spot.

Over the month of July, I settled into my new place and brought Ed over to help me better arrange the little furniture I had.

Since it was a studio, I had to be creative. I used a trio of book-cases as a partition between my living room space and my bedroom space. I found a bedframe for a full-size bed at Goodwill, then bought a new mattress and box spring for it. I left my twin bed at my other apartment for the next tenant. A desk, a small couch, and a dinette set made the studio look inviting.

I liked it, anyway.

Ed hailed from Homewood, Pennsylvania. He had attended Harvard for undergrad, and unlike me, he'd been a shoo-in for Harvard Medical School, even after his interview with Dr. Alvin Pouissant. He, after all, was a Harvard alum, not some low-brow Black girl attending a women's liberal arts college who tried to sneak in through the back door. But Dr. Pinn was tenacious in her quest to find the crème de la crème of minority applicants, and she'd wooed him to Tufts.

Ed was shorter than me by a smidge, but it didn't matter. We were two birds of a feather, both of us having survived abusive homes with alcoholic fathers and battered mothers, and both having escaped "the hood." I told him about my pregnancy termination in college and he was respectful; we talked responsibly about birth control.

As we became an *item* at Tufts, we also began to reveal the damage we both still carried as a result of our difficult childhoods. We were both needy for love and validation. We were both suspicious of one another in our relationship. We were both jealous and felt threatened by other potential suitors. We were both alphas when it came to medicine.

Ultimately, our shared competitiveness was our downfall. We had many arguments over grades. Tufts was pass/fail, but you could still see a numbered grade. Ed was upset when I scored higher than he did on a test, and I was angry when he did better than me. We would yell at each other and break up, only to have make-up sex a few days or sometimes a couple of weeks later. It was a love-hate relationship in which we admired each other and were competitive with each other—not a great dynamic, as it turned out.

I loved him and he loved me. But that was not enough to save our relationship. We drifted apart toward the end of our second year. By that summer in between second and third year, we had become "just friends" . . . with an occasional relapse.

My first night on call at the hospital coincided with my trying on a different hairstyle. Some of my professors had told me that an Afro hairstyle would be a deterrent if I wanted to take care of white patients.

"You'll appear too militant, too Black Power–ish," one of my white male professors told me.

In that moment, I *felt* militant and Black Power–ish, but I knew that shaking a closed fist and yelling, "Say it loud, I'm Black and I'm proud!" would not help my escape plan. I would have to save my anger for another time, when it would perhaps make a difference. I couldn't risk having my medical degree rescinded for being "too uppity."

After considering all this, I decided to go back to relaxing my hair, telling myself that I was in need of a new look anyway.

In the hospital, I would have to deal with patients who had never had a Black doctor, and who would probably have misconceptions about my abilities. I was in Boston, where racial tension was high. And while I didn't need anyone to love me or even like me, I did need them to allow me to examine them and listen to my diagnosis.

I was on a path to fulfilling my dream. If I needed to straighten my hair to get there, so be it.

It was September 1976, the start of year three, and it was day one of my first rotation: internal medicine at Tufts-New England Medical Center Hospital.

Bright-eyed and ready to take physical examination and diagnosis to a higher level, I showed up Monday morning at 6:30 a.m.—via car, not public transit—and had straight hair that reached down to my shoulders. I knew this new 'do was going to be a lot of work to maintain, unlike my hair in its natural state,.

Very familiar with the hospital due to my first-year stay after my classroom collapse, I easily found my way to where I would meet the intern on the service. When the elevator door opened, a young man stared at me from the opposite end of the hallway.

He wore the same short white coat as I did; he had graduated from Tufts the year prior but was not quite to the point of "long white coat" status. He did have a fancy name tag, however, and his stethoscope looked more durable than the one I wore around my neck.

As he approached me, his glance went to my name tag.

"Hi, Lynette, I'm Tim, the intern on this internal medicine team. Welcome." He shook my hand. "In about fifteen minutes, we will meet the rest of the team and go on rounds. We only have ten patients assigned to our team right now."

"Rounds" was a period where the medical team visited each patient and discussed their care. These were morning rounds. At the end of the day, there would be evening rounds.

Within a few minutes, the rest of the team arrived: the head doctor, adorned in a long white coat with his stethoscope in a pocket; a second-year internal medicine resident; and a first-year internal medicine resident. With Tim and me, we were a team of five.

From seven to eight thirty, we rounded. We entered a ward and stopped by the bed of the patient closest to the door. The chief doctor asked the second-year resident to "present" the first case, i.e., the first patient. As we stood at the foot and sides of the patient's bed, he began.

"Mrs. Johnson is a sixty-five-year-old white female who presented with an increased thirst and a dry mouth. She also needed to urinate frequently and felt tired."

"Okay, Dr. Harper. Let's stop right there." The chief doctor looked at me. "Dr. Charity, welcome to the team. With this small amount of information, what is your diagnosis?"

I almost peed on myself at him signaling me out and calling me Dr. Charity.

"From what Dr. Harper said," I replied, "this woman has two out of the three main symptoms of hyperglycemia, most likely caused by diabetes."

"And what made you decide on that diagnosis?"

"The main symptoms of diabetes is polyuria, polydipsia, and polyphagia," I said.

He offered a brusque nod. "That is correct. Good start to your rotation."

The chief doctor "picked on" me a few more times that day—not in a malicious way, but I was still happy whenever he called on someone else as our rounds continued.

* * *

Once morning rounds were over, I was tasked with reviewing lab work on the patients and taking specimens—blood, urine, and sputum—to be analyzed. I was busy all day!

On evening rounds, Tim and the residents presented the cases to the night team. The chief doctor would still be the contact for them.

"So, Lynette," the chief doctor told me at the end of the day, "tomorrow night you will stay longer and observe how the team works at night."

I was ready.

My first night on call was exhilarating. They gave me a beeper! Between seeing patients with the intern, I took power naps on stretchers in my clothes. Around 3:00 a.m., I was *beeped* and told to go down to the ER to evaluate a patient.

When I arrived and opened the curtain, the intern was already on the scene.

"Ms. Morgan," he told the patient, "this is Lynette Charity, a third-year medical student. She'll be doing your exam."

The patient looked up at me. "Hello, future doctor Lynette. My name is Chesty Morgan."

Wait? What? THE Chesty Morgan?

I knew who Chesty Morgan was. She was a well-known stripper who had a burlesque act in The Combat Zone, an area in Boston that was home to strip clubs and peep shows. Chesty was five foot five with a 73-inch bust. I knew because the theater where she had her show had her picture with those measurements underneath her breasts. Some of us, curious, used to walk through the area during

our lunch break and marvel at this designated adult entertainment
district.

I didn't measure her bust during my examination, but they were
enormous. I'd been told by one of my classmates who swore to me
that he had seen her act that it consisted of two little people, dubbed
the Morgan Midgets, carrying her breasts in front of her onto a
raised stage in this theater. I'd never seen the show, so I had to take
his word for it.

Tonight, Ms. Morgan wore a hospital gown that protruded forward as she sat up on the ER stretcher, her head propped up with a
pillow. The protrusion was caused by her massive breasts!

I learned that Chesty had been performing at the Pilgrim Theatre
in the Combat Zone when she started having chest pain. I couldn't
have predicted that!

I did a thorough history and performed a full examination from
the waist up, including auscultation of her heart and lungs and an
exam of her upper back and front. She had soreness over her left
breast on palpation. There was no redness. Her EKG and chest x-ray
revealed normal findings. If she were having a heart attack, we would
have expected some changes on her EKG, and perhaps some evidence
of an enlarged heart on the x-ray.

A basic blood panel showed no evidence of anything abnor-
mal. The intern and I both decided that the weight of her breasts
had pulled a muscle on her right chest, producing the chest pain.
This could have occurred during her act. Perhaps the little people in
charge of her breasts had *mishandled* them, causing them to inadver-
tently drop and painfully stretch her chest muscles.

The intern was tasked with informing her of our diagnosis.

I stood by her as he gave her the news.

"Ms. Morgan," he said respectfully, "it appears you pulled a muscle. Two aspirin as needed every four to six hours and resting your breasts in a non-dependent position for a while will help."

"Thanks, sweetie," she cooed. "And thanks to the future female doctor. In my country, I never knew any female doctors."

"Thank you," I replied, appreciating that at no point had she said anything about me being Black.

I later learned that Ms. Chesty Morgan, a.k.a. Lillian Stello, was born in Warsaw, Poland, in 1937. After the death of her parents in a Jewish ghetto during WWII, she was sent to Israel and lived there until she met her American husband and moved to New York. I realized that she had gone through so much herself that she had no time to judge others.

After my internal medicine rotation, radiology was next. I spent four weeks looking at x-rays of all types of body parts.

When I was asked by the chief doctor, "What do you see on this x-ray?" the first thing I did was make sure the x-ray I saw was put up properly. Just like in Gross Anatomy, laterality mattered. Looking at an x-ray was like looking at a person facing you, so their left arm was on your right and their right arm was on your left. This was key.

I got good at diagnosing pneumonia and cardiomegaly, an enlarged heart. I enjoyed looking at fractures in particular. But I didn't fall in love with radiology.

Radiology was followed by a psychiatry rotation in South Boston. Let me say, I was concerned. South Boston was the epicenter of the racism in the city. It had been in the news for random acts of violence committed against Blacks over the last few years. And nothing much had changed since the unrest during my first year. As a Black female, what idiot had put me in harm's way like this?

When I arrived at the psychiatry hospital, everyone stared and seemed aghast at my presence. Once everyone closed their mouths, a tall white guy with blond hair and blue eyes approached me. I hoped that he would tell me to go home—that I'd passed this rotation by default.

"Hi," he said, "you must be Lynette Charity. I'm Nathan and I'm the second-year psych resident." He offered a muted smile. "This should be a great rotation, but we will make sure that you are headed home before it gets dark, just for your own safety."

My own safety? That did not sound good.

Nevertheless, although I was allowed to leave every day at 3:00 p.m., I was not allowed to bypass that rotation altogether.

What I found interesting during this rotation, as time went on, was that although visitors and staff sometimes stared at me, the patients I chatted with seemed colorblind. Not once did anyone I was assigned to use a racial slur or decline to talk to me. I guess they were too busy dealing with their mental health to deal with being upset by a Black female medical student.

I already mentioned that I had no interest in becoming a surgeon. Well, my rotation in surgery confirmed that disinterest. It was a demanding and demeaning rotation. Everyone on the team was a less knowledgeable version of "The Great One," the surgeon. He knew it all. All you had to do is ask him.

One day, after repairing a hernia, The Great One looked at me and said, "Lynette, you can close the skin." With that, he backed away from the OR table and sat down.

I was excited and nervous and scared. I'd practiced stitching on non-human objects, but what if I messed up? The patient would have to see his botched scar every time he looked at his groin.

The pressure.

"Lynette, this is the suture all ready to go in the hemostat," the scrub nurse said. "Take it and put in a few vertical mattress stitches to close the wound. You'll be fine. I can finish if you have any problems."

"Thanks," I said gratefully.

I took the suture and made my first pass at performing the "far, far, near, near" suturing technique. It took a while, but I managed to close one end of the wound. As I continued, I felt all eyes on me. I was new at this, but I felt everyone expecting me to just get done.

I was about to start another stitch when I heard The Great One yell, "Aren't you done yet? Are you waiting for the wound to granulate in? Let the scrub nurse finish."

I was immediately embarrassed—but also relieved.

The scrub nurse smiled at me before taking over. "Your stitches are quite good," she said. "Keep practicing. You will be a great surgeon in no time."

Was she out of her mind? I had no intention of becoming a surgeon.

My stitches and closing times did get better during that rotation. But I couldn't wait to get off the service.

The last rotation of my third year was a four-week paid elective in anesthesiology. The American Society of Anesthesiologists was trying to lure more medical students into the field. I didn't know what to expect; all I cared about initially was the money. Someone was paying me to learn. Without a blip of interest in the specialty itself, I thought, *Why not?*

I looked at locations for this four-week paid learning opportunity—and wouldn't you know it, one of the hospitals was Portsmouth Naval in Portsmouth, Virginia. The hospital was located near the downtown area. I could stay with my mother for free. And since I had a car, the commute would be easy.

There were other options, but for any other placement I would have to find housing on my own dime. It just didn't seem worth it when I had this option staring me in the face.

I'd spent four years of college steadfastly avoiding going home for holidays or summers, and now here I was, going back for my third time in three years—this time voluntarily. It was a little hard to believe. But getting paid to do a rotation sounded great—as did the chance to find my place in medicine. No rotation to date had really sparked an interest. Maybe I'd like anesthesia.

And I could handle a month with my mother. I knew I could.-

Portsmouth Naval was a hospital for active-duty military, their dependents, and military retirees. On the first day of my rotation, I drove from my mom's house to the hospital, fifteen minutes away. Upon arrival, I was given a parking pass and directed to the Department of Anesthesia, where I met the chief, Captain Richard Norton. A captain in the navy is a colonel in the army, so Captain Norton was pretty high-ranked, and he was an anesthesiologist.

Dr. Norton introduced me to several of the active-duty anesthesiologists and then had a corps person show me the women's locker room, where I changed into scrubs. To prevent people from leaving the hospital in scrubs designated for the operating room, a special color was assigned to OR scrubs: pink. Throughout the rest of the hospital, green was the color of choice. Anyone trying to leave the hospital in pink scrubs was detained and told to go change.

Wearing pink scrubs on my first day, I felt a part of the operating room staff. Once dressed, I was directed to the operating rooms, where I put on a surgical mask and bonnet, and some booties over my outside shoes. Once I saw how often various liquids spewed out from different orifices onto the floor, I welcomed the protection of a shoe covering.

My first day consisted of an orientation. Dr. Norton explained the role of the anesthesiologist in the surgical arena. He escorted me into various rooms to observe anesthesiologists in action. I must admit, I observed many of them sitting down. I took that as a good sign, since all of the patients were resting comfortably while the anesthesia machine was doing its thing.

By three o'clock, I had observed a hernia operation, several abdominal procedures, and an open-heart surgery. It had been a good day, and I was already being allowed to leave—at 3:00 p.m.!

This is almost too good to be true, I thought as I gathered my things and headed out the door.

The next day, I was assigned to a particular anesthesiologist for the day: Lieutenant Commander Jones, the assistant chief of the department.

"Okay, Lynette, today you will get the opportunity to intubate a patient," he told me. "Are you familiar with intubation?"

"Yes, sir," I said with a nod. "I've intubated a few dead people at the end of a code. They let us practice and view the anatomy." I felt pretty impressed with myself as I responded.

"Well, intubating the dead is a start," he conceded, "but you'll need to learn how to intubate the live patient, the moving patient, the patient that might be bleeding out of their mouths or puking. Very different." He told me about muscle relaxants and how those helped. He was calm as he discussed what sounded like pretty chaotic moments in an OR. "But sometimes it's necessary to just get the breathing tube in," he added.

I liked him immediately. He seemed genuinely invested in helping me learn the craft.

And I was a fast learner. I became adept at intubation fairly quickly—at least, that's what I was told. From intubations, I proceeded to learn how an anesthetic machine worked, and all about the different anesthetic gases, IV fluids, and the pharmacology of all things anesthesiology.

I loved it! I had not felt this exhilarated in any of my previous rotations. It was only the second day of this externship, but I felt committed to becoming an anesthesiologist.

I spent my first week in the OR in the main building. At the beginning of week two, I got dressed as usual and headed to the OR, where I met up with Dr. Jones.

"Today, Lynette, you are going to another building, where the Obstetrics Department is located," he said. "The anesthesiologist over there is going to show you how to insert an epidural and a spinal. You will also see some surgery. Some women require a caesarean section to deliver their babies."

I knew about C-sections from my rotation at Women & Infants Hospital in Providence, Rhode Island.

Off I went to the other building to meet Dr. Davis, a woman

anesthesiologist. She was also a lieutenant commander, which corresponds to the rank of major in the army.

As soon as I walked in, Dr. Davis flashed me a big smile. "Hello, Lynette. Nice to meet you."

Dressed in pink scrubs with a matching "designer" bonnet and pink OR shoes, Dr. Davis was stylin'.

"First, let's get you dressed," she said. "Then let's go see who's in labor."

What was amazing about this whole externship experience was that it was mostly hands-on. Yes, I did have to attend some lectures on the techniques of intubation and other aspects of anesthesia, but it was almost a see-one, do-one after that. And this approach did not frighten me in the least. I felt comfortable with my observation skills and my ability to mimic what I saw. It's true that I was not successful in inserting my first epidural or spinal, but it didn't take me long to figure out the anatomy and feel the distinctive *pop* for an epidural and the distinctive *pop-pop* for a spinal. (I was reminded constantly that you did not want a "wet tap" during an epidural. That meant that you'd gone too far. In performing an epidural, you did not want to see spinal fluid.)

On the second day of my time in obstetrics, I got a wet tap. The patient immediately complained of a headache. If enough spinal fluid leaks out from a hole in the dura, a membrane that keeps the fluid in the spinal canal, the brain fibers get stretched, resulting in a headache. I felt so bad when this happened. This woman was already having a baby; now she also had a headache, and I was the one who'd caused it.

As soon as the woman complained of the headache, Dr. Davis jumped in, patient and supportive.

"Okay, Lynette," she coached me. "The way we fix a wet tap is by taking some blood and injecting it where the hole is. It's called a blood patch. When the blood clots, it seals the hole."

She was not upset, clearly. I worried that the patient would be—but this, I found out, was one of the compromises patients at teaching hospitals made. The doctors had to learn their craft, and that meant mistakes would be made.

That particular patient received a successful epidural, had her baby, and got a blood patch and some extra IV fluids. At the end of it all, she thanked everyone. At no point did she look at me and say, "You idiot! Look what you did. You are not anesthesiology material. Can't even do a simple epidural. Just leave." But I felt that way.

I made it my mission to never get another wet tap, and during my week with Dr. Davis, my mission was successful. I did get a few more over the course of my career, but considering how many I performed over the years, I can't be too hard on myself.

The last week of my four-week externship, I continued learning anesthesia and being given more responsibilities. The whole time, Dr. Norton was invested in making sure I developed all the knowledge and skill sets needed to become an anesthesiologist. I felt better prepared than many who might be considering an anesthesiology career.

"You're a fast learner, Lynette," Dr. Norton said with a smile as we wrapped up our time together.

After I said my goodbyes to all the staff on my last day, Lt. Jones surprised me with a ride in his private plane. It was amazing—and

I was so excited to share the experience with my mother that I got a speeding ticket on the way home. I winced when I saw that it was $35.

"Lynette, can't you stay awhile longer?" Mama asked on the Sunday after the conclusion of my externship. I was packed up and ready to head back to Boston.

"No, I can't, Mama," I replied without hesitation.

I knew she liked having me there, but it was July 1977, and I was anxious to return to Tufts to share my epiphany with all my friends: when the time came, I was going to apply for a residency in anesthesiology.

As soon as I got back to campus, I interviewed with Dr. John Hedley-Whyte, the chief of Anesthesia at Beth Israel in Boston. Dr. Norton had contacted him and given me a glowing recommendation. I was told it was quite unusual to get an interview having not even applied to a residency, but I recalled having had an interview at Chatham without having filled out any paperwork beforehand, so it didn't seem strange to me. I was enjoying this word-of-mouth tactic. It worked for me.

We met at the Brookline Country Club, an all-white male establishment. I did not know this until I showed up. My first hint was the curious look I received when I first walked in. The gentleman, a Black man who was clearly on staff, opened the door said, "May I help you?" in a way that said, *Girl! I don't know what you thinkin', but you ain't comin' in here!*—or perhaps, *I'm terribly sorry miss, but you are not the correct gender or color for this fine establishment.*

I was rescued by Dr. Hedley-Whyte, an English gentleman in the true sense of the word, as well as a noted published anaesthetist—what an anesthesiologist is called in the United Kingdom.

"She's with me, old chap!" he remarked before grabbing me by the arm and leading me into the dining hall.

No one followed and no police were called, but I could tell by the whisperings during our lunch that Dr. Hedley-Whyte had committed an egregious no-no. He appeared not to care.

During our lunch in this posh, white men–only eatery, we talked about my anesthesia externship. As Dr. Hedley-Whyte told me that Dr. Norton felt I was an exceptional candidate for his anesthesiology residency, I tried valiantly to eat the beef tongue sitting on the plate in front of me. I wanted to wrap it up in a napkin and discard it later, but the napkins were cloth and being accused of stealing a napkin would not have looked good, so I slowly ate it as I tried not to throw up.

"So it's set!" Dr. Hedley-Whyte exclaimed as I forced down the last of the tongue.

I was to start in the fall of 1979, following a one-year internship.

"I would suggest that you match at any hospital of your choosing for your internship, except the BI," Dr. Hedley-Whyte suggested. "They can be quite mean knowing that you've already been accepted into a residency. Best to not give them that chance."

The "BI" was what everyone called the Boston Beth Israel hospital. I resolved to steer clear.

As I left the dining room, all eyes were upon me. Actually, I think no one had stopped staring from the moment I entered. But that didn't matter. I was so thrilled I was practically floating. I wanted to stop at the door, turn around, and shout, "I'm going to be an anesthesiologist!" In that moment I felt I could have mimicked Julie

Andrews in that opening scene from *The Sound of Music*. I could have twirled around in the restaurant and shouted, "This country club is alive with the sound of Lynette Charity, MD, whoopin' and a hollerin' in JOY!"

But why draw even more attention to this Virginia colored girl in a white man's world? Besides, the police would surely have been called if I'd put on such a spectacle. So I left with little fanfare—but inside I was about to explode from happiness. I'd finally made it.

Well, almost. I still had my fourth year to complete.

Chapter 27
Sam

BY APRIL 1978, my externship and my interview with Dr. Hedley-Whyte were little more than great memories. My fourth year was winding down. I continued to live in my studio apartment in Mattapan, but I would be leaving it soon: I had been accepted into an internship year at Eastern Virginia Medical School Hospitals in Norfolk, Virginia!

Yep, I was going home again—but only for one year, and then I'd be back in Boston for my residency. In six short weeks, I would receive my medical school diploma and officially become Lynette D. Charity, MD.

I was now dating Sam, a fourth-year medical student attending Boston University School of Medicine. We had met at the beginning of our fourth year while doing rotations at Newton-Wellesley Hospital in Newton, a suburb of Boston, and had hit it off right away. We were eight months into our relationship, and everything seemed to be going well.

We went out on a date one weekend evening. The night started out well: we had an enjoyable dinner at a Chinese restaurant nearby. Upon our return to my apartment, Sam stopped outside to have a cigarette, saying he'd meet me inside afterward. I didn't much like that he smoked, but his positives outweighed that one negative.

When Sam entered, I was already undressed and lying in the bed, covered only by the top sheet. He smiled, revealing his beautiful set of teeth, and quickly undressed.

He was a dark-skinned, well-endowed, hunk of a man. I looked forward to being grabbed up by his massive arms and just held. It was the cuddling with him that I loved the most. He made me feel . . . safe. All my worries about my life seemed to melt away while I lay on his chest and he held me tight.

Now naked, he plopped onto the bed and kissed me the way only Sam could, and I immediately smelled and tasted the cigarette he had just smoked.

Eww!

I forced myself to ignore the bad taste, because I just wanted to be swallowed up by him. He kissed me again—first on the mouth, then everywhere else. He was so gentle. We both took our time enjoying and exploring and sharing the exhilaration of our sexual connection.

Afterward, we lay in each other's arms for a while before either of us spoke.

Then, as he rubbed my back, Sam asked, "Lynette, why do you need to go to Virginia? Why didn't you try to get an internship in Boston?"

I had explained to Sam several times that it had been recommended that I not do an internship in Boston, specifically the Beth Israel, and that had led me to the decision not to apply to any Boston hospital. I had also explained to him more than once that it was cheaper to stay with my mom than it would be to continue to rent an apartment. It seemed the practical thing to do. I wasn't sure why me leaving was so important to him.

I stroked his sweaty chest, stopping at each nipple and giving it a pinch. He moaned. I kissed his sweaty chest, and then I kissed him.

"I just needed an internship, Sam," I cooed. "It's just a year, and then I'll be back for my anesthesiology residency." I don't think I sounded very convincing.

He grabbed my face in both hands and in a scolding voice said, "You're going to go off to that internship and meet somebody and forget all about me."

"That's ridiculous!" I replied. It was the first response that popped into my head. I didn't know what the future held. I certainly had no plans to forget Sam or go searching for yet another "Mr. Right" anytime soon; that said, how I felt about him was visceral, sensual, but I didn't see myself marrying him. I'd worked hard to become a doctor, and my goal now was to be the best damn doctor in the world. I had no time for a husband and children and the white-picket-fence life.

I never told him that, of course.

"Besides, you know how they treat interns in the hospital," I said, trying to reassure him. "I won't have time to meet anyone."

He sat up on the side of the bed with his back to me. He appeared deep in thought. I kissed his sweaty skin just between the shoulder blades. He pulled away.

"I need a cigarette," he said, and stood up, revealing his massive, chiseled body in all its nakedness. He was built like a tank and his thighs were massive. In fact, *massive* is the best word one could use to describe everything about Sam. I watched as he bent over his pants, which lay across a desk chair near the bed, and rummaged around in the pockets.

Nice ass! I thought, admiring him.

He sat back down on the bed with his pack of cigarettes and a matchbook in hand.

He was quiet there on the edge of the bed. Without saying a word, he shrugged, shook his head, and put a cigarette in his mouth; then he struck a match and put it to the tip of the cigarette.

I watched, incensed, as he puffed the cigarette tip aflame and inhaled and then blew out the smoke.

As he blew out the match and put it down on the floor, I exploded, "Sam, what are you doing? You know my rule. No smoking in my apartment." I sat up on the bed behind him. "Put that out!"

Sam took another drag off his cigarette, turned to face me, and blew the smoke into my face. He stared at me and smiled.

What the . . . ?

I hesitated for just a moment before snatching the cigarette out of his mouth and stuffing it into a Coke can on the bedside table.

He smiled again. Or was it a sneer? He lit another cigarette. Now more angry than surprised, I grabbed the whole pack of cigarettes, jumped out of bed, and started tearing each cigarette to smithereens. "You should know better!" I yelled. "You're gonna be a doctor! And I told you, NO SMOKIN' in here!'

As I ripped apart his pack of cigarettes, Sam grabbed me from behind, his massive arms holding me in a bear hug as he tried to wrestle his precious cancer sticks out of my hands. Tobacco was flying.

"Lynette, stop it!" he shouted as we grappled. "What's the point? You're leaving this apartment soon. Give me back my damn cigarettes!" And with those last words, Sam wrenched me around, punched me in the gut, and rescued what was left of his pack.

"Oomph!" I groaned with an exhale. Shocked, perplexed, and gasping for air, I slowly descended to the floor. Holding my abdomen, I fell forward onto the bed and then slid off the bed onto the floor, landing in a fetal position heap.

As I lay on the floor, Sam tried to salvage what he could.

"Do you know how much a pack of cigarettes costs, Lynette? You had no right."

Maybe I had no right—but damn! It's my place and you hit me to salvage your cigarettes?

As I lay on the floor naked, gasping for breath, I tried to collect my thoughts. This side of Sam I had never seen. This was a man willing to hit someone over a pack of cigarettes! And not just "someone"—the woman with whom he had just had sex and for whom he supposedly cared a great deal. The more I thought, the more I reeled. If he had the capacity to hit me, he had the capacity to hit *any* woman! My shock quickly turned to anger. This behavior could not be tolerated. Whatever I felt for Sam dissolved in that moment.

I got up and put on my robe. "Sam, get dressed and leave, please," I said, still slightly winded. I held my abdomen.

"Oh, babe, sorry about that. Lost my cool. You were tearing up my cigarettes!"

"Sam, get dressed and leave now or I will call the police and have you arrested."

"What?" His eyes widened. "Babe, you don't mean that. Come on. I guess I was a little upset that you seemed okay leaving me. When I get upset, I need a cigarette."

"Sam, I am going to the phone. If you are not out of here in five minutes, I'm calling."

He stood by the bed for a moment, and then he got dressed and left.

And just like that, Sam and I became exes. There was no way to forgive someone for that kind of transgression. Abuse is abuse. Unforgivable.

After Sam left, I sat back down on the floor and rubbed my stomach. I contemplated crying, but decided that was a waste of time. Instead, I reviewed the incident over and over in my head, dissecting it like I would a cadaver in the morgue. As I took my mental scalpel and peeled away the layers of that evening, I could make no sense of why a man like Sam would hit a woman. I wondered if I had been his first. Or had I just not ever given him a reason to hit me until that night?

I found myself reviewing my childhood, my young adulthood, and my future in a way I never before had. Memories of past relationships that went south emerged. Memories about prior mental and physical abuse by men.

My only role models growing up were the men in my family: a father who was an abusive alcoholic and a maternal grandfather whose abusive behavior caused his wife to divorce him. In my neighborhood, many women were abused by their boyfriends or their husbands. Many had several children from different men. What drew them to these men? What drew me to men who treated me as *less-than*? Why did I love them?

I thought about it until my head hurt. And since I came to no real conclusion, I made a decision. Well, maybe a reaffirmation. There would be no more Sams or Walters in my life. Relationships with men had never gone well for me.

I cleaned myself up. I put on an Al Jarreau album. I started preparing for my move after graduation. I decided I would stick to my original plan, the plan I'd concocted on a dark evening in the summer of 1961 when my father hit my mother so hard I thought he'd killed her.

My plan was to become a doctor. Nothing else mattered.

Chapter 28
A New Beginning

ON MAY 21, 1978, I graduated from Tufts University School of Medicine. I had escaped! Maybe I sported a wide smile as I walked across the stage. Maybe I shed some tears of joy. Maybe I celebrated with my classmates. I don't remember. Even pictures I have of my graduation evoke no memories.

Looking back, I vividly remembered my first day at Cradock, my first day at Chatham, and my first day at Tufts. New beginnings. But my graduation memories were all fuzzy. Maybe endings were not my thing. Maybe I'd known that once these milestones were achieved, I would succeed and move on, regardless of the obstacles I had to overcome. How else do I explain my lack of memories of these events?

I packed my car and headed south to Norfolk, Virginia. As I drove, I couldn't help but think about my past. I had come a long way, baby. Giving myself a pep talk, I told myself that I had made it. I wasn't going to be that welfare mother with a gold tooth and several children by different men! I was a medical doctor, and I would now receive the respect I deserved.

It took me two days to get home. I was in no rush. I had four weeks before my internship would begin. I relived the excitement I felt while in that anesthesia externship. I allowed myself to remember the good, the bad, and the ugly of my relationships. I needed to reinforce my resolve to focus on this new career. I strongly hoped that this internship would keep me so busy that sleeping would be my top priority during my free time.

A new beginning, Lynette. Stay focused.

July 5, 1978, was the first day of my internship. I walked through the doors of the first of four hospitals I would rotate through over the year. I carried my dark brown hospital bag in one hand, filled with my Littmann stethoscope, a reflex hammer, a tuning fork, flashlight, tongue depressors, and some size 6 sterile gloves I'd pilfered as a medical student.

My short white coat, the attire of a medical student, intern, or resident, was draped over my shoulder. In three years, I'd get the coveted long white coat worn by the physicians who had completed all their specialty training.

Here I was at the Hampton VA Hospital—the hospital where my father, a World War II veteran, was first diagnosed and treated for his metastatic esophageal cancer in 1975.

I considered what I would say if someone said to me, "I had a patient whose last name was Charity. Any relationship to you?"

Maybe I'll lie. I wondered why that was my instinct. Why was I afraid to just say, "Yes, he was my father"? Maybe I wanted him to stay buried, all memories included. After some deliberation, I decided I'd tell the truth, but if asked for more details, I would say, "I'd rather not."

Out with the old. In with a new beginning. Stay focused, Lynette.

In the foyer, I looked around for some assistance. Everyone appeared to be in a hurry. All manner of hospital staff was walking, jogging, even running to get where they needed to be. They avoided eye contact with me as I stood looking for directions.

I saw an orderly pushing an empty wheelchair. He saw me and put his head down and made a U-turn.

I continued to scan the area for help and finally saw a sign, in big block letters, at the front service desk. It read: ORIENTATION FOR INTERNS, SECOND FLOOR.

I made my way to the elevators and entered the first car that arrived after I pushed the number 2 button. The elevator doors opened on the second floor. There were several other newly minted MDs dressed in short white jackets walking around in a clueless state. I had found kindred spirits.

I suppressed a smile as I thought, *This is going to be a great year!*

"Those of you who have not had a tour, please come forward," said a woman with a name tag that read NURSE JOHNSON pinned to her white uniform. The white uniform complemented her medium-brown skin. *A Black nurse—and she's in charge!* I marveled at seeing this woman. I had encountered no Black nurses in my four years at Tufts.

I approached Nurse Johnson and said hello.

"And you are?" she asked in a southern drawl.

"I'm Lynette Charity, ma'am," I replied.

"Well, *Dah-tur* Charity, welcome to the internship program here at Eastern Virginia Medical School Hospitals. I'm Nurse Johnson, head nurse here at the Hampton VA. Let's take a tour, shall we? Oh, and here's your name tag."

It felt weird and exhilarating to be addressed as Dr. Charity, southern-styled or not. As I put on my white coat and attached the name tag that said Lynette Charity, MD, I marveled at how far I'd come. A few weeks earlier, I'd been a fourth-year medical student *scut monkey*, doing menial tasks such as running blood/urine/sputum samples to the lab, and now I was Dr. Charity, with the power to utilize a medical student *scut monkey* to do *my* bidding! I'd moved up in the world.

Weird. And exhilarating.

My impression of Nurse Johnson was that of a proud mama bear who every year prepared her new intern cubs to leave the den and manage on their own as confident physicians. Not an easy job, I suspected.

"Now, Dr. Charity, I think you calling me 'ma'am' may have given you away," she said as we began our tour. "Are you from the South?"

"Yes, ma'am—I was born at Norfolk Community Hospital," I replied, feeling the southern accent that I had repressed for many years resurfacing.

You can take the girl out of the 'hood, but you can't take the ma'am *or the drawl outta the girl.*

"A local. Well, welcome home," she said with a twinkle in her eye. "I hope you'll decide to stay after your internship. We could use more Black doctors here."

"We'll see?" I lied. I wasn't in the *welcome home* mood. I was in the *let me get through this internship so that I can get back to my life in Boston* mood. I hoped she wouldn't find out that I had no intention of staying after my internship. I could only imagine what she'd say.

"Okay, Dr. Charity. Let me show you around."

Nurse Johnson walked me all over the hospital. We visited wards and the intensive care units.

The surgical ICU. *Did my father spend time here after his cancer surgery?*

The medical ICU. *I think Mama said that Daddy was in this unit for a while.*

The more I tried to disassociate this hospital from my father, the more the hospital evoked thoughts of him—his cancer, his surgery, his death.

Stay focused, Lynette.

My tour was two hours long, but it seemed longer.

As we walked down a corridor leading to the cafeteria, she announced, "I bet you're hungry. The cafeteria food is pretty good." She stopped at the door. "Let me tell you a little about the selections we have before going in . . ."

As she began reciting the menu, starting with hot entrées, a door opened in front of me.

Time slowed down as a man entered the hallway. When I saw him, I stood still, frozen by the sight of him. I did a total-body scan of this man as Nurse Johnson chatted about the food served in the cafeteria: "Now our cold entrées consist of . . ."

Her voice became distant.

The man had dark, thick, curly hair and hazel eyes that sparkled through his dark-rimmed eyeglasses. The sun coming through a window caught his eyes at just the right angle and I'm telling you, they sparkled. His eyeglasses were perched on a roman nose. He had full lips and a two o'clock shadow. He wore gray slacks, a blue blazer, and a once-white shirt with a blue tie. *Is that a mustard stain on that tie?* Now, I couldn't attest that for certain, but from my vantage point, it looked like mustard to me. His stethoscope dangled precariously out of the left pocket of his blazer. *Why isn't he wearing his short white coat?* There was a plastic protector inserted in the top pocket of the blazer. The pocket protector held pens and a set of calipers used to read EKGs. His shoes were black, and he wore one black sock and one dark blue sock.

He looked in my direction. I gasped quietly.

Oh no, I've been found out! Arrest that woman for ogling while on a hospital tour.

But no—false alarm. Phew! I watched, unnoticed by him, as he turned and walked away from me.

But now I was miffed. *How could he not have noticed me?*

He had a swagger. Or was it a saunter? I moved my head from side to side as I observed him sashay down the hall.

Nurse Johnson was still sharing about the cafeteria menu, now talking about salads and desserts. Her conversation remained far away, muffled as though I had in earplugs that shut out most of the sound.

As the mystery man *sauntered* away from me, I turned toward Nurse Johnson and raised my hand. "Excuse me? Nurse Johnson?"

"Yes," she replied, raising her eyebrows slightly at the interruption.

"Who's that?" I said pointing to the disheveled yet handsome male walking away from us.

She looked in the direction of my finger. "Oh, that's Dr. Sado. He'll be your senior resident."

A senior resident! That meant he was in his third year after internship and two years older than me. (I later learned that he was actually only one year older, since Eastern Virginia medical school was a three-year program.)

I looked at him again, then turned to her and said—feeling absolutely no awkwardness at my question—"Does he have a girlfriend?"

With that question, I saw a shift going on in in Nurse Johnson's head. She looked . . . *confused.* Was it because the question had nothing to do with cafeteria food?

After what seemed to be a very *pregnant* pause, she replied, "I . . . I don't . . . think so. Well, let me just say I've never seen Dr. Sado at any of the hospital get-togethers with a girlfriend."

Great! A smile formed on my face that spread from ear to ear.

There was something about this man—about this white, nerdy doctor with hazel eyes that sparkled.

What had just happened to me? *There were going to be no more Walters or Sams, remember?*

Yet something told me he would not be like the others.

An inner voice shouted, *Lynette! Don't you dare.*

Another very calmly said, *Lynette. Dare, but be aware.*

I officially met Dr. Anthony S. Sado after lunch. I sat in an auditorium while we newbie interns were parceled out to various senior residents.

"Hello, Lynette," he introduced himself. "I'm Sid."

Seeing him up close I saw that he was indeed handsome, but also disheveled and possibly colorblind, since he wore one black sock and one dark blue one.

"Hello," I responded as I shook his hand. It felt sticky. And up close I could now see that it *was* a mustard stain on his tie. I didn't mind. In the words of my Granny, I was *smitten*.

And so, my internship began. Rather than a year to get through, it now showed potential. The philosophy of *never say never* was at play here.

When I shared my desire to get to know Dr. Sado better with some of the staff, I was advised that pursuing him was a bad idea. Not just because he was my senior resident and such fraternization was verboten—could, in fact, lead to removal from the program—but also because he was white, and I was . . . *not* white.

I paid them no nevermind.

I pursued Dr. Sado my first month at the Hampton VA with the same drive I had exhibited throughout my medical doctor quest. I enlisted the help of the nurses. It was a team effort, and it appeared that they also saw something in both of us. They dropped hints.

"Dr. Sado, have you noticed how Dr. Charity looks at you?" Nurse Vandiver asked him one day within earshot of me.

I pretended to be engrossed in a patient's bedside chart.

"Huh? What?" was his reply.

It was now the third week of my internship. I'm still not sure why I was so hell-bent on dating this man. I had just sworn off all things male. That decision was supposed to be final. Why, then, was my heart telling me something different?

The Monday of the fourth week, Sid approached me after morning rounds. He had a hard time looking me in the eyes as he spoke. He appeared nervous.

"Lynette, you wanna go out on Friday after work?" he asked as he looked down at his shoes. "We both have the weekend off."

"Sure, Sid!" I said excitedly. *Good work, nurse friends!*

That Friday, after signing off to the evening team, I followed Sid to his apartment complex. I had not returned my mom's Chevy Nova after graduation as promised; I still didn't have enough money to purchase a car of my own. Mom had agreed to let me keep using it.

Sid drove a silver Volkswagen Beetle. Seeing his car brought back the memory of me and my four friends driving to NYC to see *The Wiz*.

When we got to his complex, the Hague, I parked my car next to his. He got out of his car and approached my driver's-side window.

"My apartment is a mess, but you're welcome to come up while I go to the bathroom," he said. "Then we can go out. Oh, and I have a roommate. His name is Jim Hatcher. He's probably not home right now, but I thought you should know."

Saying his apartment was a mess was an understatement. When

we walked inside, I saw that there were clothes strewn everywhere and the living room was littered with discarded takeout food cartons. Oh, and there were roaches. The roaches didn't bother me much—they were part of living in Virginia—but if the apartment had been cleaner, maybe, just maybe, there would have been fewer of them.

I had strong enough feelings for this man that his messy apartment was not going to deter me. That said, I stood at the door while he went to use the bathroom.

"I'm taking you to Brennagin's," he yelled out from the bathroom while he urinated. "It's a steakhouse. I think you'll like the food."

Men are so different. I had always wondered at their willingness to urinate in a public bathroom surrounded by other men urinating; I felt somewhat uncomfortable urinating in a closed stall if another woman was in the stall next to me. But I knew at that moment that I would forego my anxiety and urinate at the restaurant rather than use the bathroom in this apartment. There were two, but I wasn't sure if Sid's roommate was any cleaner than he was.

I heard the toilet flush, but wasn't sure if I heard the faucet turn on for the washing of hands, before he exited the bathroom and said, "Okay, let's go!"

When we arrived at his car, Sid opened the door for me. What? Okay, he got a brownie point for that. It would have been okay if he hadn't done it, but it was an unexpected, nice touch. And after I got in, he gently closed the door behind me.

I was amazed by how much space there was in a Volkswagen Beetle when just two people instead of five occupied the space.

When we arrived at Brennagin's, Sid requested a booth away

from the door and in a quieter area of the restaurant. We both ordered prime rib.

Our get-to-know-each-other conversation unfolded quickly in between bites of prime rib, mashed potatoes, and creamed spinach. He was from Central Falls, Rhode Island. His father was Turkish. His mother, who had died from breast cancer shortly after he graduated from medical school, was Syrian, but had lived most of her childhood in Brazil with her divorced father and her adult life in Worcester, Massachusetts.

Sid was animated and engaged in his storytelling. His shyness and awkwardness melted away as he spoke; it was as though the floodgates had been opened and the raging waters of a most interesting life were being allowed to escape.

When it came time for me to share my story, he listened intently. I told him about the pregnancy termination in college and my encounter with Sam, and he seemed genuinely concerned.

After our delicious meal, we shared a dessert.

"When we go back to my place, let's take a walk around the area," Sid said as we slid out of the booth. "We can talk some more while we walk. Okay?"

I wasn't ready for the date to end, so I said, "Yes, let's take a walk."

As we walked, we both shared more about our lives. Eventually, the hour grew late, and we both acknowledged that it was time to go home.

"Let me walk you back to your car," Sid said. "This has been very nice, Lynette. I'd like to show you more about the area at a later time, if you like."

"That would be very nice, Sid."

I knew that if we were to keep seeing each other, we'd have to be discreet. Sid was still a senior resident, and I was still an intern. Our "friendship" was taboo, as would be a relationship between and officer and an enlisted person in the military.

We reached my car and there was a moment where we both paused, unsure what to do next. I decided to take the initiative: I kissed him.

Not waiting for a reaction, I opened my door and got into my car. "See you on Monday," I said. "This was very nice for our first date."

As I shut the door and started the car, he stood almost motionless, just staring at me.

I waved. He waved. And I drove off, looking forward to our next time.

I spent the weekend thinking about all things Anthony Sidney Sado.

Monday morning arrived with no time to recap our date from Friday night. The day was filled with all things medical—IVs started, ICU procedures on my patients, and writing SOAP (subjective, objective, assessment, plan) notes. I performed a successful emergency intubation that had everyone impressed. And there were death summaries to dictate. The previous intern had left me with several. It was my job to take stacks and stacks of hospital charts documenting treatment over the course of months and condense them to a one-page death summary—no easy feat.

I saw Sid very little that day, and when I did I couldn't gauge his response.

I worried that our date had been a bust.

Why was I pursuing this man? What were my expectations?

I had fulfilled my dream of becoming a doctor. Maybe now, with that goal achieved, I felt slightly lost? What was I going to aspire to next? Was my pursuit of this man filling a void? The escape plan hatched on my porch as a nine-year-old had led me to persevere through segregation, discrimination, racism, and sexism. Was overcoming the prejudice of an interracial relationship next?

Two more days passed, during which Sid and I were very professional with one another. On Thursday, however, he approached me.

"Hi, Lynette. Sorry I haven't talked to you since we went out. It's been busy. I stay focused on the patients when it's busy." He cleared his throat. "So, sorry again. I enjoyed our date. Shall we go out again or are you done with me?"

I most certainly was not done with him.

Sid and I went out again—and again and again. It was wonderful. By mid-internship, I had moved in with him, his roommate, and the roaches, and had purchased a light blue '78 Chevy Nova of my own.

My income for my internship year was $10,000 dollars. The car purchase price was $5,500 dollars. Sid cosigned the car loan so they would give it to me.

Toward the end of my internship, we announced our engagement to be married.

At no point did I feel we were moving too fast. He was the one.

At the end of June, my internship complete, I drove back to Boston to start my anesthesiology residency. Sid remained in Norfolk, finishing up his internal medicine residency and then joined me Boston.

We returned to Virginia for the wedding. On October 6, 1979, we married at Queen Street Baptist Church in Norfolk. In attendance were relatives, friends, colleagues, and a few naysayers—the ones who'd said it would never work out. It was a beautiful thing.

At the time, I was unaware that we were making history. Interracial marriages had been illegal in Virginia until 1967. The landmark and unanimous civil rights decision by the US Supreme Court in the case *Loving v. Virginia* ruled that laws banning interracial marriage violated the Equal Protection and Due Process Clauses of the 14th Amendment of the US Constitution. Richard Loving, who was white, and Mildred Jeter, who was Black, had come before me and Sid. They'd married in 1958 in Washington, DC, where their union was legal—only to be arrested and sentenced to a year in prison when they returned to Virginia, wedding license in hand. They were released when they promised to leave Virginia. After almost a decade of living away from family, they decided to fight the law, and they won—paving the way for couples like me and Sid.

There was no time for a honeymoon. We married on a Saturday and planned to drive back to Boston early Sunday morning. I had to be back to my residency on Monday. Even getting married was not a justification to take a vacation during medical training.

Sid and I packed up his part of the apartment at the Hague—with a few cockroaches included—and with Sid driving a packed U-Haul and me as his copilot, we made a stop to say goodbye to my neighborhood yet again.

When we pulled up in front of my childhood home, my mother came out to greet us. She took a Polaroid picture of us kissing on the lawn, then we both gave her big hugs and promised to visit.

Since my father's death, my mom had gotten a job and opened

her own checking account. I was proud that she was finally taking care of herself instead of someone else.

While she and Sid talked, I sat down on the porch at 512 Taft Drive and took a moment to reflect on my life. I took in a deep breath, and when I exhaled, I felt such a sense of accomplishment. It had been eighteen years since that fateful day that made me want to escape. So much had happened in that period of time. My escape plan had not been set in stone, thank goodness; obstacles that might have derailed me had ultimately given me fortitude.

My seventeen-year journey from first seeing myself as a medical doctor to actually completing that journey had not been linear; there had been several missteps along the way. But I'd always managed to regain my footing, and in the end I'd escaped from my life—because I *had* to. I was so afraid of a life in Victory Manor that I had to stay the course to freedom.

How did I do this? I still wonder. Forging a document, taking whatever I needed from my high school education without a fear of not fitting in. Pleading with the universe to help me and then receiving that help. I was smart, I grant myself that bravado. My IQ of 136 was considered "moderately gifted"—not too shabby. At least while navigating through obstacles, I was able to do the work to move forward. Of course, doing the educational work was never a problem for me. My own mental health, which to this day causes me some angst, was always my biggest obstacle.

As I sat there on my mother's porch, Granny's mantra, "Pay them no nevermind," jumped into my consciousness. *Powerful words, Granny*, I thought, grateful to her for the lesson.

I knew that being open to helping hands when I least expected them had been so important to my success as well. I was thankful to my family of origin, warts and all. And my extended chosen family, from Cradock to Chatham to Tufts, had all been so important in my plan and to me as well, even if I hadn't always realized it right away. Thanks to all of them, I was now and would ever be Lynette D. Charity, MD.

Sitting there, I wondered—*Where will my next journey take me?*

Wherever that proved to be and whatever challenges might come my way, I knew I would be ready.

Acknowledgments

I'D LIKE TO thank my mother, Anne Elizabeth Washington Charity; my grandmother, Dorothy Mae Cotton Washington Ferron; my great-grandmothers, Mary Elizabeth Cotton and Annie Mae Washington Holloway; my great aunt, Hunter Sue Washington Goodman. Without their guidance, I would not have found my purpose in life. Thanks to Peggy Donaldson, and my professors and classmates at Chatham College for Women, for helping me become a "World-Ready Woman." My thanks to Dr. Vivian Pinn, for saving me from my demons and believing I could become a medical doctor. To the women at She Writes Press, my sincere thanks. Lastly, to Linda Joy Myers and National Association of Memoir Writers for making my memoir a reality.

About the Author

photo credit: Robb Williamson

LYNETTE CHARITY, MD, is aboard-certified anesthesiologist with over forty years' worth of experience "putting people to sleep." After growing up in the segregated South, she graduated with honors from Chatham College for Women in Pittsburgh, PA, then went on to earn her medical degree from Tufts University School of Medicine. She has practiced nationally and internationally, and as a US Army doctor, achieving the rank of Lt. Colonel. Also a keynote speaker, humorist and author, Dr. Charity competed in the semi-finals of the 2014 World Championship of Public Speaking in Kuala Lumpur, Malaysia, and won a third-place trophy for her speech. Now a septuagenarian living in Gilbert, Arizona, her mission is to help others go after their dreams through sharing her story of overcoming obstacles of racial bias, gender bias and age bias.

Looking for your next great read?

We can help!

Visit www.shewritespress.com/next-read
or scan the QR code below for a list
of our recommended titles.

She Writes Press is an award-winning
independent publishing company founded to
serve women writers everywhere.